BEAUTY
AND
OTHER FORMS OF VALUE

MACMILLAN AND CO., Limited
LONDON · BOMBAY · CALCUTTA · MADRAS
MELBOURNE

THE MACMILLAN COMPANY
NEW YORK · BOSTON · CHICAGO
DALLAS · ATLANTA · SAN FRANCISCO

THE MACMILLAN COMPANY
OF CANADA, LIMITED
TORONTO

BEAUTY

AND

OTHER FORMS OF VALUE

BY

S. ALEXANDER

O.M., Litt.D., F.B.A.; Hon. LL.D., D.Litt., Litt.D.

HON. FELLOW OF BALLIOL AND LINCOLN COLLEGES, OXFORD
HON. PROFESSOR OF PHILOSOPHY IN THE UNIVERSITY OF MANCHESTER

MACMILLAN AND CO., LIMITED
ST. MARTIN'S STREET, LONDON
1933

COPYRIGHT

PRINTED IN GREAT BRITAIN
BY R. & R. CLARK, LIMITED, EDINBURGH

PREFACE

THE following work is mainly an essay in Aesthetics. The study of beauty is, I think, the best or the easiest way to approach the study of value in general. The introductory chapter explains how much I feel the need of such a study. There is no pretence of completeness, and I have thought it best to introduce as little critical matter as possible. There is more of it still than I could wish, especially in Part II.

A large part of the book consists of papers, or passages from papers, which have appeared during the last ten years. They have, however, been made the basis of a continuous work. The sources of the passages used are indicated as the passages occur. I am deeply indebted to those who have allowed me to make use of these previous writings: to the Manchester University Press, the Clarendon Press, the Aristotelian Society, the British Academy, the Editors of the *Bulletin of the John Rylands Library*, *Philosophy* (formerly the *Journal of Philosophical Studies*), and the *British Journal of Psychology*, and finally to my own publishers, Messrs. Macmillan, for permission to reprint some pages of an earlier work.

S. ALEXANDER

MANCHESTER, *May* 1933

CONTENTS

vii

CONTENTS

CHAPTER X

PART II. TRUTH AND GOODNESS

CHAPTER XI

CHAPTER XII

CHAPTER XIII

INTRODUCTORY

TRUTH, goodness and beauty have long been described as the supreme values, and the word value with a convenient ambiguity is applied either to the character which makes them valuable or to the valuable things themselves, the true, the good and the beautiful. They are, however, only special cases of value. To say nothing of economic value, value has a much wider extension than this famous triad. We set a value on things for all manner of reasons—for their rarity or from sentiment or for their usefulness. Nor does value belong to what concerns man only. Food is valuable to the animal and moisture to the plant; though perhaps only from our human point of view, for we need not suppose that an animal, and still less a plant, regards these things as valuable but only feels them so or acts as if they were so. We may even go further and say that there is value below the level of organic life and that anything has a value for another if they matter to one another: that the iron filings are valuable or a value to the magnet, because the magnet has what Mr. Laird,[1] who is responsible for this extension, calls a 'natural election' for the filings.

Other attempts have been made to assert the ubiquity of value. But it is plain that there may be some use of metaphor in these extensions. The same question arises in the attempt which is made to find mind everywhere in the universe. The stone or the atom may have a mind as well as the man. Is such mind the same everywhere, or do we mean only that in everything, and per-

[1] J. Laird, *The Idea of Value*. Cambridge, 1929.

haps even in the world as a whole, there is something corresponding or analogous to mind in man? The plant's mind is *prima facie* a different sort of mind from ours, and this is still more obviously true of the stone or the atom. Indeed Leibniz was content to recognise different grades of minds and leave the matter in this form. Still it may be true on further inquiry that, without any admixture of metaphor, being mind is the same property everywhere, that everything has in Mr. Whitehead's language a subjective and an objective pole, is bipolar; and that the different sorts of minds differ not in respect of their character of mind but in respect of the different sorts of bodies they have. If this were so, to establish this result, to say that everything has mind or life, would be a real discovery. Some such conclusion seems to be winning general acceptance at the present moment, without any very clear apprehension of the issue involved, or of what it is to be a mind.

In like manner if we are to maintain that there is value everywhere, it seems to me that we must first inquire carefully what value is, and rescue the word from the ignoble and somewhat scandalous condition into which it has fallen from careless and light-hearted use. It is so easy to say that there is value everywhere, and to understand this to mean that there is goodness or truth or beauty everywhere. The two propositions are by no means identical. Value may be an ingredient of everything, and perhaps even the most important ingredient, but it does not follow that goodness and truth and beauty are. We are easily inclined to this confusion because these highest values are so precious to us practically that we like to believe that they exist in things, or are to be taken for granted theoretically without an analysis of them which may seem sacrilegious. But we

have to keep our passions out of scientific or philosophical inquiry and preserve what has been called
'ethical neutrality' (Russell). Life demands from us
that we should be prepossessed in favour of goodness
and her sisters. But we must study these practical
prepossessions without theoretical prepossession.

Two methods are possible. The first, and perhaps
the more natural one, is to start with a hypothesis as to
value in general, such as Mr. Laird's, or if we confine
ourselves to human value, with a proposition like Mr.
Perry's,[1] that value is what interests us; and then proceed to the highest values. The other method is to
examine the highest values first and then inquire
whether and how far features found in them are to be
found lower down in the scale of values in general. I
propose to follow the second method, though it is the
less systematic, not because it avoids the employment
of hypothesis, but because it seems better adapted to a
tentative inquiry. In the highest values the nature of
value is exhibited upon larger lines and the subject is
more familiar, and it may be easier to see what value
is in these highest forms of it. I do not mean that the
lower can only be understood in terms of the higher.
That remains to be seen; and will, I think, be seen to
be untrue. But it is still true that the lower may be
easier to discover after we have considered the higher.

I propose therefore to begin with the highest values,
and for reasons which will appear later I propose to
deal at greatest length, and first, with beauty. The
following is to be primarily a study in aesthetics and
then, since knowledge and morals are a kind of art
though not of fine art, deals with the nature of truth
and with ethics.

[1] R. B. Perry, *General Theory of Value*. London and New York, 1926.

PART I
BEAUTY

CHAPTER I

VALUATION

VALUATION is the act of mind whereby we attach value to an object or regard it as valuable, and presumably in the same sense as we call an object pleasant because it gives us pleasure. The valuation of an object is thus secondary to the apprehension of it. We not only see a picture or a landscape but we judge it to be beautiful. The judgment of value is thus superimposed or founded on apprehension or judgment of an object. Now what distinguishes our judgments of the beauty of an object, the truth of a proposition, or the goodness of an act, is that the object valued (where the word object is used to cover propositions as well as things) is apprehended for its own sake. It is not merely contemplated as it presents itself in the course of practical or even theoretical life, but for itself, and its value is therefore called intrinsic. Even if our judgments are personal—I think this picture beautiful or this action good—we still contemplate the respective objects for themselves. What the relation is of such personal or subjective valuation to objective valuation in which we judge the object to be beautiful or true or good not merely because we personally think it so; this is a topic which will concern us in the sequel; and I am much mistaken if we shall not arrive at the conclusion that without such objective valuation we should hardly assert subjective value. Be this as it may, wherever we assert these highest values, we are contemplating the object for itself or intrinsically. The question is how do we come to perform

7

such acts of more than practical apprehension. It is safe to presume that we do so because of some impulse or motive in our minds. For our minds are through and through impulsive or conational. It is not therefore enough to say that when we look at a landscape for itself we admire it and call it beautiful. We have to ask what makes us want to contemplate it for its own sake. What is that impulse which adds to the mere looking at the landscape the act of looking at it for itself and finding it admirable? What is it that leads us on or diverts us from mere practical seeing to aesthetic seeing? We may feel sure in advance that we may apply to beauty with proper changes what Hume said of virtue, that "no action can be virtuous or morally good, unless there is in human nature some motive to produce it distinct from the sense of its morality".[1]

We have first of all to satisfy ourselves that mere apprehension is always primarily an action and that the object we apprehend we apprehend as the outcome of such action. We do not first know or cognise an object and then act upon it, but we cognise it through and in acting upon it. We know through doing. Take a simple apprehension of colour. The physical illuminated object acts physically upon our eyes and by a physiological process the eye turns to the object. So far the response is of the same kind as the motion of the filings to the magnet or the rebound of an impinging body from a body which it has struck. But the eye is not merely physical but is the organ of a living and conscious body. Shelley's sensitive plant opened its fan-like leaves to the light, and nobody would doubt that this is a physiological reaction of the plant to physical stimulation by the light. But the animal's, and our, visual response is a more complicated reaction, the reaction of a creature

---

[1] *Treatise*, Book III. Part II. sect. i. (ed. Selby-Bigge, p. 479).

with a nervous system, which has the character of what Sir Henry Head calls 'vigilance'. In this wakeful response of our eyes to the exciting object we are aware of the object as coloured and we ourselves are in the condition of colour-apprehension. To keep the statement simple I have described the reaction elicited physically by the object (which in the first instance is not seen at all but merely excites the eye physically or physiologically) as one of turning the eye to the object. That is a very insufficient description, and if that were all, the object would not be apprehended as coloured but merely, I suppose, as visible. The eye turns to the object equally whether the object is blue or green or yellow. In each case the physical excitement produced by the green or blue light stimulation (or if you will, by rays of such and such wave-length) ends in a well-differentiated efferent response, and these responses, whether appropriate to blue or green, issue externally by the 'common path' of direction upon the object. Neglect these differences for the moment. In every case the external object physically excites a physical response; but in creatures with minds the response is of such a character that at once the creature is aware, and the thing which before was merely a physical object is revealed in its appropriate characters; as blue or green, or hard or soft, or sweet, or fragrant.

I am deliberately abstaining from metaphysics, and assuming that there is a world of physical things which we get to know by our minds, and asking how we get to know them. It may be that physical things are in the end mental existences. That makes no difference. We may still, as Berkeley himself said, talk with the vulgar and think with the learned. Whatever the ultimate truth may be for metaphysics, it still remains that physical things have a different status from creatures with life or mind, and we have still to ask how the things called minds come to apprehend the other things, perhaps also in some sense minds, which are called physical things. If anyone chooses to impeach this procedure as unphilosophical, I demur. I admit I am not writing philosophy, or only in the looser, more general, sense of that word, but maintain that I commit no sin against philosophy. I do not much care whether this particular inquiry or the book as a whole is called philosophy or science, or what it is called, so long as it is true; and it will contain philosophy enough before it is finished.

We become aware, then, of external things and their characters, because they evoke from us physically, or provoke us to, or compel us to, or extort from us, they being the things they are and we the creatures we are, certain responses in which we are aware of them, and they are revealed to us. Like other creatures and things, we live in a world upon which we act at the suggestion of our surroundings, but our responses are cognitive as well as conational, because we are the creatures we are. The truth of this general statement is clear enough when we consider less simple cases than mere sensation. I do not see the apple to be good eating, but it tempts me, a mere son of Eve, to eat it, and I find it good and nutritious. So true is the saying of Spinoza that things are good because we desire them; we do not desire them because they are good. When on a dark night I am mounted on my bicycle and a motor-car bears down upon me with all the effrontery of its blazing headlights, I do not evade it because I recognise it to be dangerous, but it terrifies me so that I swerve into the ditch, and so I am aware of it as dangerous. William James tells the story of how his boy, standing near the edge of a railway platform, rushed in terror, as an express came thundering through the station, to his father's side. The boy's action was extorted from him by the terrible train, but he was aware of it as terrible through the terror it induced, and the acts appropriate to that terror.

We fail to realise the truth of the general statement because experiences are rarely so simple as in the instances I have taken. One complexity even in sensation has been just mentioned, the small difference in the response according as a colour, say, is red or blue. Also our responses are complicated by our previous experience or our present condition. The physical thing touches off a response and compels it, but we ourselves interfere with the simple effect of the stimulus from without. To the impulse or conation engendered from without we add all manner of impulses engendered from within. Hence the object as in ordinary perception comes to us not merely in the character which excited the response but with characters corresponding to the efferent processes linked up with the main efferent impulse. We shall see later how important and vital a part this increment to the mere compulsion from without plays in the creation of beauty. Our behaviour to external things is so complicated with our ideas or thoughts about them that it is no wonder we imagine that our actions are determined by our cognitions of things. And in our later experience such ideas about things are actually present in our minds and do, of course, affect our reaction to the things.

Even here we need to remind ourselves that ideas and images and thoughts are merely the objects that correspond to certain impulses and conations of our own. I have not room in this place to suggest a systematic survey of the objects, from sensory elements up to thoughts, which enter into our experience. It may, however, be shown that these are the names of the objects of various conations. That an idea for instance, an image held before the mind, is revealed to the mind through a desire or a conation of the nature of desire, and that the different look of the object in sensation and in image is the different revelation to the mind of the world outside it according as it is evoked by a present physical object compelling an act of tactual or visual or other grasping, or corresponds to a conation initiated from within. Remembered or expected objects are in some form desired objects. But the complete exposition of this thesis, which I have attempted sometime elsewhere,[1] would for my actual purpose carry me too far away from the immediate truth that we know things under the various forms of knowledge in so far as we act upon them or respond to them by responses, either enforced from without or supplied from ourselves and in the end from our own bodies, which include our brains, or belonging to both these sources.

But to return to our immediate subject. The typical act of cognition is one which begins with an impact upon our bodies from some object in the external world and ends in a recoil of our body upon the external world. In this physical chain, mental action, that is vigilant conation, is interpolated in the shape of awareness on one side of a revealed object upon the other. Sometimes the return to the external world is delayed, as when a perceived object sets going not the grasp of the object but a train of ideas, which when it is ended, sooner or later, returns to the world in the form of an efferent response. We have here the simplest instance of diversion of the mind from direct response to indirect. No new impulse is needed to effect this delay, for the

---

[1] 'Foundations and Sketch-plan of a Conational Psychology', *British Journal of Psychology*, vol. iv., 1911.

ultimate reaction follows merely on a longer circuit in the mind or brain.

A new impulse comes into play when the response to the external object is diverted into speech, and the object being named is detained by its name for the mind to contemplate in overt attention. I say 'overt attention', for every awareness is the simple form of attention, attention being another word for the direction of the mind upon an object.[1] Speech is the beginning of that process of lifting an object out of the mass of experience in which it is imbedded—a process which ends in the contemplation of an object for its own sake —which is involved in the highest valuations, truth, goodness and beauty. A name fixes the object to which it belongs, and hence its importance for thinking, even if it is premature to hold it indispensable for thinking. Now to name an object is not like going on from apprehension of the object to related ideas or images which are of the same order as the original object. It is the excitement of a special impulse, speech impulse, which issues in sounds or vocal gestures appropriate to each object named. For speech is not merely a cry like an interjection wrung from the creature's feeling, but is a cry made significant through its reference to an object. And I desire to repeat that it is the expression of a new impulse, so that detaining an experience in overt attention is not something which is a matter of course but requires an impulse directed to that end. We may accordingly anticipate that when we find objects beautiful or true or good, it is because a special impulse has been brought into play whose satisfaction is the beauty or truth or goodness of the object in question.

Still it is a long way from the mere detention of an object in the mind which is effected by speech to the

[1] J. Ward, *Principles of Psychology*. Cambridge, 1929.

contemplation of the object for its own sake. For naming is but an incident in the practical behaviour of the mind towards the world, sharpening the features of the things we observe. We have to ask what, if any, are the motives or impulses which lead to this intrinsic contemplation of objects. Even speech itself may be considered for its own sake in the fine art of literature. We may feel sure in advance that if we take objects and contemplate them for their own sakes and pronounce them beautiful or true or good, there is some special impulse in ourselves, or some qualification of an impulse in ourselves, which makes us do it, and these impulses it is our business to identify.

CHAPTER II

BEAUTY

BEAUTY, like pleasure in Wordsworth's line, is 'spread through the world'; and those who begin their inquiry into beauty with the beauty of nature are apt to conclude that beauty is a quality of things, independent of us, which we discover as we discover the other qualities of things. But the conclusion may be premature. Nature is beautiful only to the mind which is prepared to apprehend her beauty, to contemplate her for her own sake apart from the practical delight she brings. We distinguish the mere pleasure which she gives to the eye or ear from the pleasure of her beauty. A green field is doubtless pleasant to the eye of the cow, as well as grateful to her hunger. But does she find it beautiful? "Pleased when the sylvan world displays its raptures to the feeding gaze"—those raptures are not mere delight of the eye. There has been selection of what suits the feeder. Nature is not beautiful because she pleases but, to borrow a famous phrase of Hume which we shall elsewhere find enlightening, because she pleases after a particular manner.[1] To discover in what manner, let us turn to the beauty of fine art.

Art of all kinds, including fine art, constructs the work of art out of physical materials, wood or stone or pigments or words or, as in music, tones or, it may be, bodily movements as in the dance. A poem, whatever else may be said of it, is made of words, a picture of paints, a sonata of tones. There may be beauty

---

[1] *Treatise*, Book III. Part I. sect. ii. (ed. Selby-Bigge, p. 471).

of imagery or of thoughts. But images are images of things, and so in some more difficult sense are thoughts, when they are thoughts of physical things, physical too. The objects of the mind's internal visions are drawn in the lines and colours of external things, as the brief remarks upon the subject in the preceding chapter may have served to indicate. In any case it is always well in dealing with intricate matters to take the simplest cases first. Art, then, is the construction of material works of art, and fine art of beautiful material or physical things.

Man is not the first artificer. He is preceded by the swallow which builds its nest, by the beaver which builds its dam, by the bee which constructs the hive, by the nightingale who sings to his mate. This impulse (or instinct) of construction may be identified as the impulse which in a qualified form produces in man fine art, and is the foundation of the impulse towards beauty. But such animal constructiveness falls far short of fine art. It is exhausted in practice and serves practical ends which the animal itself may be unaware of. Nest-building of birds and burrowing of wasps are spontaneous outflows of impulses whose end is the preservation of the young. The beaver and the bee construct for storage of food. The nightingale's song, however lovely to our aesthetic ears, is an incident in the practical arrangements of mating. It is not fine art, it is not even craft.

Craft is the next stage upwards from animal construction and differs from it in that the end is purposed and not merely attained. Accordingly all manner of thinking and devices may enter into it. The craftsman is full of ideas of what he means to do, on the whole and in detail. The main feature, however, of his work is that he constructs his materials for practical ends, to give his clay the shape of a pot, or to weave his yarn into the pattern of cloth. Craft is more than spontaneous construction, because the result is willed, and less than fine art. At the same time craft is at every moment passing over into fine art. The craftsman as such is not an artist. The good craftsman constructs his product as perfectly as he can, he takes faithfully the steps necessary to that end. He becomes an artist in so far as he treats his materials also for themselves, and the craftsman may be and is perpetually besieged by dreams of beauty in his work. From skill he proceeds to good taste and from taste to charm and beauty. So constantly may the faithful craftsman be mixed with the creative artist. On the other hand the artist, if he is to be a good artist, must possess craft,[1] and though a defect in his craft may be atoned for by excellence of creative handling, his work loses in artistic rank, just as contrariwise he may fail of greatness because his creativeness may be unequal to the craft of the 'perfect painter'.

Moreover, the greater part of what is commonly known as fine art is not art at all—and in future when I say art I shall mean fine art—but is craft. The paintings which cover the walls of our exhibitions are largely skilful or competent representations, good rather than beautiful, half-way between photographs, which are the artistry of the sun, and those truly beautiful representative paintings which I shall later describe as the prose of painting. The larger part of the houses and other buildings of our towns are not so much architecture, many of them are not even made by architects, but workman-like constructions, and sometimes they are even positively ugly because they defy architectural

[1] See J. Hubert Worthington, 'Address to Students', *R.I.B.A. Journal*, vol. xxxiv., 1927.

form. The greater part of our writing, in books and still more in newspapers, is competent narrative or exposition, skilled but not beautiful or artistic writing such as deserves the name of literature. And this is in no way intended in depreciation of such works of craft. For craftsmanship is not only the prerequisite of artistry but is itself precious and good and attained only by much labour and experience, and exercised only with pains and devotion.

Art grows out of craft and goes beyond it, when the worker handles his materials not, or not only, as a means of reaching a certain practical end but for their own sakes, and becomes contemplative instead of merely practical. How does this difference arise? We have seen how practical observation of things becomes theoretical when the practical issue of grasping the object is diverted into another practical issue, that of naming. But the fine art of speech goes beyond naming and introduces into speech magic and beauty. How does construction become thus contemplative? The question has to be asked, for the act of the artist, like that of the craftsman, primarily conforms to the type of behaviour already exhibited in ordinary cognition of a thing or colour. The artist is excited by some subject or other, a scene in nature, a woman, a commission to build a house, the thought of a chivalrous deed; and his excitement issues in external action, in the use of the hands with chisel or paint-brush or burin, or of the voice or other instrument for producing tones, or of the limbs in dance, or in speech. Some of these instruments of his utterance are native to him, others are acquired. In all cases he uses materials which as in building he finds ready to be used, or as in speech and singing he himself provides and constructs into certain arrangements. But the artist, unlike the craftsman, uses the materials not practically but contemplatively, for this is the meaning of the phrase which I use, 'the use of materials for their own sake', which means simply that the materials are used without practical purpose as in craft, though of course without excluding the practical purpose in the craft which underlies the art. It does not mean that the materials are considered in themselves as if words should be regarded in their history or derivation as the philologist uses, or pigments in their chemical composition, or stones as geological formations.[1] That is precisely what the artist does not do.

How is this transition effected? The answer is to be found in an old phrase which describes the work of art —*homo additus naturae*, the addition of man to nature.[2] It is because the artist mixes himself with his materials. Not only does he arrange the materials in a form which they themselves, as he finds them, have not; the craftsman also does that, which is implied in mere construction. He introduces into his materials, through the form he gives them, characters, or rather the appearance of characters, which in their practical use they do not possess.[3] He gives the bronze breath and living features to the marble, according to the Virgilian phrases, *spirantia aera, vivos ducent de marmore voltus*. He does not merely interpret as we do in ordinary perception the data of sense by his past experience of things, perceiving the orange which he merely sees as fragrant and juicy fruit, and so add to things as he experiences them characters which they do actually possess

---

[1] The artist has to consider the suitability of his materials, and to that extent the sculptor considers his marble as rock. Michael Angelo used to go down himself to Carrara to choose his blocks; and the David was suggested to him by the shape of the block given to him by the Florentine Council.

[2] Cp. *C. E. Montague: a Memoir*, by Oliver Elton (London, 1929), p. 272, in a letter to myself.

[3] I take representative art to begin with, leaving to the sequel to show that what is said here applies with proper modifications to non-representative art.

in practical experience. He imputes to his materials characters which in practical experience they do not possess. The exact import and the range of this procedure will be discussed presently. The fact is certain, most easily verified in the statue which looks living or the flat picture which looks solid. In virtue of this addition of the artist to his work, which in special cases may be replaced by subtraction, the work to be what it is, to convey its meaning, demands the presence of the artist's mind in its creation, or of his substitute the spectator in appreciation. Without them the marble has no appearance of life, and its form, however remarkable, has no significance. If we found such strange shapes scattered among shapeless blocks or masses of clay, they would be mere curiosities of nature.

Now it is the admixture to the given material of meaning imported from the artist himself, and not belonging to the material itself, which detaches the materials from their mere natural use in practice and makes them objects treated for their own sakes. The meanings which we add to the objects of sense in perceiving a sensible object, where the supplements imputed by the perceiver are verified by the thing itself in fact, have no such effect. But the imputation of meanings which do not belong to the material itself raises both those meanings and the sensible materials to which they are imputed into objects of intrinsic contemplation. Possessed by the excitement which is produced in him by the subject which occupies him, let us say the face of a 'beautiful' woman, and by the feel of the material in which he works in consequence of his excitement [1] (for the mere touch of clay or the mere sound of a word may excite him into production, as the

---

[1] See *C. E. Montague*, p. 271, and J. M. Thorburn, *Art and the Unconscious* (London, 1925), pp. 91-2.

feel of the fresh grass sets a horse upon a wild scamper);
under these excitements, the artist constructs spontaneously out of the fulness of his constructive impulse,
but, moulding his material as he does to a shape which,
to use inaccurate language which will be corrected hereafter, 'expresses' his own mind, his materials acquire
an attachment to himself which detaches them from
the mere world of nature. The constructive impulse,
once provoked, indulges itself in its own enjoyment,
the artist surrenders himself to what we may loosely
call ideas beyond the direct information conveyed by
the subject matter, and these promptings of his mind
issue into the shaping of his material. It is thus that
the materials, those he finds and the adventitious form
he gives them, become for him materials to be used
contemplatively. For I observe again that not merely
the significance added through the form is contemplated, but the material to which it is added becomes
transfigured in the process. The meadows Shakespeare
speaks of in the lovely song I shall quote presently
(on p. 23), 'painted' as they are 'with delight', are no
longer the mere meadows that please the animal's eyes,
and the words themselves are no longer mere names of
actual meadows. The marble ceases through its significant form to be mere marble.[1] The same thing holds
of natural objects when they are seen to be beautiful.
The thunderstorm when it is felt to be sublime has lost
in part at least the terrors it possesses as a natural
event, becomes a source of delight, and approaches to
the condition of a painted storm.

Ruskin rightly defines beauty in this way: "Any
material object which can give us pleasure in the simple

---

[1] Milton imagines the reverse process:

> There rapt in holy passion still
> Forget thyself to marble.

contemplation of its outward qualities without any direct and definite exertion of the intellect, I call in some way or in some degree beautiful".[1] But the saving notion of contemplation which distinguishes such contemplation from practical observation is left unexplained. We, however, after this history of its origin, are free to say that the beautiful is the object (and perhaps we may even add, the satisfaction) of the constructive impulse when that impulse has become contemplative instead of practical.

Instead of sculpture, which has been chosen because it is the easiest example, we may illustrate what has been said from artistic speech; remembering at the same time that speech may be used for its own sake, apparently, at an early period but still not strictly for its own sake but practically. For example, barbaric chants which are no more literature than the wild dances of the orgy are art. Much singing has a liturgical purpose or even a hypnotic one. Let us take the case then of speech and ask how speech becomes artistic, whether poetry or prose.[2] Speech is creative, and that fact offers such foundation as there is for a doctrine that has acquired authority in our own time, that linguistics and aesthetics are the same subject. That doctrine misses the difference of aesthetic from ordinary speech. For speech of itself is a construction for practical purpose. Either it is the means of creating theory or speculative consideration of things, and then it has the practical purpose of description, as in science. Or else it is manifestly practical, because it is the indication of our needs. To say 'I am cold' means in general 'help me to get warm'. It is a winter's night and friends are gathered together, and one says it would be comfortable

---

[1] *Modern Painters*, Pt. I. sec. i. ch. vi.
[2] The following pages down to p. 25 are taken from *Art and Instinct*, Herbert Spencer Lecture. Oxford, 1927.

to have more fire. That is constructive practical speech, and it may require not only for scientific description, but even for practical needs, much skill and niceness in the construction. Compare now those words with familiar ones:

Dissolve frigus, ligna super foco
Large reponens.

'Thaw away the cold, piling generous logs upon the fire.' The subject is indeed practical, but the words are not practical speech; they are used lovingly as words, though they express the same practical thought as before. They are not indeed striking as art; but for a striking difference take any accurate description of spring and the appearance of the fields at that time, which would be speech practical, and compare it with

When daisies pied and violets blue,
    And lady-smocks all silver white,
And cuckoo-buds of yellow hue,
    Do paint the meadows with delight.

There, at least in the last line, is enchantment, not from the thought alone but from the words.

But I have only illustrated and not explained. How do words get diverted from their practical use, and become enchanted? How does the magic get in? When physical objects, instead of being apprehended through practice, as originally they are, are apprehended theoretically, it was, we saw, because the normal response was diverted into another response and primarily into speech. But when speech itself, instead of being used as a practical means, becomes the end, there is no other response into which the speech-response can be diverted. If there were, we should be contemplating the words theoretically, as indeed we do in the science of them. Now the very thing which the poet does not do is to

contemplate his words theoretically. He makes an artistic and not a scientific use of them. Since then there is
no other action to detach words from practice, except
the action of poetic construction itself, what is it which
effects the detachment?

It is, I suggest, the constructive excitement itself
which attaches the words to the artist and detaches them
from their practical issues. The constructed object (the
word), instead of leading the mind on to its practical
effect, stimulates or serves as a signal for the continu-
ance of the constructive activity itself, and leads on to
the next constructed object (word) in the connected
work. Just as to pass from one thing to another in a
train of ideas loosens the first thing from its practical
urgency and makes it an object of theory, so the first
element in a constructional whole may lead on, through
the constructive process, to the next element, without
regard for the practical outcome. Then we have art. In
the constructive process the objects then are held or possessed by the constructor. The poet makes himself one
with his words and so holds them to himself, and detaches them from the subject matter which excited his
constructive impulse. In practical speech or the use of
speech for the practical means of description, there may
indeed be constructive passion, as anyone may attest
who recalls the effort of bare accurate description. But
it is the subject described which interests him: his use
of speech, his constructiveness, is a means to describing
the subject, which remains outside him and he a looker-
on. It is the subject which excites his constructive passion and he has to use his constructions in order to
satisfy the subject matter. The poetic excitement of
constructiveness, on the other hand, seeks to satisfy the
poet himself, at least to satisfy himself as well as be
adequate to the subject matter. And in this passionate

constructive effort he blends himself with his materials, which are words, holds them to himself, and thus constructiveness in speech becomes contemplative.

The statement that in art the artist mixes his mind with the materials demands explanation but it conceals no mystery, and implies no miracle. There is no literal blending of the mind with physical materials, as if such an idea could even be intelligible. It used to be said of a famous cricketer that he bowled or batted, I forget which, with his head. The use of his head was exhibited in the cunning direction which he gave to the ball. In the same way, the mixing of the artist's mind with his materials means that elements in the work of art, whether actual new material, or the form given to the material before him, are supplied at the initiative of the mind instead of that of something outside him. Let us take for convenience the simple case of a portrait bust, and for the moment disregard the difference of the matter which the artist uses and the form he gives to his clay. He is no photographer and does not reproduce the subject's head mechanically as it may be reproduced in marble by a cutting instrument which follows directly or indirectly the form of the head. He may be aware in himself of no ideas of the character of the person he is representing, and may to his own mind be copying the head faithfully.[1] In fact he stresses here, and omits there, so that the result embodies his vision but yet is a study of the original. The major part of the work is suggested from the model; but some elements are suggested in the working of the artist's mind. He makes his bust live by importing into the dead clay the life which he sees in the model or subject. With his hand he imputes life to the clay.

The process is familiar from ordinary perception in

[1] See again later, Chapter IV. p. 64.

which, according to James's well-known phrase, half comes from the object and half from the observer's mind. The observer interprets what he sees. But what he adds to what he sees is of the same order as what he sees, is physical and not mental. What goes on in his mind is the mental act, the conation, of which the object is the physical addition he makes to the thing he perceives. That conation is started in his mind, in virtue of his past experience, by the mental act provoked in him by the external object. He complicates that simple mental process by enlargement. The elements he adds may have been first entertained by him consciously in the form of an imaginative act. But most commonly his supplementary act does not reach the level of imagination. Rather it is 'ideal supplementation', 'tied ideas', as when we see the ice cold. Or it may not reach the conscious level at all. In every case what happens is that, for one reason or another, an impulse or conation is started internally and to that interior conation an external object corresponds, which is a modification of the actual external thing which would have provoked such internal conation. The object so brought before the mind forms part of the whole perceived external object because the conation to which it corresponds is linked into a unity with the conations evoked by the presented external thing. This is the simple process of imputation, and the imputation characteristic of the work of art is precisely of this nature. The mind is mixed in artistic creation with its materials because the impulses initiated in it in the course of construction are reflected in the materials as worked up into their artistic form.

This unmysterious statement has been conjoined or overlaid with more disputable elements in the notion of *Einfühlung* or Empathy which is connected with

the name of Lipps, according to which a man feels
himself into the work of art in a kind of sympathy
with it. The great importance of this notion is admitted;
and I regret my present inability to discuss it.[1] I
content myself with the modester position I have tried
to describe, that the artist from his personality initiates
the modifications of the material work which are necessary constituents of its artistic reality.

Such then is the aesthetic impulse, and the emotion
or sentiment which accompanies or is part of it is the
aesthetic sentiment. Such too is, I believe, its affiliation
with impulses which are found lower down the scale in
the animals. Instinct is a conception whose application
is greatly questioned at the present time, but I see no
reason why we should not adopt the usage of Mr.
McDougall[2] and call the impulse of constructiveness an
instinct. I prefer in general to use the less questionable
word impulse; and in order to avoid misconception and
irrelevant criticism I may as well say here that, wherever here or hereafter I shall speak of impulses or instincts, I mean no hidden entity such as might recall
the faculties of the older psychology, but am using a
word to cover the fact that under certain circumstances
the animal or man does for certain internal reasons do
certain acts and certain complexes of acts—that the
bird is moved to build its nest, for instance; or again
when I speak of the instinct or impulse of curiosity,
that the dog does pursue smells and examine them, or
(to speak of the impulse of sociality) that a man does
for internal causes associate with his fellows. The words
signify internal tendencies to perform certain actions

[1] Of Lipps I know only the earlier *Raumästhetik* (1897), not the large later
Asthetik (1903). A full account of the doctrine of *Einfühlung* will be found in
Lord Listowel's *Critical History of Modern Aesthetics*, just published.
[2] In *Outline of Psychology*, London, 1923, chapter v. But see also his later
The Energies of Men, London, 1933, chapter v.

which are observed. Which of them deserve the name
of instincts is a matter left to the psychologist, as likewise which are only secondary and acquired, and which
are original.

So far as the analysis goes of the psychological conditions of the apprehension, I have done little more
than repeat in another form the doctrine of Kant, the
greatest name in aesthetics, who declared that the
judgment of beauty arises in respect of an object when
the concept of it which is made by the understanding
works in harmony with the imagination which it sets
going; that describes in my language a blending of data
supplied by the subject matter itself and the elements
which are imported into or imputed to it by the mind
imaginatively. Kant began his inquiry with natural
beauty, beauty which is given to us, and accordingly
failed to ask for the impulsive basis of aesthetic apprehension, as we must ask where the object has to be
created. On the other hand Burke, by whom Kant was
so greatly influenced, and upon whom he so greatly
improved, did endeavour to trace back the apprehension of beauty and the sublime to instinctive sources.
He showed his originality in the work he wrote when
he was a very young man by such reference, and the
above inquiry follows his fortunate precedent. He referred the sublime to the instinct of self-preservation
and the beautiful to that of society, which includes in
particular the instinct of sex. Sublimity was aroused
by dangerous and terrifying objects, which threatened
existence; beauty by objects which appealed to our
tenderness. So far as beauty is concerned he thus anticipated Darwin's attempt to establish a relation between
the decorative appendages and colouring of animals
and the purposes of mating. Burke knew well enough
that the sense of the sublime is not the same thing as

terror, nor the sense of beauty mere animal tenderness. He was not misled into that blind alley. Unfortunately he does not tell us wherein the difference lies, and herein lies his failure. His merit lies in the appeal to the instincts, though he missed identifying the really relevant instinct.

Both Burke and Kant in occupying themselves so largely with natural beauty are analysing aesthetic appreciation rather than aesthetic production. Accordingly Kant did not look for an instinctive basis for aesthetic judgment, and Burke who did missed it. For from apprehending beauty in nature to apprehending it in art there is no easy road. We cannot understand from the beauty of nature how we come to treat material objects for themselves and make them beautiful, nor indeed can we understand in Kant's analysis why it is that a beautiful object should set going in ourselves both understanding and imagination and bring them into harmony. We cannot proceed from appreciation to creation. But we can proceed from creation to appreciation. As Mr. Croce makes clear, appreciation of beautiful art is to repeat the creation of it, so far as the spectator can. The work of art throws the spectator back into the frame of mind in which the artist produced it. Goethe when he was in Italy tried with small success under the tutorship of Tischbein to become a painter. The gods had given him the gift of creativeness in speech, but not the gift of handling creatively the pencil.[1] Nevertheless Goethe was thankful for his attempts to become a painter because they enabled him to understand pictures. The picture sets

---

[1] Vieles hab' ich versucht, gezeichnet, in Kupfer gestochen,
Öl gemalt, in Ton hab' ich auch manches gedruckt,
Unbeständig jedoch, und nichts gelernt noch geleistet.
Nur ein einzig Talent bracht' ich der Meisterschaft nah:
Deutsch zu schreiben, und so verderb' ich unglücklicher Dichter
In dem schlechtesten Stoff leider nun Leben und Kunst.

I borrow the reference from K. Vossler, *Spirit of Language*. London, 1932.

the spectator following the artist's hand, the poem read aloud sets the reader constructing the words into their perfection of unity, and incidentally, though, as we shall see later, this is strictly irrelevant, may induce in us the passions which supplied the poet with his words. There is therefore no difference in kind between aesthetic appreciation and aesthetic creation. The one is the pale shadow of the other, as passively at the suggestion of the accomplished work the spectator recovers the creator's mind.

Natural Beauty.—When we approach the beauty of nature[1] after learning what beauty is in art, we discover, however, that the appreciation of natural beauty is more than passive following of the artist's work. It is itself creation, creation in the less exacting form of selection. Nature is beautiful only if we see it with the artist's eye, and all of us are artists in our degree in so far as we find beauty in nature. The nature we find beautiful is not bare nature as she exists apart from us but nature as seen by the artistic eye; every landscape, as Mr. Santayana says,[2] "to be seen has to be composed". We find nature beautiful not because she is beautiful herself but because we select from nature and combine, as the artist does more plainly when he works with pigments. Coleridge's saying,

> O Lady, we receive but what we give,
> And in our life alone does nature live,

goes too far. Nature does live for herself without us to share her life. But she is not beautiful without us to unpiece her and repiece. We do this in the contemplation to which Ruskin referred our feeling for beauty, which

[1] The rest of the chapter is taken from 'Art and Nature', *Bulletin of the John Rylands Library.* Manchester, vol. ii. 1927.
[2] *The Sense of Beauty*, p. 133. London, 1896.

contemplation is but the artist's function at its most primitive stage. For just as few men have the religious passion, but most men feel the presence of something which is deity, in art while only the few are initiate, there are many wand-bearers. Yet these many are not pretenders as the Greek proverb seems to suggest. For the wand-bearers are the indiscriminate herd of us who find nature beautiful and do not even know that we are unconscious artists. It is not so strange that to the young Wordsworth nature was all in all, and that the sounding cataract haunted him like a passion. He was fledging himself for the poet's flight. The rest of us never get beyond that use of the constructiveness (which as employed about the artistic medium is art) which consists in feeling nature's beauty. Not all of us even do this; for to some nature is not so much beautiful as pleasant or healthful or full of bounty: they are nearer to the Greek view of landscape as Ruskin describes it.[1]

Small wonder that we do not know that we are artists unawares. For the appreciation of nature's beauty is unreflective; and even when we reflect, it is not so easy to recognise that the beauty of a sunset or a pure colour is a construction on our part and an interpretation. Yet the artist's exercise of his gift is also in the main unconscious or unreflective; and perhaps even the artist finds it difficult to reflect upon his art and recognise its real character.

I cannot do better than quote a paragraph from Mr. Richards:[2] "The fact that roses, sunsets, and so forth are so often found to present harmonious combinations of colour may appear a little puzzling. . . . But the vast range of close gradations, which a rose petal, for example, presents, supplies the explanation. Out of all

[1] *Modern Painters*, Pt. IV. ch. xiii. 'Of Classical Landscape.'
[2] *Principles of Literary Criticism*, p. 155. London, 1925.

these the eye picks that gradation which best accords
with the other colours chosen. There is usually some
set of colours in some harmonious relation to one another to be selected out of the multitudinous gradations
which natural objects in most lightings present; and
there are evident reasons why the eye of a sensitive
person should, when it can, pick out those gradations
which best accord. The great range of different possible
selections is, however, of importance. It explains the
fact that we see such different colours for instance when
gloomy and when gay, and thus how the actual selection made by an artist may reveal the kind and direction of the impulses which are active in him at the
moment of selection.''

The delight we take in purity of colours or tones is
another illustration of unconscious artistic vision. Pure
colours and tones do not exist in nature in isolation.
They have to be selected from the colours or tones into
which they grade. Even pure notes do not exist, and
still less pure tones without overtones. Pure colours or
tones suggest their own purity, their contrast with their
surrounding fringe of experiences, their refinement from
dross. Of this anyone may satisfy himself who is aware
of the strange beauty of a simple tone on a tuning
fork, unlike the pleasure from a musical note. Such a
pure experience is a compound one, and owes its beauty
to its artistic or artificial suggestions.

One more illustration of the silent constructive artistry
of natural beauty and I have done. The beauty of the
human face or form is often at least in part a pleasure
due to the dim stirring of the impulse of sex, and where
this happens is not a contemplative but a practical
pleasure. The disinterested contemplation of a beautiful
face of either sex carries with it suggestions of character
or of characteristic or at any rate significant form.

When we have recognised this we cease to think that in the more difficult case of lovely scenery, Grasmere or Loch Lomond seen from Tarbet, nature is beautiful of herself. She is so rather because of the significant line or, where we yield to the pathetic fallacy, because of the response of the landscape to a mood which selects from nature the shapes and colours that suit that mood. It is the mute Keats or Wordsworth or the numb Turner within us which makes these scenes lovely, though our lips shall never and could never speak a poem nor our minds direct our hands to use the brush.

If the recognition of beauty in nature is in the end artistic in character, we can now see easily enough how it differs from art. The creative artist, who alone is called artist, and rightly so, fashions his material to his purpose, and the formed material is something which he has to make to carry his artistic purpose. Making is more than practice, for practice terminates upon its object, as when I strike an enemy or pay a compliment to a friend. Making creates a new object or at least creates a form. And artistic making goes also beyond technical craft. The builder makes a house for its useful purpose. But the architect who seeks to make the house beautiful has over and above the needs of utility to consider the composition of his stones and bricks and other material for their own sakes. The poet operates with words as words and not as mere instruments for action: and the painter's pigments are his language in the same sense. And the artist has to manipulate his material so that it shall become beautiful.

Now in nature the material is already present, the gift of nature. He who finds nature beautiful does not manipulate with chisel or brush or voice the material he uses, he makes it beautiful by selection and composition and, if need be, imaginative addition. In this

D

way, like the artist, he imputes his mind to nature.
But he needs no skill but that of his imagination. The
hardest part of the artist's work is done, the execution or
technique by which he works out his creative impulse
into reality. The artist reacts to the subject which in-
spires him by moulding his chosen medium to suit his
impulse, and that material is stone or words, and even
when he creates drama, his material is not mere men
but the dramatic speech and acts of men. But the
material for natural beauty is actual trees and animals
and lakes and men. There is no medium chosen by
convention, a word I use without disrespect, still less
for belittlement; for nature herself, according to the
thought of Polixenes in the play, imposes the convention. These actual real things the admirer of nature
moulds to suit his imagination, and makes of the landscape a composition; makes the marigold go to bed
with the sun and with him rise weeping; makes of a
human form an athlete or even sees him as a Greek
disc-thrower or spear-bearer. For though this last is but
one of the ways in which we make a composition out of
natural objects, some part may even be assigned in our
judgment of natural objects to the influence of familiar
works of art.

CHAPTER III

PRIMARILY, then, beauty or the beautiful is what satisfies the impulse to beauty as it has been described—the constructive impulse diverted from practice and become contemplative. We can now proceed to describe the qualities of the beautiful whether in art or nature in virtue of which it pleases after this fashion. We can use the nature of the impulse as a key to lay open the characters of the object which corresponds to it and gratifies it, instead of doing as writers in aesthetics are apt to do, without convincing success, who endeavour to analyse the nature of the object itself.

In the first place, the beautiful as that which satisfies an impulse become contemplative is disinterested. This feature is the foundation of its objectivity which will fall to be discussed later at more length. Even the subjective valuation of beauty is unselfish. To say 'I think this beautiful' does not mean that it is beautiful for me alone. I am not thinking of myself, but modestly declaring that the object satisfies my sense of beauty. In essence the beautiful is shareable, even though it makes no claim to be such, because it is not personal and practical.

This feature has been unquestionable ever since Kant first made it plain. There is more difficulty in the next proposition, that the beautiful is in a certain sense illusory, or rather contains an element of illusion. But this follows at once from the nature of the process which creates beauty. The artist introduces into his materials

35

(that is into the form of them, since he does not make
his materials but only gives them form, and, even when,
as in song, he does actually supply the materials, he
gives them form as well) elements derived from his own
personality and expressed in turn in the material form.
To revert to the easier case of sculpture, the Hermes
looks not merely marble but alive and divine and playful. Hence beauty attaches, as has been long an
aesthetic commonplace, to the appearance and not to
the practical reality of the work of art, which is beautiful only if the mind is there which can add to the palpable material the features which the artist has embodied in it. In the sense in which illusion means a
mistaken interpretation of the reality, the work of art
is not, in the strict use of the word, illusory. For in
perception of a real object the elements we impute in
our interpretation do actually belong to the object perceived; the fragrance we do not see in the orange, the
cold we do not see in the ice, belong to the thing we
perceive and are verified if we smell the orange or touch
the ice. Correspondingly, in illusion proper, as when
we take a reflection to be a real thing, the imputed
characters really do belong to the object we fancy, but
are wrongly imputed to the object which is actually
present. But the features we impute in art to the
material do not belong to it, are in general foreign to
it. The marble which looks alive is itself a block of
stone; the figures of Giotto, if I may take the example
made familiar by Mr. Berenson, press upon the ground
they tread on, as the figures of the lesser artist Duccio,
he says, do not; "the baseless fabric of this vision" has
magic which the mere words by themselves have not.

In truth the work of art owes its reality to its illusori-
ness, and consequently illusory is an unhappy epithet.[1]

---

[1] Schiller's phrase 'aesthetic semblance' (so Bosanquet renders *aesthetischer*

The work of art asks not to be believed as we believe in things of the practical world in which we live, submitting ourselves to it.[1] In art, according to Bacon's phrase, we submit to ourselves the shows of things. We create an autonomous world, a blending of the physical with ourselves, and therefore a new reality within the so-called real world; neither believed nor disbelieved but entertained, and therefore not acted upon. I quote the words of Mr. A. C. Bradley which have become classical: "Its nature (*i.e.* poetry's) is to be not a part, nor yet a copy of the real world (as we commonly understand that phrase) but to be a world by itself, independent, complete, autonomous".[2]

The examples I have taken have been from representational sculpture and painting. I am not raising at present the question of the nature of formal painting or sculpture, though I have been assuming throughout that what the artist deals with, and it is obvious enough, is the form of his materials, the relations of line and plane and surface and volume and colour and light and shade. What is plain in examples drawn from the plastic arts is plain also in examples from literature, and especially poetry, that the literary artist imports into his words characters which are foreign to them as words of practical use. In the first place, as we have seen, it is not only the materials he introduces but those which he finds that become objects of contemplation. The meaning which in customary speech is attached to the sound of the word is in art blended or fused with the sounds. The sounds not only have meanings, that is they refer to things, but they are charged with their

---

Schein') is perhaps preferable, besides its authority. I take this opportunity of recording my indebtedness to Bosanquet's writings in Aesthetics.

[1] See R. G. Collingwood, *Outlines of a Philosophy of Art* (Oxford, 1925, pp. 11 foll., and *Speculum Mentis* (Oxford, 1924), section iii.

[2] *Oxford Lectures on Poetry*, p. 5. London, 1909.

meanings and indissolubly one with them. For words
or other expressive products become the material of
art when they are used not for the sake of the things
which they mean but in themselves and for their own
sake.[1] It is therefore mistaken to hold all spoken words
to be aesthetic; they are in general purely semantic.
Language becomes aesthetic only when it in turn becomes an object, and as such is revealed to the speaker
charged with its meaning. It now not merely means its
meaning and serves as a guide to the thing it means,
and as in general happens, passes out of the mind when
the mind is directed upon the thing through it; but is
held there and becomes itself the thing which occupies
the mind, and no longer merely has a meaning but is
charged with meaning or fused with it.

I must dwell a little longer upon this; for a word
charged with meaning becomes a different thing from a
word *with* a meaning. There is no mystery about meaning. A thing (*e.g.* a word) *means* the real things or
qualities or patterns of things for which it stands. But
in art the word or marble or drawing has welded into
its being the things which it means. Its meaning is part
of it in the same way as in the perception of an orange
the round, yellow form does not merely stand for the
juiciness of the orange but is actually qualified by it and
fused with it into one. In the marble block the Hermes
does not merely mean life and divinity but is divine
and alive, in so far as we appreciate it as a work of art.
Its imputations, which come to it from the appreciating
mind, and, unlike those of perceived objects, do not
belong to it as a physical thing, are, for the appreciating
mind, part of its nature. The artist or the spectator do
not ask if the Hermes is really alive; they raise no

---

[1] The following down to p. 41 is taken largely from *Art and the Material*,
Adamson Lecture. Manchester, 1925.

question of true and false;[1] they see it so. This which is
so clear with the statue is true also of language in art.
The words are no longer mere sounds, but are alive
with the qualities they mean.

Secondly, besides this the artist gives his words, or
some of them, a meaning which they do not of themselves possess, and, paradoxical as it may seem that
words take on in art qualities they do not of themselves
possess, that is the fact; a fact not stranger in itself than
that the dead marble seems alive. It may not be single
words; it may only be whole phrases, and it is always
the whole phrase, the run of the words in their unity,
which is predominant in producing the result,[2] or it
may only be the poem as a whole. Certain it is that in
a poem the words are new things altered from their
common use; enchanting they may be, but they are
always enchanted; magical in both senses of that word.
Any illustrations from great poetry will serve:

> St. Agnes' Eve—Ah, bitter chill it was!
> The owl, for all his feathers, was a-cold;

the enchanted version of the scientific or historical fact
that it was a cold night, so cold that the birds felt it
through their feathers. Or Hamlet's dying words to
Horatio:

> If ever thou didst hold me in thy heart
> Absent thee from felicity awhile,
> And in this harsh world draw thy breath in pain
> To tell my story:

the words are bewitching music, as Mr. A. C. Bradley
says; my point is that they are bewitched. Or this of
the flowers in *Winter's Tale*:

> Daffodils,
> That come before the swallow dares, and take
> The winds of March with beauty.

[1] R. G. Collingwood, as cited in note on p. 37.
[2] See later, Chapter IV. p. 70 f.

These are examples of easy or facile beauty, as the critics call it. Here is difficult beauty, again from *Winter's Tale* (Leontes to Camillo):

> Dost think I am so muddy, so unsettled,
> To appoint myself in this vexation; sully
> The purity and whiteness of my sheets,
> Which to preserve is sleep, which being spotted
> Is goads, thorns, nettles, tails of wasps?

Or an example of artistic humour, Lamb's comparison of the silence of a Quaker's meeting with "the uncommunicating muteness of fishes".

There may be, as in some of the above passages, some strangeness in a word which makes the passage magical. But consider, (as an illustration of the first point that words owe their aesthetic use to being not merely significant but one with their meaning), in its context, a familiar line in which Wordsworth seems to approach most near, not to prose, but, according to his own distinction, to scientific description:

> And never lifted up a single stone.[1]

The line does not merely describe the old man's grief: the grief is, for the aesthetic appreciation, actually in the words. Paraphrasing reduces words to useful and significant description, turns them into bare words again.

Sometimes it is not so much by way of addition but by way of subtraction that the strangeness enters in, as in the virile leanness of the style of Swift or even more so in that of Hobbes, where art reduces expression to a bare skeleton with a character of attractiveness foreign to skeletons. In prose as distinguished from poetry the strangeness may be hardly more than the

---

[1] One or two of these instances are taken from Matthew Arnold's introduction to Wordsworth. The example of difficult beauty is cited by Mr. Abercrombie as an illustration of Shakespeare's later style.

rhythm which belongs to artistic prose. The enchantment of poetry may likewise be due in some cases
entirely, and in all cases partially, to its mere rhythm
and metre, devices as these are for securing the unity
and as it were organic life of the poem. For rhythm and
metre are dependent upon the co-operating mind; they
do not belong to the words intrinsically even though
the words are regarded not as printed or written marks,
which they never properly are, but as spoken sounds
with their meanings. Their artistic value comes from
the intelligence of the speaker or reader, who may
speak the speech trippingly on the tongue or mouth it
as your players do, when we might as lief have them
spoken by the town-crier.

But the statement which seems so easily defensible in
the plastic arts and in literature seems paradoxical when
extended to the formal arts of pure music and architecture. I regret that I must in answer anticipate to a
certain extent what more properly belongs to a later
chapter (Chapter V.), when I shall deal with the contrast
of form and representation. But, to confine myself to
music, in pure music there is, it is maintained, no other
meaning than is contained in the tones themselves.
Music means nothing but the music. How can we then
declare that in music characters are introduced from
the mind which are foreign to the tones themselves?
For the view that music means only tones and their
relations I appeal to the authority of Eduard Hanslick
in his famous book, *Vom Musikalisch-Schoenen*.[1] He
was moved to anger by the doctrine that the subject of
music was emotion, its aim to render the emotions
through sound, and he insisted that it was concerned
solely with tones and had no interest outside them,

[1] 1854, 13th ed., 1922: Eng. transl., *The Beautiful in Music*, 1891. The
following pages down to p. 45 are taken from *Proceedings of the Aristotelian
Society*, N.S. vol. xxx., 1930, 'Beauty and Greatness in Art'.

though tones might suggest emotion. Whatever meaning it had was derived from the 'dynamic' element in
tones, their swiftness, weakness or strength, their rising
and falling; in a word, their movement. He even allows
himself to say that music can in this sense imitate the
movement of a physical process.[1] Lotze went much
further, and thought that great music corresponded
to the great movements in the world of things. But I
doubt if Lotze was not surrendering to the impulse to
find a subject for music outside music itself; and in
any case Hanslick's expression 'imitation' is not to
be pressed. The movement he mentions explicitly is
the movement of the separate tones themselves. But
such movement, not always in the separate tones but
amongst the tones, is the form of the music, and in
the spirit of Hanslick's treatment we may say that the
only subject matter in music is the sound-form itself.

But granted that music means only its tones and is
not representative, what room is left the artist to introduce his mind except in the selection of the tones? I
answer by another question. Though in Hanslick's
language the subject of the music be the movements of
tones and among the tones themselves, do these movements belong to the tones themselves in their material
character? Possibly the mere strength or weakness or
the rise and fall. But certainly the movements among
the tones, their flow, their harmony, melody, rhythm,
are these not characters introduced into the tones by
the artist; to which, indeed, the tones lend themselves
but which have meaning only for the constructive hearing? Tones themselves do not flow into one another any
more than lines do; I doubt if they can even be in
strictness said to rise and fall except for the imagination—'it had a dying fall'. It is of no use to answer that

[1] *Loc. cit.* p. 26.

even the tones themselves exist only for the mind which uses the ears. That may or may not be true philosophically; I think it is not true; but even if everything we perceive exists only in the mind, we must still distinguish between the mind as it sees or hears and as it apprehends relations of meaning which are constructed by and depend on the sustained action of the mind for their existence. Consider for a moment the simplest rhythm. Tones are repeated at certain intervals of time. The number of times they recur in a given time is a physical fact (or a mental one if you like). But their order as tones[1] exists only if it is noticed or experienced by the mind, like the belt of Orion, to use an example of Sir Arthur Eddington's, which is a fancy of ours; and to choose notes in that order is an illustration of the constructiveness of the mind, and to notice their rhythm is not merely to hear them in what the outsider would call a certain order but to hear the order itself, and receive a pleasure different from the pleasure the separate notes may give us.

It is so easy to overlook the active part the mind may play and attribute to mere sensible experiences, like tones themselves or colours, characters which do not strictly belong to them though conveyed to us through them. A pure tone, for instance, seems something very simple, and physically it is easy enough to describe, a tone unmixed with others. But, as before observed,[2] its purity as a musical value is the noticed contrast with an impure tone, or its noticed freedom from admixture. Tones harmonise in virtue of certain physical characters they possess, their vibration numbers and, perhaps, that their partials do not beat with one another. But

---

[1] I say 'as tones', because they have also a temporal order. All things have order of some kind, (see *Space, Time, and Deity*, vol. i. bk. ii. ch. v.) but some orders may depend on relation to the mind.

[2] Above, p. 32. I owe the remark to Bosanquet.

do we hear the harmony? We hear harmonious tones;
but it is the pleasure they give us distinct from the
pleasures appropriate to the separate tones, that is to
say, it is the pleasure of their relational form which
makes us attribute to them and their physical combination a quality which we call harmony. In arabesques, to which Hanslick so aptly likens music, the lines
themselves do not flow, but have geometrical characters which we so interpret for our delight, by apprehending their relations. Milton, who was a musician, has
touched in words, so familiar that I leave them to a
footnote to remind the reader,[1] these intricate relations
of tones to one another which give form to the whole
but are the increment, in terms of tones, to the tones
themselves from the side of the creative or from that of
the appreciating mind.

It may still be answered, granted that the rhythm
and melody and harmony of tones are made by the
composer who selects the tones for this purpose; yet
when the music is once composed the form belongs to
it and not to us.[2] No, it still has to be noticed by the
hearer through the aesthetic or formal or, I should say,
constructive or reconstructive act with its relevant
pleasure. And thus the form needs sustainment from
the hearer's mind, as much as it needed creation from
the composer's mind. The appreciative reconstruction
may be more or less passive, may require more or less
effort according to the familiarity of the forms employed
and the degree of musical education of the hearer.[3] The

---

[1] In notes with many a winding bout
Of linked sweetness long drawn out;
With wanton need, and giddy cunning,
The melting voice through mazes running,
Untwisting all the chains that tie
The hidden soul of harmony.

[2] For this objection see A. C. A. Rainer, 'The Field of Aesthetics' (*Mind*,
N.S., vol. 38, 1929, esp. p. 179).

[3] See R. M. Ogden, *Hearing* (London, 1924), chs. vi. xiii.

beauty accomplished in the finished work stimulates
the hearer to hear it in such and such a way; just as the
accomplished objects in nature, the landscape or the
face, stimulate us so to select from them or add to
them as to see their beauty. Hence the unlimited possibility of different interpretations even of pure music
by the executant, a freedom independent as I suppose
of whether he treats his music, as some do, with an
emotional bias or a tendency to interpret by help of
pictorial bias. I admit that to call the harmony foreign
to the material is to use strange language, which was
suggested by the palpable foreignness of the subject to
the material in representative painting or sculpture. If
the only art we knew were that of absolute music I
could not say, as I shall say,[1] that the subject in art is
foreign to the material. But that is because here in
pure music the subject is identical with the form, and,
of course, the form is not *foreign* to the material but
congruous with and only distinguishable from it.

In architecture, in like manner, though the architect
is fashioning his work out of the relations of line and
space and mass presented by his materials, empathy[2]
introduces as in music elements which do not belong
to the material in its purely mechanical character.

And if it is true that even the plastic arts of painting
and sculpture are most art when they approximate to
music and become formal, it will be true over the whole
field that the beautiful contains ingredients of what
does not properly belong to its material but is imputed
to it by the constructive mind. By beginning, as I have
done, with representative art, where imputation from
the mind is obvious, because through the moulding of
the material into a certain form the artist introduces

---

[1] Later, Chapter V. p. 79.
[2] As in the familiar Lippsian example of the column springing to sustain
the weight of the beam.

also nuances into the representative elements themselves, we have been thus helped to recognise that in a
purely formal art like pure music, there is present in
the form itself something imputed to the material by,
and imported into it from, the mind, a significance
which the bare materials have not of themselves, and
which, even when the work is finished, can only be
recovered by the reconstructive act of the appreciating
onlooker.

But the culmination of the arts in music enables us
to retrace our steps and recognise that even in representative art it is the form which contains the vital
work of the mind, and not those subsidiary readings of
the material elements themselves, taken singly, which
were rightly dwelt on when we considered plastic art
or literature. Only we must not understand form as
mere arrangement in space or time, but as the system
of relations in which the parts of the material are unified; the form of a picture is dynamic as much as that
of music, the form of a poem is not merely an arrangement of sounds, nor even of sounds with their meanings,
but the interplay of them. Accordingly when I dwelt
on the strangeness which words may possess in a poem,
I have now to remember that they owe their strangeness to their function as elements in the formal whole;
and that it is for this that they are chosen even when
they are strange in themselves taken singly. Music
enables us to see the secret of beauty in the arts, whose
beauty is hidden under wrappings which fall off in the
highest art.

It follows in the third place from these observations
that the work of art has significant form. The phrase
belongs to Mr. Roger Fry and Mr. Clive Bell,[1] and

---

[1] R. Fry, *Vision and Design*. London, 1920; *Transformations*, London, 1926.
Bell, *Art*. London, 1914.

the importance of the conception is great. The whole of
what precedes about the part which mind plays in the
beautiful may in fact be regarded as a commentary
upon the conception, as it presents itself to me: the
work of the mind lies in significance imported into the
material through its form. If it be asked of what is the
form significant[1] the answer is that the significance lies
in the form itself, understood as has been just explained, but that if the art is representative the form
may be described also with reference to the subject, it
means dancing girls, or Venus rising from the sea, or a
natural scene, while in formal art it can only be described by its own pattern. This statement is, however,
subject to what will be added in Chapter V. about the
relation of the two kinds of art, that formal art is the
limit of representative art, where the represented subject has become the formed material itself. Replace the
word significant by 'meaningful', and the difficulties
of the phrase 'significant form' perhaps disappear.

Fourthly, the work of art presents the character
anciently ascribed to it of unity in variety, a character
it shares with the true and the good. This character of
the beautiful, which is obvious to inspection, it possesses because of the unity of the act of construction
of the work out of its many and various elements.
That act gives to the work of art an organic character
which fits it to be an individual existence in that autonomous world of which it is a member, even as in the
real world of external nature things maintain themselves as individuals in virtue of their organic unity.

But in nature the unity of things is given to us, however it has been brought about. In the work of art it is
made by the artist and is accounted for by the impulse
or instinct of constructiveness in its qualified form, by

---

[1] I was guilty myself of raising this doubt in *Art and Instinct*, p. 23.

the aesthetic impulse with its inherent aesthetic sentiment or emotion. Even in natural beautiful forms
we reconstruct what is given to us, and in admiring
the exquisite adaptation of the animal or plant to
the performance of its functions, we interpret it in the
likeness of our own constructiveness, and find it beautiful because of the pleasure which it so gives to our
aesthetic sense. For it is one thing merely to observe
such adaptation as an existing fact and another thing
to admire such adaptation; when we admire it we
are introducing our own sense of design. We do so even
more obviously, when we admire a manufactured object
like a locomotive because of its success in performing
its end and call it beautiful.

In affirming the existence of this sentiment, I regret
to find myself at variance with Mr. Ivor Richards,
with whom I should for my own sake wish to agree. In
a well-known passage[1] he writes: "When we look at a
picture, or read a poem, or listen to music, we are not
doing something quite unlike what we were doing on
our way to the Gallery or when we dressed in the morning. The fashion in which the experience is caused in
us is different, and as a rule the experience is more
complex and, if we are successful, more unified. But
our activity is not of a fundamentally different kind."
Quite so: we dress because we want or have to do so,
and the stages of the process are the means of effecting
our purpose. In the making of the work of art, we obey
another impulse, and it is important to put our finger
upon it. For Mr. Richards, if I render him rightly,
the aesthetic experience is nothing more than an equilibrium established between the mental states of whatever kind in which the artist or the spectator of the art

---

[1] *Principles of Literary Criticism*, p. 16. London, 1925. The following down
to p. 50 is taken with alterations from the article 'Beauty and Greatness in Art'
mentioned above.

reacts to the subject or topic on which in a poem he writes or in a picture he paints. Now without the aesthetic impulse it is difficult to see how the mind intent upon its topic could settle down into that particular balance or equilibrium of reactions which is the so-called beautiful state of mind. Still harder is it to understand how it could guide the hand with its brush or chisel to produce the picture or statue. We shall find the same problem facing us in morals in different material. There is perhaps a certain suspicion (however little justifiable) of preciosity in the idea of a special aesthetic sentiment or emotion, a suspicion which can, however, hardly be suggested where it is recognised that every man is in his degree an artist and shows his artistry in ability to appreciate a work of art or natural beauty. It is not quite so common or so well developed as the habit of dressing but it is singularly inexclusive.

Now I quite understand that in morals a repulsion should be felt to theories that right conduct is fixed by reason, a method of action which for all its grand name no man can verify the existence of in himself, in his experience of determining right conduct; and that in the revulsion from such theories we should think (as once I myself thought) that the passions balance one another and secure an equilibrium which issues in the virtuous action. But what is it which impels us to balance one motive against another? For motives have not hands and do not pull the man divers ways so as to produce a resultant. The balance must be effected by some other passion though it is not reason. Just so, that out of a mind intent upon a certain subject that subject should be induced upon marble or canvas or in the medium of words in the only way possible, that is, in the form of the marble or the pigments or the words —this can only be, or at least this is so, effected, be-

E

cause some passion is excited in the mind which is
satisfied by external creation, and which, being intent
upon the subject, makes use of the mental tendencies
corresponding to that subject in order to guide itself
in its work.

I cannot help thinking that what I should like to
believe is an oversight on Mr. Richards's part, but is,
I fear, a real antagonism, comes from his describing
a work of art as an experience; and so the poem which
is a poetic experience is part of the ordinary world of
experience, though an isolated and fragmentary one.
Experience is so tricky a term. A table is an experience
to a man who sees it, but a table in a picture is that
and more. What I desiderate in the statement that a
poem is an experience is the words themselves; or in a
picture the pigments of it; and hence the work of art
on this view becomes a condition of the mind and not an
external thing which, by the mind's action, has been
formed to be full of meaning. Beauty on the one view
is a property of the mental state; that is, it is these
mental reactions to the subject matter (really a set of
bodily experiences) in so far as they settle down into
a unity. On the view I am urging beauty is, as it is
commonly supposed to be, a property of the work of
art, and not something mysterious or indescribable, but
simply that formal disposition of the physical material
in so far as it produces in the mind a special pleasure
by satisfying a certain impulse in the mind to produce
such external objects.

It is commonly recognised that the subject matter of
fine art, unlike that of science, is particular or rather
individual and not general or universal, concrete and
not abstract, sensuous and not intellectual. This fifth
feature of the beautiful in art is usually stated as a
result of simple inspection of the subjects of art, with-

out much illumination of the question why such subjects choose art for their embodiment. In reality it follows from the material character of art, and corresponds
in the subject matter to the particular character of the
material; just as the harmony in the beautiful corresponds to the unity of the act by which it is created.
For fine art is not thoughts or images but individual
material things, is made of words or tones or pigments
or stone which are necessarily particular. The work of
art is a particular concrete thing, and everything that
it means is embodied in this particular material. The
artist's subject matter is such as can be so embodied,
and in the final shape it assumes, after all the elaboration it has undergone in the artist's mind, is that picture of things which is arrived at in the interplay of so-
called artistic vision and 'expression': an interplay in
which, if a priority must be given, the so-called expression determines the vision rather than the vision
the expression. The full force of this statement awaits
justification in the succeeding chapter. All attempts to
describe the vision of the artist, even such a description
as Mr. Bergson's, are in the air, till we recognise that
his vision is reached in the effort to express his mind by
particular material means. Start on the other hand with
the truth that a work of art is a particular material
structure, and the concrete insight of the artist into his
subject matter becomes intelligible.

The work of art may imply thought to any extent,
only not as thought, but as reduced to particular
images or perceptions conveyed through a particular
piece of material. Hence allegories, whether in literature or in other arts, are felt to be incongruous patch-
work, though the text may, as in the *Faery Queene*,
taken by itself apart from the allegory, be exquisitely
beautiful. Scientific work, especially mathematical

work which is purely conceptual, may indeed possess the appearance of beauty, because of the inner coherence which it shares with fine art, or may resemble a piece of architecture. But it is called beautiful rather by analogy than intrinsically.

Literature may seem to present a difficulty. Are not words the names of concepts, and does not literature accordingly produce its effects by a combination of concepts? The answer is found in what was said above of the use of words in literary art, not as symbols of their meanings, but as particular words, spoken or written, charged with meanings which have become as particular as the words themselves. In verification whereof we may note the varying grades of success with which a poem attains its end, when it deals with intellectual subjects, according to the degree in which its thoughts are fused with its words. Long extracts are not necessary; but contrast, for all the splendour of the rhetoric, Pope's "All are but parts of one stupendous whole", etc., with its incomplete and half-hearted fusion of thought and speech,[1] with the far greater passage of Wordsworth's *Tintern Abbey* upon the same topic ("a sense sublime of something far more deeply interfused", etc.), or this again with some of the philosophical *longueurs* of Wordsworth's own *Excursion*. Philosophical or scientific poems are successful in proportion as they attain this fusion; Lucretius, for instance, in a greater degree than Bridges' *Testament of Beauty*.

---

[1] Accordingly, if I may stray for a moment into literary criticism, Pope is, I should say, most of a poet (and I do not doubt that he is a poet) in the Satires and Epistles where this fusion is completest.

CHAPTER IV

THE artist's work belongs to the order of creative as distinguished from that of passive imagination. The second we have not only in ordinary memory or expectation, but in one species of what is commonly called constructive imagination, in day-dreams or reveries or in dreams in general, that is, the comparatively idle play of fancy—comparatively idle, for there are no hard and fast lines of distinction in these matters of the mind's action; and dreams in particular are, some of them at least, as is well established, directed by a hidden purpose. The difference of such passive imagination from the creative sort is the absence from it of purpose. In passive imagination, images flare up in the mind, more or less like the perceptions we have had, or in new combinations which have had and will have no real existence. In the creative imagination of art, on the other hand, a new reality is created (not to linger on what has been already urged) which possesses, or may, if successful, possess beauty. And it is done by moulding the material of the art to express a purpose. Not the purpose of creating beauty, for that is the last thing the artist thinks of. As the scientific inquirer aims not at truth but at the solution of his problem, the artist aims to express the subject which occupies his mind in the means which he uses. His purpose may be dictated by passion but is still a passionate *purpose*. The artist works spontaneously: the poet sings, indeed, like the bird because he must, but with a directed passion, not as the

bird-wooer sings without forethought and predestin-
ately in the pursuit of his natural ends. 'Purpose' conceals no mystery. Even where it is most conscious it
means that action, provoked from without, is controlled
from within the agent's mind. Such controlling factors
are present in the work of art, not necessarily and perhaps rarely in conscious form, most often as a dominant
passion, which guides the artist more surely than conscious ideas, but yet unifying his choice of words or
colours or sounds into an expressive whole.

In attempting to trace his procedure in detail, we
must begin by noting certain distinctions which may be
regarded as provisional. The work of art consists of
materials which assume a certain form, two things
which are separable only in thought and not in reality.
Further, in the actual substance or contents of the work
of art, we note its topic or subject or subject matter or
meaning, a face for instance, or a party at cards, or a
landscape in storm, which occupies the artist's mind
and is the stimulus to or occasion of his production.
The subject may and does change between the incep-
tion of the work and its completion; in the final shape
which it assumes it is embodied in the work of art. In
representational art it is distinct from the rest of the
work; in non-representational art like music, there may
be no other subject but what is contained in the formed
material itself. We may thus conveniently distinguish
the mere subject of a work of art from what it means
and says to the artist, or the spectator, though in non-
representational art the two things coincide.

The topic or subject interests or agitates the artist
and throws him into an excitement in which we can
discriminate two sorts of elements, the passions appropriate to the subject and the passion proper to the
artist. At the risk of some confusion in the double use

of the word material, I shall call these respectively the material passions and the formal passion. The formal passion has been already identified. It is fed and controlled by the passions aroused by the subject, but is, though dependent on them, superadded to them, as their fine flowering into something they do not themselves contain. The difference is most obvious from illustrations. It is a long way from saying passionately 'I love you and always shall' to saying

> As fair art thou, my bonnie lass,
> So deep in love am I;
> And I will love thee still, my dear,
> Till a' the seas gang dry,

where the words of the poem are not a mere half-practical gesture appropriate to the material passion, but are handled for their own sakes, and with that strangeness which enters into the proportion of beauty.

A second example is even more familiar:

> And Ruth said, Intreat me not to leave thee, or to return from following after thee: for whither thou goest, I will go; and where thou lodgest, I will lodge: thy people shall be my people, and thy God my God: where thou diest, will I die, and there will I be buried: the Lord do so to me, and more also, if aught but death part thee and me.

where the material passion of the devotion of the alien daughter to her husband's mother and the images and thoughts suggested by this emotion can be distinguished from the white heat of artistic excitement which, fed by these ideas and feelings, issues or, if the metaphor be pardoned, overflows into a perfection of words which reveals the situations appropriate to her devotion as perhaps she could not herself describe them.[1]

In conduct Aristotle has put the same point once for all when, in describing bravery, he contrasts that virtue

[1] From 'Artistic Creation and Cosmic Creation', *Proceedings of the British Academy*, vol. xiii., 1927.

with the impulse to show pluck and face danger, and says that in true courage there is the impulse towards the beautiful (τὸ καλόν). It is this, I suppose, which is what the Herbartians meant when they spoke of the aesthetic and other feelings of value as formal. It is as necessary to recognise their special existence and status and the special impulses to which they belong as it is not to forget that, except in taking up and assimilating the impulses which feed them, they cannot operate. You cannot be generous without having something to give, were it only the widow's mite, and were the act only a thought or wish; nor pursue science without data; nor hardly indite a ballad to a mistress' eyebrow without some basic tenderness. I say hardly, for the material passions which gather round the subject and are felt by the artist himself may be replaced by thoughts or images he has of them, but need not feel himself except in sympathy. Not all poems are lyrical, and we cannot therefore accept the ruling of Mr. Croce that art is essentially lyrical; it is lyrical of the artistic impulse, but not necessarily except in lyrics and perhaps not always there lyrical of felt passions. Some have even supposed that Shakespeare's sonnets were some of them exercises in gallantry after the Italian fashion of the time. Improbable as this may seem from the internal evidence of the sonnets themselves, the point is well taken, and as before explained there are whole regions of poetry where the poet cannot be supposed to experience in his own person the passions he describes, but only to know them by that divination which artists possess above other men.[1]

---

[1] Browning's comment on Wordsworth's sonnet on the sonnet is well known:

With this same key
Shakespeare unlocked his heart. Once more!
Did Shakespeare? If so, the less Shakespeare he!

('House', *Collected Poems*, vol. ii. p. 479).

We have, then, to determine the part played in the artist's creation by images, and it is all the more needful to do so because of an opinion commonly entertained that the artist translates into material forms the images he has already in his mind.[1] Thus Mr. Lascelles Abercrombie (himself a poet and therefore particularly valuable to hear) writes:[2] "The moment of imaginative experience which possesses our minds the instant the poem is finished possessed the poet's mind the instant the poem began. For as soon as there flashed into complete existence in his mind this many-coloured experience with all its complex passion, the poem which we know was *conceived* as an inspiration. . . . So that it is also possible to consider the inspiration of a poem as distinguishable from the verbal art of it: namely as that which the verbal art exists to convey, and which can be distinctly known as such, however impossible it may be to describe it or express it at all in any other words than those of the poet." Even Mr. Croce, who identifies the image or intuition of the artist (or anyone else) with expression, and laughs at those who fancy they could themselves be Raphaels or Shakespeares if they had but the skill to express their beautiful imaginations, still urges that the artistic experience, though it is essentially expression, is purely mental, and that the actual physical embodiment of the experience is a technical matter and merely serves the purpose of communication. I do not desire to press the words of these writers, and in what I shall say I shall sometimes say what they would take for granted. But I believe there is at least much obscurity in their doctrines and even in the end error.

It is vital to distinguish again among the images

---

[1] From *Art and the Material*, Adamson Lecture. Manchester, 1925.
[2] *Theory of Poetry* (London, 1924), p. 58.

which have reference to the work of art images excited
by the subject matter from images of the artistic product itself. Now as to the first set, there can be no doubt
that such images precede in the artist's mind his work.
The subject matter calls up such images in proportion
to the artist's wealth of experience. They are images
about the subject matter and along with them there
may be unconscious thoughts or feelings which, like
the express images, control and feed the constructive
impulse. Here we note the relevance of what is said by
psycho-analysis. Dante's love for Beatrice Portinari was
part of the motives which supplied his art, and doubtless too the unrest hidden in an artist's unsatisfied life
may be a reason unknown to himself for seeking satisfaction in a world of seeming.[1] Under this head of preliminary mental work about the subject belongs the
stage through which the artist passes, which has been
described so well by Graham Wallas as incubation, *à
propos* not of art but of thought.[2] But all these images
or thoughts or vague unconscious stirrings are but
servants of the creative impulse, and they issue into
outward expression in the material only *via* that impulse. There is no direct road for them to voice or
hand. Neither are they images of what the artist means
to say or paint; they are not images of the artistic
product; nor is it they which are translated into the
material.

On the other hand, images of the product itself if
they existed might be said to be translated into the

[1] The reason why I apparently neglect the work of the psycho-analysts on art
is not merely that it lies so much outside my capacity and knowledge, but a
different one. In his *Introductory Lectures on Psycho-analysis* (Eng. transl.,
London, 1922) Mr. Freud speaks of the artist as seeking in art and phantasy a
refuge from the unsatisfied longings of real life which he has not the power to
gratify; and saving himself by true art from possible neurosis. I recognise the
interest and importance of this, but it still leaves open the question why art is
chosen for this purpose and what its nature is, and it is this I am concerned with.
[2] *The Art of Thought*, ch. iv. London, 1926.

material. But to speak generally (the qualifications must come later) there are no images of the product at all. The poem is not the translation of the poet's state of mind, for he does not know till he has said it either what he wants to say or how he shall say it. The imaginative experience supposed to be in his mind does not exist there. What does exist is the subject which detains him and fixes his thoughts and images and passions and gives his excitement a colour and direction which would be different with a different subject matter. Excitement caused and detained by this subject, and at once enlarged, enlightened and inflamed by insights into it, bubbles over into words or the movements of the brush or chisel. When the artist has achieved his product he knows from seeing it or hearing it what the purpose of his artistic effort was. He makes the discovery of what were the real directive forces of his action. All that he was aware of before, so far as he was aware of them, was the thoughts and emotions of the subject matter directly produced or indirectly suggested, and doubtless often presented in imaginative form. These combine with, or in part are identical with, the more or less unconscious movings and emotions yielded by his 'vision and faculty divine' and with the gathered expertness of his technical flair, to guide his hand or his voice or speech into the movements which end in the material work of art.

Two conclusions follow from this statement, which have been anticipated. The external work being an organic part of the creative process, it ceases to be possible to hold that the external material is needed merely in order to communicate the artistic experience to others. That experience would not exist except for material embodiment, which may of course be replaced by finished imagination of it, about which more presently. Next,[1] it follows that Wordsworth was, I must believe, mistaken when he said that there are many poets in the world, who have "the vision and the faculty divine; yet wanting the accomplishment of verse"; as if verse were a charm superadded to the real poetic gift. His own words about the poet give a truer view: "he murmurs by the running brooks a music sweeter than their own". Poets and all artists, it will be admitted, are more sensitive to things and persons than ordinary men. Such greater sensitiveness does not, however, make them poets. You have only to compare the magnificent lines describing the mystical absorption of the youth in the spectacle of nature, in the same poem,[2] with Spinoza's scientific account of the 'intellectual love of God' in order to recognise that two great men may have like emotions and the one be a poet and the other a philosopher, and the expression of each be perfect in its kind, but that of the one a poet's work, and that of the other a philosopher and scientific man's. In the second case the words only catch fire from the subject matter; in the other the words are themselves on fire.

What the exact character of the excitement is which is the proper impulse to creation, it may be difficult to say. It may be something of a shock to realise how

---

[1] The following pages of the chapter are taken in large part from *Brit. Journal of Psychology*, vol. iv., 1927, 'The Creative Process in the Artist's Mind'.

[2]   Sound needed none,
Nor any voice of joy; his spirit drank
The spectacle; sensation, soul, and form,
All melted into him; they swallowed up
His animal being; in them did he live;
And by them did he live; they were his life.
In such access of mind, in such high hour,
Of visitation from the living God,
Thought was not; in enjoyment it expired.
No thanks he breathed, he proffered no request;
Rapt into still communion that transcends
The imperfect offices of prayer and praise,
His mind was a thanksgiving to the power
That made him; it was blessedness and love.

lowly in character it may be. To judge from the glow that accompanies productive work of inferior kinds, such as everyone has experience of who tries to write a brief essay, or even a letter, and make the result as artistic as is open to him, the excitement is mainly a feeling of unrest which keeps one in suspense, but a directed suspense like that we are aware of when we try to remember a name which we have forgotten but know that it is connected with this, that and the other circumstance, and we feel ourselves straining towards it but unattaining. Over and above this, the impulse is felt mainly in bodily repercussions, in the visceral organs and the organs of secretion, about the heart and down the back and all over the body. It is a directed restlessness for it varies according to the topic, but what it is the indication of, what hidden movings urge us forward into the customary outlet of words or other forms of artistic material, is not disclosed until we have in semi-blindness achieved the desired product.

The truth of the above description[1] of what goes on in the mind in artistic production may be tested in various ways, two of which are only approximations to a real test. We may take our own selves, all of us artists in our degree, and observe ourselves in modest efforts to produce something artistic or beautiful, say an ordinary essay of a student who tries to make a finished composition. He does not, if I may trust my own experience, try to think out his work in an artistic form, but steeps himself in the subject, 'moons' over it, as we say, and when his interest is sufficiently strong lets himself go, and the words come of themselves. Anyone who happens to be blessed or cursed with the gift of humour, and practises it to some degree as a fine art, may test his own procedure. A person or topic releases

---

[1] From *Art and the Material* to p. 63.

within him a hidden spring of gaiety, flavoured perhaps
with a slight sub-malicious ingredient, and the spring
issues forth into jest. It is his gaiety which produces the
words, and no image of what he means to say. Hence it
is that the jester so rarely laughs at his own jest. His
laughter has preceded the jest and has been done with;
for him it is part of the cause of the jest, and not, as for
the hearers, the effect.

Or he may take a finished piece of art, and, observing
himself, think himself back into the artist's situation.
Any work of art will serve as a test. For instance, the
scene in Meredith's *Vittoria*, where the prima donna
sings the song of Italian freedom in the opera-house of
La Scala at Milan. In the agitation which such a passage throws us into (so violent that some readers can
hardly proceed beyond this point in the book) it is perfectly possible to distinguish (however much they are
interwoven) the passionate sympathy with the actors
in the situation from the proper aesthetic excitement,
felt in the fitness of the words both of the narrative and
the song to express the situation. It is not necessary to
suppose that Meredith or Shakespeare actually felt the
emotions of his characters, but only that he understood
them. Doubtless such emotional sympathy may be, and
probably often is, present as well, but, if it is, it is present to add fuel to the excitement of the proper creative
tendency, the tendency, I mean, to expression not in the
ways of anger or remorse or love, but in the ways of
speech or movements of the hand directing brush or
chisel. Herein is the answer to the old controversy raised
by Diderot (upon which Molière before him had ex
pressed an opinion in the same sense as Diderot[1])
whether the actor should feel himself or not into the

---

[1] *Impromptu de Versailles*, Sc. 1: "You show what an excellent comedian you
are by expressing so well a character contrary to your own humour".

emotions of his personages. With different actors the conditions of success will vary. Some may be content with the semi-intellectual excitement of understanding their parts, another may be able more readily to imitate his part by feeling its emotions, or at least may have his imitative procedure heightened by the simulation of the passions themselves.

But the only satisfactory test is the judgment of artists themselves, helped out by observation of their behaviour in creation, and since it is the business of artists to create and not to psychologise, there may be difficulty in extracting their answer to questions which seem to them strange and perhaps unimportant or, in the old sense of that word, impertinent. An inductive inquiry of this sort I have failed to perform by direct inquiry from living artists. Artists have, however, left incidental reports of themselves, like the familiar ones of Mozart, and Goethe's comparison of his own condition in writing some of his poems to somnambulism, which favour the doctrine stated here. Other records of artists' experiences have been collected by M. Dessoir in his book.[1]

I have, however, to confess my own failure of energy in the research. Two young writers of imaginative literature whom I consulted told me that in their best work they do not know beforehand what they mean to say; one of them admits that sometimes the work is thought out consciously beforehand with much labour and never with so satisfactory a result.

An opportunity which I have had of observing an artist, and a great one, at work appeared to me to bear out my sketch of the creative process. The artist, a sculptor, was unacquainted with his sitter, and could hardly have formed any preconceived idea of the kind of

[1] M. Dessoir, *Aesthetik u. allg. Kunstw.*, Stuttgart, 1906, Pt. II. ch. i.

character he was trying to produce in the clay. He in fact denied that he had, but declared that his sole object was to study the form of his sitter's head in every detail. To judge from his behaviour, which I was privileged to witness, he was utterly absorbed with the head he was modelling, and his excitement about it was manifest at every stage—first, when he was sketching the head each successive bit of clay was dabbed on to the growing shape, as if he were indulging in a violent pugilistic encounter with it, a gymnastic display which testified to his intentness on the exact delivery of each increment; and later when, the general form being modelled, the smaller knife was used to perfect the detailed structure, here removing clay or indenting lines, here adding tiny portions of liquid clay with as much delicacy as the painter uses with his brush, the sculptor's face marked the strenuous effort to transfer his subject into the clay. And yet this meticulous study of the sitter resulted in no literal copy of him but was full of the artist's vividness and rather a reading of the original than a transliteration of it. Plainly it was not only the aspect of the head which worked in the artist's mind; these forms were moulded by him, as if they passed through an alembic. His eyes saw differently from another man's and his hand was obedient to his eye. Therein lies, as I suppose, the personality of the artist, that he selects or adds or accentuates so as to bring out what is significant in the form. A direct answer to my question I could not elicit. But this particular artist seemed to think that both procedures might occur with him, both the semi-unconscious one I have suggested to be typical and the conscious forethought of some particular result, so far as he was guided by knowledge of the history of his art. My general impression was that I was witnessing absorbed observation of the sitter and that that observation, after filtration through what for want of a better word has to be called the artist's genius (for what this loose word means is mainly the unclear and undefined prompting of personality), ended in a creation which was far more significant than an ordinary observer like myself would have judged the original to be.

It is time to qualify the over simple account I have given of the artist's process of creation, which I have only suggested as an account of what happens in general and is the fundamental character of the artistic process. Even so far as I have gone in my inquisition it is clear that both processes are employed, execution by the relatively blind impulsion of the creative gadfly, and transcribing from pictures in the imagination. I set aside first, to repeat myself, those cases in which an artist of exceptional experience or skill produces his work in his head. Leonardo may have seen the picture of the Last Supper in all its details before he put the pigments on the wall; Wordsworth composed his poems on his walks, giving the simple peasants the impression of a mooning creature; the deaf Beethoven must have made the Choral Symphony in his imagination, and perhaps most musicians trust from the nature of the case to their imaginations. One eminent painter referred to in my correspondence formed so exact a picture in her mind of a portrait that when she came to put it on the canvas and desired to alter it, she found she could not. Is it not evident that the imagination in such cases is the work of art itself, and embodies the materials of the external work (I will not say the physical work) and possibly even the necessary movements of the hand? There is no more difference between it and the external work than there is between a sum done in the head or on paper. The question still arises, How is this image reached? You would not say from a precedent image of

F

itself. And if not, then how? The case is irrelevant
psychologically, for in such an image the work is
already achieved.

I set aside such cases. Moreover, even when the artist
does not do the whole work in his head, he may do parts
of it in this way, and tends to do so the more in proportion to his experience and his acquaintance with the
history of his art. But there is another way in which he
may use images, not of the finished product, but of the
subject matter, realised in such detail that it may seem
he is merely transcribing his picture into words or
colours in the same sense as a man of science describes
a natural phenomenon or an animal form. Perhaps it is
such cases which are in the minds of those who say
that the external embodiment in the material form is
merely a matter of technique. In other words the artist
merely describes in his customary medium a fully realised picture of his subject matter. The supposed case is
not so likely to occur in painting or sculpture, for there
the more vividly the artist pictures his subject, say his
landscape, or the person he is modelling or sculpturing
in stone, the more his image approximates to a picture
of the finished product, and the situation is the one
already mentioned. In poetry, however, the poet often
seems to be merely describing, as it were scientifically,
a picture in his mind. It may be doubted whether even
in purely descriptive poetry he really does so, unless
exceptionally. In general the picture and the words
mould each other: the picture may be transcribed in
words, but the words as they flow alter the picture. One
of my correspondents urges that when Wordsworth
wrote of the daisy

> The beauty of its star-shaped shadow thrown
> On the smooth surface of this naked stone,

the picture preceded the words. *A* picture doubtless,

but was even that not altered in the transcription? 'Smooth' and 'star-shaped' seem to exceed the mere picture. When Tennyson writes

> The lizard with his shadow on the stone
> Rests like a shadow,

the phrase 'rests like a shadow' betrays the effort to turn the mere picture in the subject matter into words. If I am right, even these pictures fall back into the rank of subject matter in which the artist is absorbed but whose real character is only fully revealed when the words are spoken (or imagined). The lines which immediately follow the words quoted from Tennyson are:

> The purple flowers droop, the golden bee
> Is lily-cradled.

The poet is working from a picture; but is it likely that the 'cradling' of the bee in the lily was part of the picture or suggested by a fresh one? It was wrung from him by his delight in his picture, and completes the feeling from which he worked.

Moreover, as the details are transcribed (and let it be granted they are literally transcribed) they affect and are affected by the rest of the composition, and either themselves must undergo change, or they alter the total. The sculptor I observed when he introduced a touch with his knife into the clay model's nose or eyes, found he had affected the unity of his model and so he was always working over the whole head at once.

The artist proceeds by stages, filling up his general impression into fulness. Partly, as I have said, he works from new images in the manner conceded. Partly he works by what a correspondent calls *tâtonnement*, perpetually correcting the product. It may be asked, Does not his correction show that the work achieved falls short of his ideal, of some image in his mind of the perfect work? The answer I suggest is that it falls short of his ideal but not of the alleged image. If he had that image in his mind, his failure could only be a matter of technical unskill. He goes on correcting because his work does not satisfy the impulse which drives him into his work, with all those complicated sources from which that impulse is drawn which I have so inadequately sketched.

But it is precisely because the artist's working is so various that I desire to have more data. The variations of procedure attested at first hand are certain to be of more importance than rough and possibly incorrect or at least unguarded dogmas laid down by a person who is not himself an artist. Such material would be the only satisfactory basis of a thorough psychology of the matter.

There remains a further problem which arises from the existence of that 'eidetic' imagery which has been so interesting and important a discovery of recent years. Children up to about fifteen in large numbers, and adults in much smaller numbers, appear to possess images of what they see which in some respects resemble the images of memory but in others resemble after-images. The image has the substantiality of a percept, the person sees the object or scene very much as if it were really before him; it has a hallucinatory character. Now it is natural to think that artists may be individuals who retain this gift which other persons lose after youth. "Many men", says Rossetti,

> Many men are poets in their youth,
> But for one sweet-strung soul the years prolong
> Even though all change the indomitable song.

And Mr. Kroh,[1] who gave the first systematic account (not the first account) of these facts, has made a study

[1] O. Kroh, *Subjektive Anschauungsbilder bei Jugendlichen*. Göttingen, 1922.

of certain German poets past and present, one of them being Goethe, and concluded on internal evidence that they were eidetics. It by no means follows that all artists are so; a passage is quoted describing Goethe's impatience with Schiller because when Goethe described the *Urpflanze* from a vivid picture which he had in his mind, Schiller, who perfectly understood him, called Goethe's topic merely a notion. Let us assume, however, for the moment that all poets and other artists have such pictures in their minds. It might well be asked, Does the artist, does the poet for instance, do anything more than read off his image as a scientific man would read it off? I believe I have really answered the question in advance. The real problem would in the first place be to explain why the artist comes to possess such highly finished pictures; in other words the artistic creation lies behind the eidetic image used. In the next place, I incline to think that though eidetic artists have these vivid pictures which simulate reality, these pictures are but an additional gift they possess in conceiving the subject matter. The well-known case of Reynolds's friend who painted from a single sitting of his subjects is typical. The eidetic image took the place of the reality. There is even one case quoted of an engraver who projected his image on to the plate and merely traced the outline with his tool. Whether the result was good or bad we are not told. But the case is surely exceptional. In general, when the artist paints from his image or describes it in words, he is moulding it, in the product itself, into something of which the image supplies him with the subject but whose complete idea is revealed in the product itself.

For completeness' sake, I will return for a moment to the organic character of the material work of art, confining myself to poetry. If the doctrine be correct,

the mere sound of the words is vital to the art. Yet
words have meaning and it is never possible to dis-
sociate the meanings of words from the words themselves. Two conclusions follow which I may expound
briefly by illustrations. In the first place, no subject
however trivial or mean is beyond the reach of art.
Success depends upon the handling, though no doubt
the higher the subject the greater the work if the words
are commensurate. To illustrate triviality of subject in
a perfect poem I will cite a stanza from a well-known
seventeenth-century poem, hardly daring to quote it
because under our modern conditions it requires an
effort to realise the picture:

> Her feet beneath her petticoat
> Like little mice stole in and out,
>   As if they feared the light.
> And oh! she dances such a way,
> No sun upon an Easter day
>   Is half so fine a sight.

Miss Austen's novels are compact of delicate trivialities,
and how great is their art!

Secondly, there is a regular adjustment of sounds to
meaning, and verse is far from being a superadded
charm, but is an integral, possibly the chief constituent.
The burden of Mr. Saintsbury's work on prosody is
this theme. Metre and rhyme are not mere adjuncts of
poetry. The periodic recurrence of sounds or groups of
them is part of that process by which the unitary purpose of a work of art is effected in its material. We may
take it that, as Mr. Middleton Murry says,[1] poetry
differs from prose by its greater, at least its intenser,
passion; that passion finding vent in words is ordered
and controlled by rhythm and metre and rhyme. But
I am more concerned with the blending of the de-

---

[1] In his book *The Problem of Style*. London, 1922.

light of sounds, isolated or in their periods or in their cadence, with the thought or subject matter. Indeed it is mainly through poetry that we realise the charm of words. I come myself from no mean city but, its name suggesting smoke and damp, few persons perhaps think of the word as charming. They have only to re- peat the words of the Jacobite song, 'Farewell, Man- chester, noble town farewell', to realise how beautiful a word it is. In good poetry there always is this con- sonance of thought and song. Where either element is found alone we have defect—the tinkle of words or the aridity of bare ideas. Illustration would be endless, but it would be taken, not from the deliberatively imitative passages,[1] where sound of word recalls sound of nature, but from great music like that of Prospero's speech in *The Tempest* or the cadence of Cleopatra's "Give me my robe", etc.;[2] from the rolling catalogues of names in Milton, or the organ music which accompanies Adam's prayer, or the fragrance and softness of the words them- selves describing Eden in Book V. I will cite two ex- amples; the first, to reprove Wordsworth's doctrine by his own practice, shall be the famous skating passage in the *Prelude*:

> So through the darkness and the cold we flew,
> And not a voice was idle; with the din
> Smitten the precipices rang aloud;
> The leafless trees and every icy crag
> Tinkled like iron; while far distant hills
> Into the tumult sent an alien sound
> Of melancholy not unnoticed, while the stars
> Eastward were sparkling clear, and in the west
> The orange sky of evening died away.

[1] *E.g.:* When Ajax strives some rock's vast weight to throw,
            The line too labours and the words move slow.

or   The moan of doves in immemorial elms
             And murmur of innumerable bees.

[2] The remark comes from Mr. Murry.

The second, where the purpose in the blending is more deliberate, is from the stanza describing the concert in the garden of Acrasia in the second book of the *Faery Queene* where the unison of sounds is expressed by the linkage of the lines:

> The joyous birdes, shrouded in chearefull shade,
> Their notes unto the voyce attempred sweet;
> Th' angelicall soft trembling voyces made
> To th' instruments divine respondence meet;
> The silver sounding instruments did meet
> With the base murmure of the waters fall;
> The waters fall with difference discreet,
> Now soft, now loud, unto the wind did call;
> The gentle warbling wind low answered to all.

I may summarise the preceding pages briefly thus: (1) The impulse to creation is based upon the material passions provoked by the subjects, but is distinguishable from them and is formal. (2) The process of creation arises from the excitement caused by the subject matter, and images play a large part in the awareness of that subject. These are not images of the work of art, which are in general only got through actual production. (3) Images of parts of the work of art may precede the actual production, but that this is a subordinate feature of the creative process. When there is complete anticipation in idea or image, the work of art has been already produced. (4) Eidetic imagery which is probably frequent in artists belongs to the images of the subject matter not of the product. (5) The material of the art is a vital part of artistic process. In poetry for instance the sound of the words, their rhythm, metre, etc., are integral to the work, and perhaps the element of prior value.

Creativeness having been described, we can now advance to a 'philosophical' feature of it[1] which is implied

[1] From *Art and the Material*.

in what precedes. All cognition is discovery in which its object is revealed to the mind. The work of art being the expression or embodiment in material and contemplated for its own sake and not merely as a sign, however much it owes its form to the artist, reveals to him his own meaning, and the artistic experience is not so much invention as discovery. In sculpture, where the block already exists, it is easier to recognise the truth of this. In Michael Angelo's unfinished statues of slaves in the Academy at Florence we can feel the artist not so much making the figure as chipping off flakes of the marble from the figure which is concealed in it, and which he is laying bare (*vivos* ducunt *de marmore voltus*). Has he not said himself that there is no thought which the sculptor expresses in marble that does not exist there already? R. L. Nettleship[1] applies to the sculptor the words of Browning:

> The thousand sights and sounds that broke
> In on him at the chisel's stroke;

and the words describe how the sculptor's discovery, elicited by his own creative art, surprises him with the definition of his own mood of mind; in the same way as with no foreknowledge of the truth but with the passion to find it and to use the methods calculated to attain it, the scientific thinker is surprised by the discovery in nature of the law or fact which he is seeking. What is true of sculpture is true also of poetry. Shakespeare discovered *Hamlet* in the English language as the sculptor discovers his figure in the block. Full as that language is of the knowledge of nature and man for which it stands, of history and thought and emotion, Shakespeare, with his artistic excitement over the subject of Hamlet's story and with his profound insight into

---

[1] In his essay on Plato's Education in *Hellenica*.

Hamlet's imagined nature, could discover there in the language of English folk the selection and combination of words which were fitted to be the expression of his excitement, and in their turn surprised him as they surprise us with the imaginations they embody. Great artists know or believe that they are inspired from something outside themselves. Why should we suppose them to be deceived? It is true that to make the discovery the gifts of Shakespeare were needed; that is why great artists are rare. But equally the gifts and skill of Newton were needed to discover the law of gravitation in its first form, and other gifts and skill have been needed to discover that law in its later and preciser form. You cannot discover Hamlet unless you have Shakespeare's mind. But equally unless you have eyes you cannot discover the green trees. "Ripeness is all." Except for the features which make the artist's act creative, there is no difference in kind between the discovery of the tree by perception and the discovery of the Slave in the block or of Hamlet in the English language. The artist's creativeness conceals from us his real passivity. Every artist is in his degree like Shakespeare, who was a reed through which every wind from nature or human affairs blew music.

CHAPTER V

FORM AND SUBJECT MATTER

THE elements described on p. 54 as entering into a work of art, the material, its form, its meaning or subject matter are the basis of well-known differences in art. The difference of the various arts is founded on the different materials they use. The relation of formed material to subject or meaning is the foundation of the difference of formal and representative art. In another way it is the source of the difference between beauty and greatness in art.

That different material implies a different art requires no comment nor exemplification. Interest for us lies in the traditional question how far it is possible to assign separate provinces to the arts, that is, to sculpture and painting and literature or even in architecture to the various materials used in that art. The problem is famous through the doctrine of Lessing, who uses the Laocoon to distinguish what is possible in sculpture from what belongs to literature. Of the two reasons why Laocoon does not shriek in the marble as in Virgil's description, one the distortion of the shrieking face, and the other that sculpture portrays and fixes permanently a moment of time and is therefore unsuitable to express a transitory and impermanent occurrence like a shriek—the second is in this form of doubtful validity.[1] For sculpture is no more limited to a moment than painting, and it is certain that a picture may

[1] Compare Schopenhauer, *W. a. W. u. V.*, bk. iii. § 46.

75

depict continued movement. Mr. Berenson[1] belauds
Botticelli as supreme in depicting pure movement.
Instance his Judith returning with the head of Holo-
fernes, in the Uffizi, or the more famous picture of
the dancing maidens in the 'Spring'. That sculpture is
confined to what can be shown in the moment is hard
to maintain in the face of the pictorial plaques of
Ghiberti in the Baptistery doors, or of his Sacrifice of
Isaac which gained the same sculptor the preference
in the eyes of the Florentine judges over his competitor
Brunelleschi just because of its superior animation in
exhibiting one moment in a felt history. Some sculp-
tors hold that no subject falls outside the scope of their
art.

The question belongs more properly to an art critic
than to such an inquiry (philosophical, if you will) as
the present. On the other hand, certain forms seem to
the unlearned eye more suitable to one material than
another. Architectural designs with large blank spaces
may be mean in terra-cotta which might have dignity
in stone, and marble would seem less suitable to the
charm of Tanagra statuettes than terra-cotta. This
would seem to suggest that where such demarcations
are possible, not as between one art and another but
as between materials open to the same art, it is the
greatness or lightness of the subject which determines.

The creation of the artist is form, that is, formed
material, whose beauty lies in its form. The material
may be of itself pleasing like marble or silk, and such
pleasure may occupy an appreciable place in the total
effect of a beautiful work upon the mind, without being
in itself a part of the beauty. The form consists in relations between the parts of the material, and is not

---

[1] *Florentine Painters of the Renaissance.* New York and London, ed. 3,
1908, pp. 69–75. The examples do not come from this passage.

identical with shape, though it includes shape. For instance, the form of a statue is not merely the shape of a living man but a shape so modified or formed as to convey the meaning life. When we are said to represent the form of some external thing or topic, say in paint or marble, the relations within what is represented are reproduced in the marble or picture under the conditions set by these materials. The design of the pigments or the stone becomes through the artist's work the form of the man as he is presented when the work is finished. It is only in this sense that there can be a copy of anything in the artist's material. Ruskin was mistaken when he said that the form of the model and the work are identical. Naïvely enough he treats the different form of a picture as compared with a statue to the accident of its being two- instead of three-dimensional. But clearly there is no identity between the form of a poem or a sonata with that of its subject if it has one, though there is correspondence of relations.

Now art can be either formal or representative because the material with its form is always distinguishable from the subject matter. The art is formal when there is no subject matter distinct from the material itself; it is representative when the designed material refers to a subject matter. Pure or absolute music is formal because its subject is exhausted by the tones themselves as the musician designs them; and we have seen that his design introduces into the tones tonal meanings which the tones do not themselves possess. It has a meaning which is tonal. Representative painting refers in addition and because of its formed material to a subject matter which it represents.

In both cases the work may be called significant in the terminology of Messrs. Fry and Bell. It is not

random collocations of tones or pigments. What the
meaning of pure music may be in a particular case may
be difficult to describe by the layman, though not by
the musical appreciator, for whom the form signifies
the relations or pattern of the musical elements. In
painting and sculpture the layman finds his task easier,
for the relations of the elements with which these
artists work have also their reference to subject matters
different from the pigments or stones which are their
material.

The saying of Pater that the other arts tend towards
the condition of music is true, not merely of certain
species of these arts but of these arts at any time and
in any kind. For all the arts are beautiful in so far as
they establish satisfying relations of form; and music
does but show overtly and unmistakably the character
of art in its essential expression. Architecture comes
next in purity to music, in creating satisfying relations
of the masses, and spaces, and lines and planes with
which it is conversant.[1] But it contains also the representational element of use; the forms of its materials
mean also houses and temples. Poetry, and literature
generally, is from the outset representative because
its words are not mere sounds to be musically composed
but are charged with meanings, that is, with reference
to the things denoted. Laura Matilda's poetry in
Rejected Addresses may be charming music but is not
poetry at all. Painting and sculpture are *prima facie*
representative, but what they are, their contents or

---

[1] Always understanding that these relations in architecture as elsewhere are
the relations as they appear to the eye. As Mr. Geoffrey Scott pointed out in his
book *The Architecture of Humanism* (London, 1924), the cupolas of the Duomo
at Florence and of our own St. Paul's appear to be self-sustained, though in the
actual building they are supported in addition by metal rings which bind the
structure but are not seen. He adduces this instance in comment upon the claims
of so-called 'functional' architecture. A too complete revelation of the actual
play of the masses employed might detract from the beauty of the structure.

substance, is certain designs of colours, lines and the like.

Thus the real nature of the work of art is illuminated best from music because there its nature is exposed. But in another point of view it is easier to approach the formal arts from the side of the representational ones. In a picture, as just now indicated, the subject matter which is at first the exciting topic of the artist's mind is foreign to the medium in which he works. As he reaches his goal, though the subject matter still remains distinguishable from his material, the subject matter has become so altered from its initial condition that its form and that of the medium correspond, or the system of relations in the two is the same, so far as is possible under the conditions. We have seen that what the painter does is so to fashion his pigments that they reveal both what he means in paint and what he means in subject matter. Suppose now that his attention to his subject matter diminishes towards the vanishing point, his subject, instead of being the subject in its own real nature, say a woman, will be the form of the subject. As Mr. R. G. Collingwood has wittily said, a painter may be interested either in the volumes of a woman or in her femininity.[1] At the actual vanishing point his subject will have become nothing but the formal relations of his paints. Or if he be a sculptor, his subject will have become the form of his clay or marble, and his picture or statue will have retained in its form only a minimum of representational reference. The subject of reference has become the 'content'.

Thus it would seem that the formal and the representative arts are not so divided as to be different in

---

[1] *Journal of Philosophical Studies*, vol. iv., 'Form and Content in Art', July 1929.

kind. Pure music has a subject matter though one not outside the material of its tones: the element of foreign reference is at a minimum or non-existent. In representative art the formal element is still the essence of its beauty, but there is the added reference to the foreign subject; but that foreign subject is so transformed in the artist's vision as to correspond to the material form and be implied in it. There is thus no quarrel between formal and representative art, and in every art (under proper qualifications) there is both a subject and a material form, only in music the two coincide.

We should expect accordingly species of art in which painting, sculpture and poetry make experiments towards a musical character; where, in other words, the artist works with the forms appropriate to his materials and makes those materials his special concern and source of significance for his forms. How far these experiments are likely to be successful or have been hitherto attended with success, I do not know. Pure painting, pure sculpture, pure poetry are on their trial; anyhow, the experiments now being made are experiments in finding significant form in these media themselves.[1] Success will depend, as I suppose, upon whether the reference to the foreign subject can be prevented from creeping surreptitiously in. Correspondingly, experiments have been made in music itself to combine musical form with representational reference, in what is called the symphonic poem.[2] The more successful these various experiments, the more conclusively will they show that formality and representation are not utterly heterogeneous. In perfectly formal art, in pure music, the subject matter has become the form of

[1] See some valuable remarks on this subject by Max Eastman, *The Literary Mind* (New York, London, 1931), pp. 79 ff.

[2] Ernest Newman, *Musical Studies*. London, 1910. A good instance is Strauss's *Heldenleben* (which I should venture to call musical prose. See Chapter VI.).

the tones themselves. In representative art it is still the design of the materials which constitutes the beauty, but there is an added reference to a topic now moulded into complete conformity with the formal character of the materials.

This last phrase leads on to a point of great import-ance which justifies the antagonism, sometimes ex-tremely exaggerated, to the claims of representation in art. It constitutes the difference between true repre-sentative art and illustrative art. In the 'Birth of Venus' or 'The Last Supper' there is a subject matter which, though foreign to the material, has become em-bodied in the material. In mere illustration the subject is not so much assimilated or woven into the formed material as suggested by it. The limit to artistic repre-sentation is found at the point where suggestion over-powers form. The portrait whose interest consists in its recalling the original, or the subject piece which with excellent craftsmanship serves mainly to tell a story, like perhaps the Pinturicchios in the Siena Cathedral or many a picture of Ghirlandajo, are instances.

It is a step from such illustrative art to where the suggestion becomes plainly practical, and the work merely serves to excite sense or sentimentality, or be-comes photographic or even it may be pornographic. The foreignness of the subject is here patent because it has not been redeemed by subjection to the formal laws of the artistic material, but operates as a piece of practical experience, an appeal to what I have called material passions, not here employed in service to the artist's constructive passion, but asking expression for themselves. The passions may be commendable or in-nocent or the reverse. At any rate the art which serves mainly to suggest the objects of these passions or senti-ment is merely illustrative and, excellent perhaps as

G

craft, is not art. It is perhaps in their justifiable zeal
to reject such pretensions that the advocates of formal-
ism sharpen their diatribes against representation. But
those diatribes are not relevant to representation as such
but only to inartistic representation.

It follows from the foreignness of the subject matter
to the formed material that the beauty of art does not
depend upon the choice of subject. What the choice of
subject affects is, as I shall explain at greater length in
a later chapter, not the beauty but the 'greatness' of the
work.[1] Any subject is available for beauty if it be
treated beautifully. The subject may be repulsive, like
the plague at Athens which forms a subject of Lucretius's fifth book; or a picture may have so disgusting a
subject as Tintoretto's picture in San Rocco of the
ministrations of that saint in the hospital, though I am
not pretending that that picture belongs to great art
nor even to the best work of its master. Or like Michael
Angelo's 'Last Judgment' in the Sistine Chapel it may
have a subject unbearable in itself, and yet belonging
to that species of beauty which is called the sublime,
which writers on aesthetics used to be so fond of con-
trasting with the beautiful. The difference lies not in
the beauty but in the character of the subject, according as it charms of itself or overpowers and at the same
time exalts. Upon this subject I may content myself
now with referring to Burke and Kant and to Mr.
A. C. Bradley's essay.[2] The difference is a real one but
irrelevant to the nature of beauty; a consideration which
accounts for, though it does not excuse, the somewhat
contemptuous treatment of the 'kinds' of art recognised
by his predecessors in aesthetics by Mr. Croce. Architecture may range from the humble though beautiful
cottage to the Parthenon; poetry from Peele's dialogue

---

[1] Chapter VIII.   [2] See further later, Chapter IX.

of Paris and Oenone ("Fair and fair and twice so fair",
etc.) with the substance of gossamer, or the enchanting
song of Spring quoted above on p. 23, to the splendour
of "the baseless fabric of this vision", or "the glories of
our blood and state".

The issue becomes acute when the subject represented raises questions of morals. But this issue is best
reserved till later.[1] It is clear enough that the beauty of
art has nothing to do with the vice or virtue of its subject. On the other hand, it is arguable that when a work
of art excites or tends to excite reprehensible passions
the reason may be that it fails of beauty because of the
excess of suggestion unelaborated into the artistic form;
because of the introduction into the work of personal
interests instead of interests which are through the art
made impersonal.

> But since he died and poets better prove,
> Theirs for their style I'll read, his for his love.

The contrast is given in these lines.

[1] See Chapter VIII.

CHAPTER VI

UPON the proportion between the formal and the representative element in art depends the difference between poetry and prose, a difference which, it will be seen, is not confined to literature, where alone it has been named, but is found in all the arts.

A. IN LITERATURE

I propose to speak only of beautiful poetry and beautiful prose or, if the adjective be preferred, artistic poetry and prose: making use of the distinction drawn already in a previous chapter between art and craft, between making a competent and useful thing which exactly fits its purpose and making it beautifully, between technical skill and artistry, between good workmanship and design and that touch of rareness which makes not merely good but fine and lovely. Much poetry and prose is not art. Many poems are not poetry, though written in impeccable verse, and long poems are always apt to drop in places into what is only not called prose because it is metrical. By far the greatest part of prose is merely good workman-like writing, and in no sense art. I am not intending to depreciate craft, and still less the value and difficulty of attaining it. To write good workman-like English is a very difficult thing to acquire, as all of us know who have not been

---

[1] The following chapter is reproduced with some changes from *Philosophy*, vol. vii., 1932.

trained at school as the young are trained in France to express themselves well in the mother tongue. It is unjust to speak of hackwork. The Grub Street writer may be an excellent craftsman who deserves more reward than he gets. But there remains the difference between his work and that of such literary men as Southey and Goldsmith, who add the touch of delight: the first in a recognisable degree, the second in the remarkable degree which makes him a model of prose of the unadorned kind, though it still leaves him a less great artist in prose than Swift. I am concerned to exclude from consideration a mass of good stuff in all sorts of art as well as in literature which is not really art, and to ask what is the difference between beautiful prose and poetry.

The most natural answer is that there is no difference except in the form; poetry is metrical as well as rhythmical, prose has its rhythm, which has lately been studied with peculiar success, but is not metrical, that is, does not repeat its rhythms with regularity as poetry does. Perhaps in the end there may be no more to say than what the Maître de Philosophie in Molière said to M. Jourdain, "What is prose is not verse, and what is verse is not prose". A friend of mine defined poetry to me once as whatever can best be expressed in verse. That is not saying quite the same thing as Molière's teacher, for my friend said 'what can best be expressed', and when you ask why best, you raise the question whether there may not be something in the subject or the way it is conceived which compels the choice of verse or prose as the case may be. On the other hand, there is the view of Mr. Herbert Read,[1] "that the difference between poetry and prose is a qualitative difference". According to him the distinction is "a

[1] *English Prose Style*, p. xii. London, 1928.

material distinction . . . poetry is the expression of one form of mental activity, prose the expression of another form". I think him right, though I am not so sure that he has stated the difference correctly or finally when he says that poetry is 'creative expression', prose is 'constructive expression'. Granting that beauty lies always in the form of a work of art, we must admit that there is room for variety to arise in virtue of the substance of what is embodied in the work. Such a difference in beautiful words or beautiful language—a difference which some, like Mr. Read, describe as a difference in the mental activity involved, which I prefer to describe as a difference in the subject, or the treatment of it which makes the subject itself different, a difference which is of course reflected or expressed, or even may be said to have its only real existence in the choice of the words—is the difference between beautiful poetry and beautiful prose.

The strict antithesis indeed to prose is verse. But this is clearly not the same thing as the antithesis of poetry and prose. For it is at least arguable that some prose is really poetry; and there is no doubt that some verse is not poetry at all, but is prose with the more external form which poetry generally assumes. Yet when this is put aside, there is still much to be said for the formal view. There is no hard and fast line between poetry and prose. There is the whole scale of gradation from manifest prose like Swift, through imaginative prose such as you may get in Newman or Burke, whose work is undoubted prose, and poems near to prose like much didactic or satiric poetry (Pope or Juvenal), to undoubted poetry. Or again, there is the fact that an artist like Molière used to write his comedies first in prose and then versify them, except when he was pressed for time, as in the latter part of the *Bourgeois*

Gentilhomme and in the whole of *L'Avare*. It was once said in Johnson's hearing that Pope for his *Essay on Man* was supplied with the matter by Bolingbroke, and all that Pope did was to turn Bolingbroke into verse. Johnson, who was both a great writer himself and an excellent critic, doubted the report, and held that all that Pope received was the "philosophick stamina, but that the poetical imagery was Pope's own". Now Johnson was himself a writer of poems, which, though not great poetry, were poetry, and knew something about what poetry was. Yet allowing its weight to Johnson's judgment, we should still find it hard to mark any difference between Molière's verse and prose but one of form, and his art raises acutely the question whether real drama, whether in prose or verse, is not to be called poetry. Those who hold poetry and prose to differ only in form have still to contend with the popular conviction that there is a poetic vision of things. They will have to explain what poetic vision is unless they deny its existence. Wordsworth, we saw, minimised the importance of words for the poet, as if verse were a mere matter of technique. But before I have done I hope to indicate why it is that this poetic vision finds its expression in verse rather than prose.

Perhaps the best way of approaching the subject is to ask ourselves what kind of topics are naturally in a developed language treated in prose and what in poetry. I say a developed language, for in the early condition of a language like Greek, for instance, all subjects are treated in poetry. Thus early philosophy, such as that of Empedocles or Parmenides, was written in poetry. Poetry precedes prose as the language of literature. Prose treats of science, and history from the mere chronicle or newspaper up to the great synthetic histories, which are both narrative and scientific or philosophical, which not merely describe events as they happened, but reveal their meaning and the play of character and tendency expressed in the events. I may take so late an instance as Mr. Trevelyan's *History of England under Anne*.[1] Narratives and science are then for the most part written in prose. Poetry, on the other hand, in its most obvious forms is lyric or dramatic, the direct outpouring by the poet of his own heart, or the equally direct outpouring by his characters of their hearts. But besides these poems there is narrative poetry or epic, that is, descriptive poetry of various sorts, which may be interspersed with dramatic episodes, like the prayer of Adam in Milton or the speeches of the heroes in Homer. Now narrative poetry comes nearer to prose than lyric or drama. And again there are intermediate forms of prose which are nearer to poetry than history is. We may, I think, say provisionally, prose is most clearly prose when it approaches to bare narrative or history, and poetry most clearly poetry when it approaches to drama or lyric; and as I suggested just now, lyric may be regarded as a special form of drama where the speaker happens to be the poet himself.[2] Further, when science and chronicle are included, we have to remember that as bare science or bare faithful reports they belong to craft and not to artistic prose at all. Let us say then that prose tends to be narrative, and poetry to be dramatic, but there are all manner of intermediate forms of both prose and verse. There is oratory, including sermons, and there are the didactic and satiric forms of poetry which I mentioned a moment ago. Now in trying to find out what makes the differences of prose and poetry, the best and, indeed, at first sight, the only way is to proceed inductively, if I may use somewhat grand lan-

[1] London, 1930–2.   [2] A remark as old as Plato.

guage, that is, to compare actual passages of admitted prose or poetry, and amongst these to set beside one another more or less parallel passages, in which the topic is more or less the same. We may then be able to detect what it is that gives the peculiar flavour of prose or poetry to the contrasted pieces. Many other passages might doubtless have been chosen besides the following, which are nearly all familiar ones.

I. SCENERY

From Plato's *Phaedrus* (Jowett's translation).

S. But let me ask you, friend, have we not reached the plane-tree to which you were conducting us?

Ph. Yes, here is the tree.

S. Yes indeed and a fair and shady resting place, full of summer sounds and scents. There is the lofty and spreading plane-tree, and the agnus castus high and clustering, in the fullest blossom and the greatest fragrance; and the stream which flows beneath the plane-tree is deliciously cold to the feet. Judging from the ornaments and images, this must be a spot sacred to Achelous and the nymphs; moreover there is a sweet breeze and the grasshoppers chirrup; and the greatest charm of all is the grass like a pillow gently sloping to the head. My dear Phaedrus, you have been an admirable guide.

Ph. [I always wonder at you, Socrates; for when you are in the country you really are like a stranger, who is being led about by a guide. Do you ever cross the border? I rather think that you never venture even outside the gates.

S. Very true, my good friend; and I hope that you will excuse me when you hear the reason, which is that I am a lover of knowledge, and the men who dwell in the city are my teachers, and not the trees or the country. Though I do indeed believe that you have found a spell with which to draw me out of the city into the country, as hungry cows are led by waving before them a bough or a fruit. For only hold up a book before me and you may lead me all round Attica and over the wide world.]

I include the bracketed part, though not strictly relevant, partly for its delight, partly because as Socrates does not feel the country, he goes naturally into prose.

From *Midsummer Night's Dream*.

> I know a bank whereon the wild thyme blows,
> Where oxlips and the nodding violet grows;
> Quite overcanopied with luscious woodbine,
> With sweet musk-roses and with eglantine:
> There sleeps Titania, some time of the night,
> Lulled in these flowers with dances and delight;
> And there the snake throws her enamelled skin,
> Weed wide enough to wrap a fairy in.

They might be speaking themselves, the flowers and the rest of the scene!

From Tennyson's *Oenone*.

> And at their feet the crocus brake like fire,
> Violet, amaracus and asphodel,
> Lotus and lilies. And a wind arose,
> And overhead the wandering ivy and vine
> This way and that in many a wild festoon
> Ran riot, garlanding the gnarled boughs
> With bunch and berry and flower, through and through.

From Wordsworth's *Prelude*, I. 438 (repeated from p. 71).

> So through the darkness and the cold we flew,
> And not a voice was idle; with the din
> Smitten, the precipices rang aloud;
> The leafless trees and every icy crag
> Tinkled like iron; while far distant hills
> Into the tumult sent an alien sound
> Of melancholy not unnoticed, while the stars
> Eastward were sparkling clear, and in the west
> The orange sky of evening died away.

II. PICTURE OF A WOMAN

From Steele (*Tatler*, No. 49).

Aspasia must therefore be allowed to be the first of the beauteous Order of Love, whose unaffected freedom and conscious innocence give her the attendance of the graces in all her actions. That awful distance which we bear towards her in all our thoughts of her, and that cheerful familiarity with which we approach her, are certain instances of her being the truest object of love of any of her sex. In this accomplished lady love is the constant effect, because it is never the design. Yet though her mien carries much more invitation than command, to behold her is an immediate check to loose behaviour, and to love her is a liberal education; for it being the nature of all love to create an imitation of the beloved person in the lover, a regard for Aspasia naturally produces decency of manners and good conduct of life in her admirers.

From *The Faery Queene*, II. iii. 24.

> Her ivorie forehead full of bountie brave
> Like a broad table did itself dispred,
> For Love his loftie triumphs to engrave
> And write the battels of his great godhead;
> All good and honour might therein be red:
> For there their dwelling was. And when she spake,
> Sweet wordes, like dropping honny, she did shed,
> And twixt the perles and rubins softly brake
> A silver sound that heavenly music seemed to make.

III. On a Poet

From Dryden.

To begin then with Shakespeare. He was the man who of all modern and perhaps ancient poets had the largest and most comprehensive soul. All the images of nature were present to him, and he drew them not laboriously but luckily. When he describes anything, you more than see it, you feel it too. Those who accuse him to have wanted learning give him the great commendation. He was naturally learned; he needed not the spectacles of books to read nature; he looked inwards, and found her there.[1] I cannot say he is everywhere alike; were he so I should do him an injury to compare him with the greatest of mankind. He is many times flat, insipid; his comic wit degenerating into clenches, his serious swelling into bombast. But he is always great when some great occasion is presented to him. No man can say he ever had a fit subject for his wit and did not then raise himself as high above the rest of poets:

> *Quantum lenta solent inter viburna cupressi.*

From Wordsworth's *The Poet's Epitaph.*

> But who is he with modest looks,
> And clad in homely russet brown?
> He murmurs near the running brooks
> A music sweeter than their own.
>
> He is retired as noontide dew,
> Or fountain in a noon-day grove:

---

[1] This is the point I shall develop.

And you must love him ere to you
He will seem worthy of your love.

The outward shows of sky and earth,
Of hill and valley he hath viewed;
And impulses of deeper birth
Have come to him in solitude.

In common things that round us lie
Some random truths he can impart;—
The harvest of a quiet eye
That broods and sleeps on his own heart.[1]

But he is weak; both Man and Boy,
Hath been an idler in the land;
Contented if he might enjoy
The things which others understand.

From Meredith's *The Spirit of Shakespeare.*

Thy greatest knew thee, Mother Earth; unsoured
He knew thy sons.   He probed from hell to hell
Of human passions, but of love deflowered
His wisdom was not, for he knew thee well.
Thence came the honeyed corner at his lips,
The conquering smile wherein his spirit sails
Calm as the God who the white sea-wave whips,
Yet full of speech and intershifting tales,
Close mirrors of us; hence had he the laugh
We feel is thine: broad as ten thousand beeves
At pasture.

IV. A Battle

From Trevelyan's *Blenheim* (*England under Anne*, vol. i.), p. 383.

The morning hours slipped by, and still with impassive countenance he watched the men he treasured fall under the cannon shots. Messenger after messenger galloped off to hasten Eugene, struggling through marsh and woodland far away. But till his colleague was ready to attack, the Duke would not give the word. What were his thoughts as he lunched among his staff in the open field, perhaps for the last time? He well knew it was the day that either made him or undid him quite: his fortunes could not survive defeat. And with his own ambitions the liberties of England and Europe had come to the

---

[1] Wordsworth here says the same thing about himself as Dryden says of Shakespeare.

last hazard, to be decided, not in any famous city or crowded meeting-place of men, but here in a naked plain of reaped stubble, be-tween villages and farms of names unknown—that tallest spire was called Blindheim, the guides said—places where unlettered peasants had for ages tilled the soil and for ages more would till it, caring nothing what the great world in its madness had come there to do that day—save only that their poor houses and barns would assuredly be burned. Yet in this uncouth rustic spot, the texture of Eighteenth Century civilisation and thought was to take its colour for good or ill. Hasten Eugene! Flesh and blood can no longer stand still under this carnage of a cannonade, and the very gods are impatient to see the invisible event.   Here at last comes his messenger galloping from the north. He is ready and we are more than ready. It is past noon, but August days are long. Cutts the Salamander is to lead the British and Dutch again at Blindheim. And everywhere, along four miles of the Nebel's course, the regiments and squadrons shake themselves and move down towards the marshy edges of the brook.

From Addison.

> But O, my muse, what numbers wilt thou find
> To sing the furious troops in battle joined?
> Methinks I hear the drum's tumultuous sound
> The victor's shouts and dying groans confound;
> The dreadful burst of cannon rend the skies,
> And all the thunder of the battle rise.
> 'Twas then great Marlbro's mighty soul was proved,
> That, in the shock of charging hosts unmoved,
> Amidst confusion, horror and despair,
> Examined all the dreadful scenes of war;
> In peaceful thought the field of death surveyed,
> To fainting squadrons lent the timely aid,
> Inspired repulsed battalions to engage,
> And taught the doubtful battle where to rage.
> So when an angel by divine command
> With rising tempests shakes a guilty land,
> Such as of late o'er pale Britannia passed,
> Calm and serene he drives the furious blast,
> And pleased the Almighty's orders to perform
> Rides in the whirlwind and directs the storm.

I add that these passages compare very well, because the first is not perfect prose, not the finest passage I could select from its author—a little artificial and rhetorical to my mind, though beautiful; and the second

is not first-rate poetry; and that the prose passage is the
finer of the two.

V. On Grief

From Burke's *French Revolution*.

The English people are satisfied, that to the great the consolations
of religion are as necessary as its instructions. They too are among
the unhappy. They feel personal pain and domestic sorrow. In these
they have no privilege, but are subject to pay their full contingent to
the contributions levied on mortality. They want this sovereign balm
under their gnawing cares and anxieties, which being less conversant
about the limited wants of animal life range without limit, and are
diversified by infinite combinations in the wild and unbounded
regions of imagination. Some charitable dole is wanting to these, our
often very unhappy brethren, to fill the gloomy void that reigns in
minds which have nothing on earth to hope or fear, something to
relieve in the killing languor and overlaboured lassitude of those
who have nothing to do; something to excite an appetite to existence
in the palled satiety which attends on all pleasures which may be
bought, where nature is not left to her own process, where even
desire is anticipated, and therefore fruition defeated by meditated
schemes and contrivances of delight; and no interval, no obstacle, is
interposed between the wish and its accomplishment.

From *King John*, Act III. Sc. iv.

> *Const.*　And, father cardinal, I have heard you say,
> That we shall see and know our friends in heaven:
> If that be true, I shall see my boy again;
> For, since the birth of Cain, the first male child,
> To him that did but yesterday suspire,
> There was not such a gracious creature born.
> But now will canker sorrow eat my bud,
> And chase the native beauty from his cheek,
> And he will look as hollow as a ghost;
> As dim and meagre as an ague's fit;
> And so he'll die; and, rising so again,
> When I shall meet him in the court of heaven
> I shall not know him; therefore never, never
> Must I behold my pretty Arthur more.
> *Pand.*　You hold too heinous a respect of grief.
> *Const.*　He talks to me that never had a son.
> *K. Phil.* You are as fond of grief as of your child.
> *Const.*　Grief fills the room up of my absent child,

Lies in his bed, walks up and down with me;
Puts on his pretty looks, repeats his words,
Remembers me of all his gracious parts,
Stuffs out his vacant garments with his form:
Then, have I reason to be fond of grief?

VI. ON MUSIC

From Newman, *University Sermons* (quoted in R. H. Hutton's
   Cardinal Newman).

There are seven notes in the scale; make them fourteen, yet what a
slender outfit for so vast an enterprise! What science brings so much
out of so little? . . . To many men the very names which the science
employs are utterly incomprehensible. To speak of an idea or subject seems to be fanciful or trifling; to speak of the views which it
opens upon us to be childish extravagance; yet is it possible that that
inexhaustible evolution and disposition of notes, so rich, so simple,
so intricate, yet so regulated, so various, yet so majestic, should be
a mere sound which is gone and perishes? Can it be that these
mysterious stirrings of heart and keen emotions, and strange yearn-
ings after we know not what, and awful impressions from we know
not whence, should be wrought in us by what is unsubstantial, and
comes and goes, and begins and ends in itself? It is not so; it cannot
be. No; they have escaped from some higher sphere; they are the
outpourings of eternal harmony in the medium of created sound;
they are echoes from our Home; they are the voice of Angels, or the
magnificat of Saints, or the living laws of Divine Government, or
the Divine Attributes; something are they besides themselves, which
we cannot compass, which we cannot utter—though mortal man,
and he perhaps not otherwise distinguished above his fellows, has
the gift of eliciting them.

From Browning's *Abt Vogler*.

But here is the finger of God, a flash of the will that can,
    Existent behind all laws, that made them and, lo, they are!
And I know not if, save in this, such gift be allowed to man,
    That out of three sounds he frame, not a fourth sound, but a star.
Consider it well: each tone of our scale in itself is nought;
    It is everywhere in the world—loud, soft, and all is said:
Give it to me to use! I mix it with two in my thought
    And, there! Ye have heard and seen: consider and bow the head.

Of the two great passages the prose is I should say

the greater. Yet the poem's failure to express the effect
in words and leaving it to the reader to imagine that
he hears and sees is itself significant for our purpose.

Now what seems to me to be the net result of this imperfect comparison of passages is this. The secret of
prose is suggested by the proximity of the less imaginative or impassioned prose to bare history or
chronicle. Think of the Blenheim piece or the Plato
landscape. It is that in prose we have a subject given
to the artist which he analyses or dissects. The situation may be a real one as the Battle of Blenheim, or it
may be imagined by the writer like a novel of Jane
Austen. But what the artist is doing is to unpiece it,
and at the same time bring the pieces again together
into a picture of the whole situation. He would not be
an artist did he not thus reconstruct. In this twofold
work he may use all instruments to produce vividness
in his picture. Sometimes his instrument is, as with
Swift, plain speech unadorned, quiet but forcible, not
rich, but as abundant as the subject requires. The plain
style may, as with Swift often and Hobbes always, be
leanness, not poverty of style; strong and sinewy, spar-
ing of words, every one of which, however, tells, and
this is perhaps the highest achievement of prose. Sometimes, as in Goldsmith or Newman or Froude, the art
lies in the simple ease and grace with which the language fits the subject as a glove fits the hand, to borrow
a phrase used by W. James about Mr. Bergson's admirable prose. Other models are the simpler passages of
Plato and almost every part of Pascal. You have to
contrast such language with the language of ordinary
life or of mere chronicle to get some idea of the consummate art it involves. For in practical language, or
in newspapers for instance, the object is to satisfy some

useful purpose, to get things done, to keep readers in-
formed of actual passing events. But the artist is concerned not with practical uses, but to bring home his
subject energetically, even if quietly, to the reader.
Only it is done by description and analysis. The same
thing is true even of impassioned prose like Burke's.
His aim is to persuade, and he may employ a wealth of
imagery which we are apt to call poetic, because the
poet, who is a creature of imagination, is full of it, though
he uses it differently. The one instrument which the
prose artist does not use, or uses only accidentally or
rarely, is poetry, for he is unbuilding and building up
again, but his chief interest is in the unbuilding. Thus
there is in the prose an element of purpose. The subject
is given, and though the material in which the writer
works is words and nothing else, the subject intended
by the words is given to him, although he may have
imagined it and given it to himself. The life of the
passage comes to it from the subject which is waiting as
it were to be described.

But now, to point the meaning of this, consider the
poetry. It too describes and analyses, but the analysis
is rather the instrument than the end. What is salient in
the poem is the whole picture, and so the poem is something concrete like a living thing, which lives in itself.
The poem is in its essence dramatic. There is given us
a live being in whose life the poet makes us live. The
prose-writer gives it to us to see, and gratifies our desire
to know and recognise things. He may, like Carlyle, be
vivid and picturesque. But it is one thing to present
the subject vividly before the mind, another thing to
put the mind within the subject so as to live its life.
Now the poet is not giving us things to look at, but
presenting us with new existences. "Grief fills the room
up of my absent child." That is not a picture of grief,

H

but is grief enacted.[1] Let me stop to illustrate by two other passages. A few words will by their force and vividness produce in the reader a thrill of astonishment or horror, or whatever it may be. But the manner is different in prose and poetry. Contrast Newman's "He has committed a great transgression; he has attempted to poison the wells"—in the preface of the *Apologia*—and Wordsworth's famous "We had crossed the Alps", as they occur in their respective contexts. The first is a most vivid and impressive article in the indictment of Kingsley. The second is the very experience occurring again under the conditions of the reader. That is why Mr. Read calls poetry creative, and that is what is true in his statement. The poet is making through his words a living event or character.

Elsewhere[2] I have attempted to contrast with one another the prose of Pascal's *Pensées* with the poetry of Bridges' *Testament of Beauty*. They are particularly useful to contrast, because the *Pensées* so often approaches poetry, and sometimes in isolated passages, like "The eternal silence of these infinite spaces terrifies me," breaks out into actual poetry, and yet remains prose, while Bridges' poem so often approaches prose and sometimes actually falls into versified prose, and yet is throughout poetry, even if not so manifestly so as Lucretius. The characteristic note seemed to me to be what I have said. And for the real poetic character of Lucretius, quite apart from his splendid lyrical passages, how his treatment of the atoms is so different from a science of them because it makes the atoms living beings and their meetings the behaviour of life

---

[1] For another case which occurs to me take the concentrated poetry of the line of Racine in which Hippolytus confesses his reluctant love to Aricia: "Présente, je vous fuis; absente, je vous trouve".

[2] 'Pascal the Writer', in *Bulletin of the John Rylands Library*, vol. xv. No. 2, 1931. Manchester.

—for this I have only to refer to Mr. Santayana's essay[1] on that poet.

Thus I take drama, which includes lyric,[2] to be the typical manner of poetry. We may pass from this to understanding why the poetic treatment of a subject relies on metre as well as rhythm. For rhythm and metre are both of them unifying instruments; they help to build up wholes. But the prosaist uses rhythms not so much for that end as because all movement and therefore the movement of language falls into rhythm in order to be sustained continuously. The poet is constrained to use every resource of rhythm, and of metre in addition, because they help to give his work the organic coherence of the living thing. Coleridge said this long ago. The poem is an organic thing, and its separate parts are not mere incidents but limbs of the whole. Rhyme and alliteration are further helps towards pulling the words of a poem together so as to make the subject a concrete and living thing.

Thus if I am right, and I do not flatter myself that I have been convincing,[3] the difference of prose and poetry is not merely one of form, but is a real difference of kind, though as with other kinds the two grade into each other by intermediate forms. They are not merely two styles of saying the same thing; what is said is different. The reason why the poet in general expresses himself in metre as well as rhythm is not that he chooses to do so but that he must. The vision which sees con-

[1] In *Three Philosophical Poets*, Harvard, 1910, quoted later, p. 145 (*Bulletin of the John Rylands Library*, vol. xv. 1931).

[2] See before, p. 88.

[3] In particular I have left undiscussed the difficult question of the status of prose drama. Poetry is essentially dramatic, I have said; but not all drama need therefore be poetry. In the same way some writings are in verse which are not poems. It would be strange to call Mr. Shaw's plays poems or Mr. Shaw a poet. Ibsen's *Brand* is a poem; can we say the same of the prose *Master-Builder*? I confess that I am not well enough equipped with knowledge of the drama to settle the question.

cretely enforces these aids to its expression. The outward form corresponds to the inward spirit. The poetic
vision, which Johnson said would make Thomson, the
author of the *Seasons*, view the two candles burning
on the table with a poetic eye, means that the subject
appears differently from the prosaist's subject, and demands of itself an appropriate form. The verse is not
the mere instrument the poet uses, so that he might
still be a poet without verse; it is as much a part of the
poetic attitude itself as the movements of the chest are
a part of respiration. When the verse is spoken, it embodies the poetic vision; when the verse fails to be
spoken, the presumption is that the vision is absent
or imperfect too, for the verse is its material embodiment.

Finally, it would seem to follow from our instances
that poetry is the higher art because of its distinguish-
ingly concrete character, which takes it nearer to the
nature of things. But poetry need not always be greater
than prose. Some prose is certainly greater than some
poetry. For greatness in art depends not on the form,
which determines its beauty, but upon the subject, or
what is often called by the un-English name of content.[1] There are no degrees of beauty, except in the
sense that works of art, poems or prose works fall short
of perfection of form in various degrees. But there are
degrees of greatness, arising from the nature or handling
of the subject.

B. In the Other Arts

So far I have taken prose and poetry where admittedly they exist, in literature, and attempted to discover the difference between them by taking pieces of

[1] See later, Chapter VIII. on "Beauty and Greatness in Art."

prose or poetry which have the same or much the same subjects and comparing them with one another. In all these pairs of passages I thought I could detect this difference: that in the poem the subject as rendered in words (for the poem is words and nothing else) acquires a life of its own, is a living thing, as it were, living its own life like an animal or plant, is organic, and, in a word, concrete. While the prose, for all its constructive unity, is not self-subsistent, but is descriptive of a given subject, even though that subject is itself created by the writer, as in a novel; and, in a word, is analytic. It is not the greater passion or vividness of the poem, for prose may be vivid, as in Carlyle, and passionate, as in Burke. It is that the poet places himself and places his hearer within the subject itself, and works from within outwards, while the prosaist describes, relatively, from without. Both of them describe, the poet as well as the prosaist. But the prosaist builds up his subject so as to bring it before your mind. The poet starts with his subject in its integrity, places the hearer's mind within it, and his exposition is the unfolding life of the subject itself.

Such are the direct and obvious method of inquiry and the provisional conclusion to be drawn from it. But there is another method to which I now proceed which is not so much comparison of poetry and prose in literature, where the distinction clearly exists, as a comparative treatment of literature and the other arts. I wish to extend the range of the inquiry and to ask whether in them there is not the same difference of kind as in literature is called that of prose and poetry, so that there are prose and poetry in painting, music, and the rest; two species in each art which can only be called by the name used in literature. If such differing kinds can be detected, we shall have fresh light shed upon what the difference is between poetry and prose in literature itself. There is a certain strangeness in the method, for we have to establish the fact that these kinds can be distinguished, and at the same time ask whether they differ in the same way as prose and poetry proper do.

I observe first that, paradoxical as it may seem to assert or suggest that there are prose and poetry in the other arts, the real paradox would be that this distinction should exist in literature alone of the fine arts, from the rest of which it is distinguished, it would seem, barely by the materials used in the several arts —words, or pigments, etc.

Next I desire to make clear from the beginning that I do not mean that certain paintings (to speak of that art for example) are attended by or suggest literary poetic ideas, in the same way that they may be romantic or classical. On the contrary, the introduction of literary poetic motives into a picture spoils the picture by mixing the procedures of two different arts. A picture which is not poetic as a picture is not made so by telling, for instance, a poetic story which may be very good in literature. What I intend to ask is whether there are not two kinds of painting which differ from each other, as literary prose and poetry differ; and I hope to persuade the reader that there are.

Thirdly, I am proposing to consider only beautiful art (of course in its varying degrees of success, for perhaps no work of art is completely beautiful), and to neglect all that immense range of so-called art which is really purely imitative and is not fine art at all but skilful craft. As the greatest mass of prose writing is not literature, but merely good literary workmanship, so in the other arts a large portion of so-called works of art are works of skill, and no more art than a photograph is art. And this no more implies depreciation of such works in the other arts than it does in literature.

Further, in suggesting that there are poetry and prose in the other arts, I do not mean that all such poetry is superior to prose. Poetry is, indeed, the higher art for a reason that will be plainer as we proceed. But some such prose may be and certainly is superior to some such poetry.

Finally, I have to ask for indulgence. The attempt to indicate the divergence of types in the several arts must necessarily be somewhat tedious, for it must take the arts one after the other and try to win attention or recognition for facts. And I labour under the special disadvantage of ignorance of—at least superficial acquaintance with—the arts. The best critic of art would be himself a practitioner in some one art. I am a practitioner in none, not even in literature, where I am content if I can attain to competent workmanship. But though I possess a fair acquaintance with literature in both its forms, I cannot pretend even to so much familiarity with the products of the other arts. My task is rather to appeal to those who know, and to submit suggestions to their judgment. I am concerned to ask them whether they would agree to the distinctions which seem to me to exist, and then further to inquire, what perhaps falls with better justification within the range of a philosopher, whether I describe the difference correctly. In any case it must remain as difficult in the other arts to say of any particular work that it is prose or poetry as it may be in literature itself.

Architecture.—The difference I am thinking of is most salient in architecture, with which I begin. Certain things I must take for granted without more than bare mention. We are concerned with beautiful archi-

tecture, and in architecture as in music beauty lies in
the relations of the material of the art. In music it lies
in the relations of tones; in architecture in the relations
of line, enclosed volumes of space, and the mechanical
stresses of the materials—stone or wood or brick, or
whatever else—employed in the building. These arrangements of line and mass and space, which are the
forms of house or church or shop, are the architectural
meaning of the building, which meaning, therefore,
does not lie in the other ideas which the building may
convey. Thus, when Hegel declared that the Greek
temple conveyed the ideas of finitude and limitation,
such as are also embodied in the Olympian gods—
human in kind, if superhuman, and each with its ap-
pointed office—while the Gothic cathedral embodied in
its soaring pillars and pinnacles the infinitude appropriate to Christian conceptions of the divine, he was
saying something perfectly true and, indeed, inspiring
about these kinds of architecture, but the ideas were
literary or historical or religious, and not constitutive
of the architectural forms, but only suggested by them.
The real difference between the Greek and the Gothic
lay in the flat roof and sustaining columns of the one,
and the vaulted roof with high shafts and walls supported by flying buttresses and pierced with windows
for the light of the other.[1] The ideas conveyed by
beautiful architecture are architectural ideas, and not
religious or literary ones; just as the ideas of beautiful
music are musical ideas and not emotions. It remains
true that as the habit of men's minds changes it will
seek out for itself architectural forms consonant with
itself. A conspicuous instance of this is the discovery of
sky-scraper architecture to suit the necessities of larger

[1] I owe this remark to my reading of a paper of Mr. R. G. Collingwood in *The
Realist*, vol. i., 1929, 'A Philosophy of Progress.'

city population and greater concentration of business within a limited area.

All this being premised, let us take examples, and contrast Salisbury Cathedral with Somerset House or even the Bush Building, or St. Mary Redclyffe at Bristol with the new University buildings there, which are also Gothic and have been much influenced at least in details by the church. Salisbury Cathedral has, indeed, the added charm of its surroundings. Still every good building is adapted to its surroundings, as, for instance, the austerely beautiful side of the John Rylands Library at Manchester is adapted to the narrow lane which skirts it, and so contrasts markedly with the more florid façade to the broad street. The cathedral has the effect upon the mind, through its own architectural form, and not through ideas imported from religion or literature, of a thing with a life of its own, as if it were a plant or tree growing out of the ground, and its self-contained life culminating at the growing top in its single spire. (It is not an architectural idea that the spire points to heaven, but a literary one, as illustrated by Wordsworth in a well-known poem, or in the phrase "a star-y-pointing pyramid".) Somerset House, on the other hand—I choose it as admittedly successful architecture—bears upon its face the purpose of its existence, the indication that its rows of windows are the windows of offices. It is so good because with all the revelation of its uses, its unity and organic character are maintained, It is prose because it is so manifestly a thing of parts and uses which are set out in their detail, while their coherence secures the indispensable unity of a beautiful design.

Now architecture, though so often likened to music, and indeed nearest to music of all the arts—the art essential to the bare physical existence of men nearest

to the most purely formal art—differs from music in
containing the representative element of use or utility.
Music has no utility except a spiritual one; architecture
has a material utility, like that of the subject matter
or story told in a painting. Now I suggest that in every
beautiful building its uses, its representative elements,
are indeed subsumed into the form, but also that in
Salisbury or St. Mary Redclyffe the building has an
autonomous life, as if it were an animal or plant created
to enjoy its own individuality, so that its uses flow from
it and are not felt; while the other buildings are not self-
contained but imply other things, *e.g.* men, to which
they are subservient in their uses. On the other hand,
when the uses are obtrusive, the building ceases to be
beautiful art, and is merely the skilful adaptation of
materials to an end and is a work of craft, as is by far
the greater number of our houses and other buildings.
This difference, I suggest, is identical with, not merely
like, by a sort of analogy or metaphor, but identical
with, the difference already indicated by way of another
approach as being that of poetry and prose in literature, and may therefore properly be called by the same
name. Because architecture has its different uses, and is
the form appropriate to that utility, it may either, as it
were, live out its uses or display them. When it does the
first it is concrete, individual, synthetic, and proceeds
from within outwards. When it does the second it is
analytic and explanatory; but its parts, so long as it is
beautiful, are held together within the unity of its
design.

Other instances that occur to me are the beautiful
prose of the now demolished Regent Crescent of Nash
or of the Royal Crescent at Bath, and indeed a large
part of the admirable house architecture of Bath, so
singularly like in the general effect it produces to the

excellent literary prose of the same century; as compared, say, with the poetry of several of Wren's churches
or Inigo Jones's Hardwick Hall at Hucknall. Perhaps
the difference may be verified in the new sky-scrapers
which are our modern substitutes for cathedral buildings. Some of them seem, from their drawings, for I
have seen none of them in their reality, to be poems,
such as the Tribune Tower at Chicago, others tell
clearly their story and are prose, according to the
difference I have attempted to describe.

But in working out the distinction there are all sorts
of difficulties. Partly we have to remember that, as
with literature, there is never perfect beauty, but yet a
building may be a poem and a more or less successful
one, sometimes a poor poem, and still bearing the distinctive marks of poetry and not of prose. Sometimes, of
course, it is bad, whether bad poetry or bad prose.
Partly we must abandon the prejudice that poetry,
however imperfect, is always superior to prose. The
admirable prose of Somerset House may be superior
to much architectural poetry. Sometimes the difference
is patent; for example, the poetry of the inner court of
the Royal College of Science, or the charming Renaissance Hospital at Milan, or the prose of the Adam
buildings in London, or of the Edinburgh University
building of the same artists.

But there are very different types of architecture,
Greek, Gothic or Romantic, and I beg to observe that
the mark of poetry is not any romantic character, for
it belongs to classic as much as to romantic architecture or other art. Again, as in literature there are different sorts of poetic prose form—epic, lyric, dramatic,
narrative, oratorical and the like—so there may be
corresponding sorts of architecture, the difference, for
instance, between Azay le-Rideau and Chambord or

Chenonceaux or the Louvre or Blois or a building of Mansart. It may be very difficult to say which is prose and which poetry in particular cases. Thus to me the Pazzi Chapel at Florence seems to be poetry, as clearly as the Rucellai or Riccardi palace is prose. But I do not know what to say of the Farnese palace at Rome or the Strozzi palace at Florence. I know a porter's lodge in my own neighbourhood (at Ashburne Hall in Fallowfield) which I think to be poetry, and an eighteenth or early nineteenth century stone house at Calver in Derbyshire seemed to me more like poetry than prose. It is, again, not merely the presence of imagination which decides. Burke's prose, to repeat myself, is highly imaginative without being poetry. And I suppose that, as in literature, there are hybrid products which are not clearly poetry or prose. Moreover, as the sky-scrapers show, it is not the particular purpose which decides; industrial architecture may be poetry. But all these matters must be left to the judgment of those who know, by whom I am content that the distinction which I have suggested and attempted to describe should be considered and approved or rejected. This remark applies equally to what I shall say about the other arts. I am rather asking a question than formulating a doctrine.

Painting.—In painting I take as illustrations of the one kind the frescoes on the ceiling of the Sistine Chapel, Botticelli's Venus rising from the sea, or the Giorgione landscape belonging to Prince Giovanelli, which was shown in the Italian exhibition of 1931, and contrast them with almost anything of Ghirlandajo, and in particular his frescoes of the history of the Virgin in Sta. Maria Novella, or, since such pictures as his are at the lower limit of their kind and might by some be

regarded as merely illustrative craftsmanship, with
such a picture as the Veronese in the National Gallery
of the meeting of Alexander and the family of Darius,
or the same artist's 'Supper at Cana', or many a picture of the Dutch School.[1] I am assuming that these
pictures which I name in the second place are good
paintings and beautiful, and beautiful because, though
they tell a story, which the others do not, the story is
completely inspired by the form, or, to use expressions
used already in respect of architecture, the ideas embodied in the pictures are pictorial ideas and not *merely*
ideas suggested by the pictures. As a satisfactory example of this second class of pictures, I add the paintings of Hogarth, whose artistic or formal excellence is
conceded. I do not know whether I should be justified
in placing beside them the late Venetian pictures of
Longhi or Guardi, more or less contemporary with his.
And comparing these two kinds of paintings, I ask
whether the first set may not be described as possessing
a self-contained life, as if they were organisms created
by the painter, so that it is not so much their subject
which pleases as rather that their subject is forgotten in
the enjoyment of their formal life, as we forget the lion's
fierceness or the cat's subtlety in delight of the lissome-
ness of their bodies and the grace of their movements.
The painter has conceived or felt in terms of line and
colour and light or shade the subject from which he
starts; and living its life from the inside has made it in
its parts and incidents live again in the picture and for
us. Whether, secondly, in the other instances the subject is not felt or conceived—still in terms of line and
colour and illumination—from without, so that the
picture depends not merely on itself but on the story

[1] Or, I might add, the Daumier picture of the St. Lazare railway station
which is reproduced in Mr. Roger Fry's *Transformations* (London, 1926).

which the spectator is told. If this is borne out, that the
one set is concrete and synthetic and the other descriptive and analytic, we may justly call the one set poetry-
painting and the other prose-painting, with the identical
difference which is exhibited in literature.

Perhaps the difference may be illustrated most easily
from portraiture. In general I suggest that Reynolds is
a prose painter and Gainsborough a poetic one, and
recall at the same time the proviso that to call a painting
prose is not to depreciate it, for some prose-painting is
higher and greater than some poetic painting. And I do
not suggest that Gainsborough, for all his poetry, can
be compared with Leonardo, also a poet if ever there
was one in painting. His poetry is rather that of grace
and charm than of depth, like the literary poetry of his
time. For the sake of bringing home the point I refer
to a comment of Fromentin on the work of Rembrandt.
Rembrandt was a great poet, whom it is far better so
to describe than to call him by the obscure name of
romantic. Velasquez was no romantic and yet was a
pictorial poet; witness his portraits of the Infanta and
Philip IV., to say nothing of the 'Venus with the
Mirror'. Now Fromentin says (in *Les Maîtres d'autre-
fois*) that there were two men in Rembrandt. One was
the perfect artist, best illustrated by the portrait of the
Burgomaster Jan Six or the earlier portraits in the
'Anatomy Lesson'. The other was the Rembrandt seen
under difficult conditions in the so-called 'Night Watch',
and in his splendour in 'The Supper at Emmaus', or the
portrait group of the 'Syndics'. Fromentin thinks that,
for all its perfection of style, the subject of the Burgomaster Six was not quite congenial, and the result is a
masterpiece of painting, but external; while the figures
of the Syndics live again. My suggestion is that Rembrandt in Six was for once painting perfect prose, per-

fect because there is nothing in the picture extraneous to the pigments, while nearly all his famous pictures are poems with varying degrees of success. His portraits are eminently pictorial poetry in the sense described; for instance the beautiful portraits of his son Titus, that of himself in our National Gallery, that of a young man in the Louvre (1651), or the lovely one of an old woman at Leningrad (1654). This is what is suggested to me by Fromentin's criticism, which I take to be that of an accomplished artist-critic, though it is, of course, not so put by the author himself.

Outside the two classes of pictures which are poems and prose, there is the whole vast range of illustrative painting in which the interest lies in the story itself that is told, and not as in prose-painting in the form or design which tells the story. Such painting does not belong to fine art, but is craft, though it may be very skilful craft. Its difference from true prose is that the ideas embodied are not pictorial, but belong to history or sentiment or religion. The pictures which alone Tolstoy would allow are religious lessons conveyed in pigments, and belong to education or edification, and not to art. The use of illustrative pictures is not in the least to be denied. So long as men are moved by recognition of what interests them, so long such pictures have their legitimate place, but they are not art. They are, of course, of the most different kinds, from really good illustrative work, through Leader's landscapes or Leighton's 'Captive Andromache' down to photographs. Competent painting has its worth like competent writing. It is, however, below the rank of beautiful prose. Once more it is to be insisted that there is real poetry or prose in a painting which in some respects good of its kind is faulty or even bad; possibly Leighton's picture just mentioned is best described as poor poetry.

In thus distinguishing prose-painting which is not autonomous but tells a story beautifully from illustration which tells a story well but not beautifully, we have been raising the question of the value of representative painting. Painting, it is still safe to say, is representative. It has a subject which is to be distinguished from the pictorial form of the subject, though the form varies with the subject, and the subject becomes different with the slightest change of the form. So it is that the pictorial poem and prose about the same topic have a different content or subject in that sense. Any variation of treatment affects the subject represented. Its representative character distinguishes painting from music, or at least from pure music. It is true that the subject may be nothing but form, as in arabesques, in which case painting approaches most nearly to music. But this is a limiting case.

The name representative painting is, however, commonly applied to painting which tells a story, and it has fallen into suspicion of late years, at the hands of those who quite rightly insist that beauty lies in the form and not in the subject. This rejection of all representative painting and refusal to count it as beautiful have been modified very considerably in the later writing of Mr. Roger Fry.[1] He acknowledges the claim of certain representative pictures to the title of fine art, but, being still unprepared to consider it a branch of painting proper, proposes the view that in such painting, besides the art of painting proper, there is another art, that of representation, which is joined with it, as in opera singing and acting are added to music. This solution appears to me a violent one, which is the outcome of the refusal to recognise the representative element in painting as such. It is, moreover, open to the difficulty that

[1] See his *Transformations*. London, 1926.

since there is representation in sculpture as well, we should have an art which works indifferently in pigments and in stone or other sculptural material; whereas each art, as we know the arts, has its distinctive material. In music there is primarily no representative element, but the material of music is the tones themselves and their relations, whereas in painting the lines and colours essentially mean things, though beauty lies not in the things but wholly in the forms which convey things. But if I am right, representative painting in the special sense, when it is beautiful and there is no element left extraneous to the form; which tells a story not for the story's sake but for the beautiful form of it; is really painting, but it is a different kind of painting. It is not a blend of painting with another art, but is prose-painting. In this way a large body of beautiful paintings will be included in fine art, as it is by the common sense of mankind. I have learnt so much from Mr. Fry, and have so profound an admiration of his writings, that it is something like a relief to me to think that by recognising much painting to be pictorial prose we are at once taking note of a difference of kinds in fine art and saving much beautiful work for what is indeed a lower place on the whole than pictorial poetry, but for a real and legitimate place.

Sculpture.—Sculpture offers, to me at least, more difficulty in testing the distinction which appears to me to exist in the two arts that have been just discussed. Partly, it is that in the standard sculpture of Greece so little of the great period remains, except in later copies, and it is just in copies that the traces of the creative hand and chisel are apt to disappear. Partly, it is that the glamour of Greek sculpture of the best time disposes the spectator, at least the unskilled one, to find

poetry in it everywhere. Yet there seems to be a clear
difference in kind between the Theseus and the Horse
of Selene from the Parthenon and, say, the admirable
Pergamon frieze preserved at Berlin. I have no reason
to doubt the story cited by Hegel that when the
Pheidian statue of Athena Promachus was unveiled
the Athenians shouted that that was Athena, not in the
mere sense as I suppose that it was a speaking and
moving likeness of their idea, but that it was the god-
dess herself in stone, filled with the Olympian majesty
and life. The Pergamenian reliefs are a story told well,
though with some rhetoric. Is the pan-athenaic procession in the frieze of the Parthenon more than prose
sculpture? Much poetic feeling seems at first to hang
about some of the lovely Athenian sepulchral stelae.
But apart from the charming domestic sentiment,
which after all is domestic rather than sculptural, they
are rather records than creations, unlike, for example,
the poetry of the lovely relief of the girl bending to tie
her sandal. We may remind ourselves that literary prose
may be lovely too without being poetry—there are
exquisite such passages in Pascal which do not rise
above prose, as one may assure oneself by comparing
them with many a passage of his contemporary Racine,
where the barest language has the intrinsic and autonomous life of poetry. The Hermes of Praxiteles is un-
doubtedly a poem, but were the Niobids of the Uffizi,
whose originals are attributed to his colleague Scopas,
even when we allow for what they have lost in transcription, more than prose art, which possibly in their
original form was more successful artistically? I venture with some trepidation upon famous ground when
I suggest that the Laocoon group may claim rather to
be good plastic prose than poetry. The Ghiberti reliefs
of the Baptistery door seem to me to be poems, however

much they violate the alleged rule that sculpture cannot
depict a continuing incident. No one can doubt that the
Antinous figure belongs to a different kind from, say,
the Zeus of Ottricoli or the Victory of Samothrace; and
the great Augustus of the villa of Hadrian is also prose.
The Ludovisi figures on the chair in the Thermae are,
on the other hand, sheer poetry.

So in general are the Donatello statues as clearly
poetry as the Campanile of Giotto or Giotto's own sculp-
tures on it. To the class of poems belong the great singing groups of Donatello and of Luca. The real difficulty is to find sculpture from the great Florentine
masters which is prose. If one steps from that great age
to the present, I should feel little difficulty myself in
referring Mr. Epstein's sculpture in general to the class
of poetry, adding that where he is faulty it is not that
he drops into prose and still less into mere illustration,
but is imperfectly poetical. The Rima relief is a good
instance of what I take to be the meaning of poetry in
sculpture, incapable as I am of appraising its real defects. Defects seem to me more palpable in his Genesis,
but they do not make it the less a poem, only the less
completely or perfectly poetical. What I have seen of
Mestrovic again is surely in the class which provisionally I call poetry, but Rodin's work I do not know well
enough to be able to judge whether some or most of it,
e.g. the burghers of Calais, is not really prose.

As in painting, there is a vast amount in sculpture
of illustrative work which is neither prose nor poetry,
but merely good (or bad) craftsmanship. The question
which I wish to submit to fit judges is whether a great
deal of really beautiful sculpture does not beautifully,
that is artistically, tell a tale, like the pan-athenaic frieze,
without restricting itself to such mere story-telling, but
making the work descriptive in beautiful form and yet

not piercing to the centre. The Augustus statue is a
good instance. Are there not in our portrait busts, besides the mere photographic ones which do not count
as art, and the real poems, such as perhaps the Pericles
or the Niccolo da Uzzano in the Bargello, many, like
certain busts of Roman emperors, which are descriptive
or analytic (like the Jan Six in painting) and yet beautiful? If I am right in these lame exemplifications, sculpture is also either poetry or prose, and for the same
reasons.

Music.—In music there would seem to be a clear
difference in kind between pure or absolute music and
programme music, which has a subject that is not itself
a musical idea. Here, as before, we may exclude from
consideration a mass of so-called music which may be
highly skilful technically, but serves an agreeable purpose, such as dancing or singing, and is at most not
beautiful but pretty. But in separating two classes from
one another of music which is fine art, as poetry and
prose, there is, besides the difficulty in the application
of the distinction to which I shall return presently, the
theoretical difficulty, that there would seem to be no
room for prose in music, because there is in music no
element of representation. For the material of music is
nothing but tones and their relations, and though these
may suggest emotions or even definite subjects, it is
not these which constitute the meaning of the tones.
They mean themselves and nothing else. Whereas even
architecture means, as we have seen, its uses; and painting and sculpture, except in their limiting cases of
arabesque and the like, always have a subject, though
that subject may in the limiting case be mere form.
Pure music is in fact, according to the statement of
Hanslick, an arabesque of tones.

The contrary opinion, that music is designed to express the emotions of the composer, arises partly from the immensely greater rôle of emotion in music than in the other arts, partly from the manifest emotional effect of all music, but partly from the mistaken belief that the aim of music, as of all other arts, is to express emotion, that is, in the main, the emotion of the artist. It would seem hazardous to demur to a proposition which is so widely accepted. Yet I venture to anticipate here a later[1] chapter and to say that no art endeavours to express the emotions of the artist in any more particular fashion than it expresses his conceptions or images or, generally, ideas; but that it endeavours to express not the artist at all but the subject matter which he has chosen to embody in his material; and that the only emotion which he can really be said to express is the artistic emotion which drives him into production, and which is satisfied by the form of the work he produces. Furthermore, if art is supposed to express the personality of the artist, that proposition would not suffice to distinguish art from any other kind of action, which always proceeds from personality. The difference of art from other such expressions is not to be found in emotion but in the fusion of the artist with his subject matter, which modifies that subject matter and makes it something that it would not be except for the artist.

Music, then, does not exist in order to express emotion, though it proceeds from emotion, and also suggests emotion to its hearers. It is limited in its material to tones and their formal relations, which have no other intrinsic meaning. For this reason it is that the other arts have been said to tend towards music when they are at their best.[2] This is, indeed, another way of saying that all art, in so far as it is beautiful, derives its beauty

[1] See later, Chapter VII.   [2] Above, Chapter V.

from its form and not from its subject, and music has nothing but the form of its materials, and therefore exhibits the true nature of beauty most plainly. When the Abbé Bremont says that pure poetry culminates not so much in music as in prayer,[1] he misses the real value of the other saying, of Pater's, though at the same time he raises the difficult and absorbing question of how poetry and the other arts at their best, though human creations, put us into relation with the universe of reality, as we are by the ways of religion put into relation with that universe in prayer.[2]

The introduction of a subject other than tonal would seem, then, to be blending music with another art and producing a mixed art like opera, as Mr. Fry proposes to say of representative painting also. If we are still to count music with a subject, or programme music, as prose, we must, I imagine, say that the subject by its emotional tone is identical with the emotional tone suggested by the music itself. In this way, though it implies some stretching of our theory, we may allow that representative music is a legitimate kind of music, though it has not the obvious legitimacy of prose-painting or sculpture. Whether the fusion of music and subject is successful, it may be hard to say in particular cases. In many cases the problem is solved by what is practically a disregard of the words of a song or an opera, of which the best instance is the sheer poetry of *The Magic Flute*, where the senseless libretto does not count. Sometimes what may seem to some representative is not so at all. Everyone knows that Beethoven, who described a phrase as "Fate knocks at the door", said also that it was suggested to him by the sound of the woodpecker. It remained pure poetry. I do not know how far Strauss's musical setting of Hoffmanns-

[1] *La Poésie Pure*, Paris, 1926.   [2] See later, Chapter VIII.

thal's poetry left the music poetry or made it musical prose. But in many instances programme music is musical prose, and the only doubt remains whether it should be likened rather to hybrid poetic prose in literature or simply treated as musical prose. Sometimes it is difficult to say, because composers call their works by names. Significantly, Schumann is said not to have given names to his songs till after they were composed. Much confusion in painting and sculpture, as well as in music, would be avoided if the artists avoided giving names to their works, *e.g.* if Mr. Epstein had not called his poetry 'Genesis', and suggested mere literary interpretations of a work which is formal or at least has no value except in so far as it is successful formally. Indeed a good test of whether a piece of plastic art is poetry or not is whether it produces its effect unnamed, as, for example, the Botticelli 'Venus' would.

I should take as pure examples of musical prose Berlioz's *Fantastic Symphony* and Elgar's *Falstaff*. I will not inquire which of the great classics are poetry and which are prose. More even than in the other arts, my acquaintance with music is too superficial. I am content to ask whether, for instance, quite apart from the relative greatness or splendour of the works, there is not a clear difference of kind between Handel's *Messiah*, or the greater part of it, and Bach's *Mass in B Minor*. Spontaneous and autonomous character is written on anything of Mozart or any song of Schubert. These are poetry. On the other hand, Tschaikovsky insisted for himself that he wrote his Fourth Symphony to a programme. It is for the musical judge to say whether that work does not bear a corresponding difference of character. There is no doubt of the poetry of Chopin or Brahms. What of Strauss? Is the Eroica Symphony of Beethoven of the same musical kind as the Fifth Symphony? Again I repeat that prose is as much art as poetry, and some musical prose may be greater than some musical poetry. Nor is every musical composition necessarily poetry throughout. It may be fancy on the part of a tyro in music to suggest that a change from poetry to prose occurs when Beethoven introduces in the last movement of the Choral Symphony not merely the voice, which is only another musical instrument, but a subject in words. Despite the splendour of the choral part, the change in character from the earlier movements is marked. And I must leave unanswered the question whether Wagner has always made musical poetry. The use of certain motifs suggests that the music has become representative. How far in such passages the composer has been better than his own theory and remained a poet, or how far he has merely succeeded in overcoming the duality of music and representation by effecting a fusion of them and so has written beautiful prose, I cannot dare to decide. I confess that large tracts of his music seem to me not poetry but prose, though splendid prose.[1] The deliberate use of motifs suggests at any rate that the composer is proceeding analytically and not as the bird sings. But a great composer may be a poet and stil sometimes change over to prose, and with this particular composer it may be of interest to know which parts of his work are the one and which the other. Here, as before, I am content to put a question and ask for an answer from those who know.

It would seem, then, from this inquiry, which I am well aware has raised as many questions as it has answered, that there is in all the other arts a distinction of kinds which is identical with, not, I repeat, merely

---

[1] *E.g.* the Good Friday music in *Parsifal*.

analogous to, but identical with that of prose and poetry
in literature, and therefore may fitly be called by the
same name. The difference we have found to be: in the
one authentic original life, in the other unity, indeed,
and organic connection, but description and analysis;
the one concrete, the other not abstract but analytic.[1]
I do not think that the result is very different from
Mr. Read's statement that poetry is creative expression,
prose constructive expression. I am, of course, at one
with him in finding the essence of the art in the medium
itself, in the words or pigments or sounds, etc., "adequate", as he says, "to the thought involved". When he
adds that poetry may inhere in a single word or two
or three words, 'incarnadine' or 'incense-breathing
morn', while prose exists only in the phrase, I think it
possible that parallels may be found in painting, for
example, or music, in the invention of a new palette or
technique, as for example by the impressionists. But I
do not feel sure, and in any case the mere group of
words forming a name may be poetry because of their
actual life as of a concrete organism. If I have spoken
so much not of words or pigments, it is because I have
taken for granted that it is these which are the work of
art and their form its beauty. And more than once I
have indicated that with these assumptions, kinds of
art may be distinguished by their subject matter or the
treatment of it.

My demurrer to Mr. Read's statement is mainly that
creativeness is an epithet of mystery (apt enough be-

---

[1] A similar (this time merely analogous) difference may be found elsewhere
than in fine art, in craft or manufacture. For example, there is a kind of biscuit
known as 'digestive', excellently agreeable to the taste and nutritious, and
conformable to the Idea of biscuit, in which yet the purpose is apparent. Compare it with Bath Olivers, whose usefulness for nutrition drops into the background. They are the poetry of biscuits, the other sort prose biscuits. They
remind you of the poetry of Oliver's contemporaries, for instance, Shenstone:
"My banks they are furnished with bees".

cause of that strange magic about poetry), and suggests that nothing further can be said. Partly my reason is that constructiveness seems to me the essence of all art, whether prose or poetry. Elsewhere in this book I have tried to find the ancestry of the sentiment of beauty in the constructiveness exhibited amongst animals, as in the nightingale's song or the beaver's architecture, and have suggested that such constructiveness becomes art when it has ceased to be practical, like the wooing song of the nightingale, and becomes purely contemplative. Poetry is the higher and more original art than prose just because it is nearer to the instinctive outpouring of song. Strangely enough, there is no creativeness here in it because it is instinctive and spontaneous. On the other hand, concrete authentic life, life as of a real living being, is a description of poetry quite in keeping with its instinctive origin. It is not, therefore, merely the philosopher's predilection for his own jargon which makes me prefer my own account to the notion of creation. Creation out of what?

Moreover, when we look more closely, prose also is creative in its selectiveness, for instance in the rigid self-restriction of some writers to the barest and fewest words, a practice so different from that of common speech or ordinary literary craft. Indeed, in so far as it is beautiful, prose always has a certain element of strangeness, because the artist is not transcribing as in mere craft, but mixing himself with his subject, according to the old formula of *homo additus naturae*. "No beauty but hath some strangeness in the proportion" is a famous apophthegm. And poetry, on the other hand, may use nothing but the plainest words, as in much of Wordsworth, and its originality and lyrical power may lie not so much in its inventiveness as rather its expression of what I have so repeatedly called authentic life

—"Rolled round in earth's diurnal course with rocks and stones and trees"; where the shock of the strange but not new word 'diurnal' helps to make us part of the actual unending motion.[1] The 'incense-breathing morn' is morning herself as she lives, and who does not feel the same intimate sympathy with the life of the flowers in the familiar 'I know a bank' which I quoted at the outset? Everything which heightens this sense of intimacy with the subject adds to the poetical effect because it removes us from even the vividest inspection of a thing to its interior. And as has been said before, metre with its repetition is a potent means of compacting words into the expression of spontaneous life.

The distinction thus drawn helps us to understand first why poetry in point of fact precedes prose as an art: analysis is nearer to reflection, poetry is nearer to the simpler, directer, experience of things; secondly, why poetry is commonly thought to be superior to prose, though prose may be the more difficult art. Finally, it throws light on the puzzling belief, so often entertained and supported by the authority of great men like Wordsworth, in a poetic vision which may be possessed by others than poets, or may be possessed by poets before they have mastered the craft of poetical writing, a belief which leads on to the separation between poetry or art in general and its expression in the artistic medium, its technique. That separation I have held to be inadmissible; poets and painters are not such except they write or paint; and I have gone further and maintained that the artist discovers his vision of things through the revelation which his use of his materials brings to him. Yet it is not probable that common testimony and the belief of artists themselves are without

---

[1] The illustration is borrowed from Mr. Abercrombie.

some foundation; and we can see now what that foundation is. Poetry in every art lends to its subjects a character of independent life. Now, it may well be that the artist is a man who is more closely sympathetic with the life in things about him than other men. Art is always concrete and individual. Science is the search for generals or universals. The artistic disposition vibrates more easily to the life about him, and feels the life of things or animates them with the life he feels in himself. Children appear often to exhibit such direct sympathy and betray it in casual expressions of wonderment,. as when a child declares a forget-me-not to be laughing. Mr. Bergson refers repeatedly to the sympathetic intuition which is characteristic of the artist, and has even questionably extended the notion to the animals, imagining, for instance, that the sphex by an intuitive knowledge stings the caterpillar in places where the caterpillar can be paralysed without being killed, and so dispenses with anatomical experience. The illustration is questionable, but the notion implied may be sound.

The poetic vision which the artist is supposed to possess may therefore well be this directer sympathy with the individual life, and the artistic nature one which possesses this simpler, more childlike habit of regarding things. Before he sings or paints, his intercourse with nature may be thus intimate. This is perhaps the vision and the faculty divine. It still does not make him a poet or a painter, but it may be that which predisposes him to artistic expression. For feeling is not art,[1] and the sensitiveness which he feels to the life of things does not make him an artist. Neither can it be said, to use a phrase of Mr. Chas. Morgan's,[2] that the 'conception'

[1] See later, Chapter VII.
[2] *Portrait in a Mirror*, p. 183. London, 1929. In an earlier passage (p. 43) Mr. Morgan, however, speaks of the artist's discipline by the material. The two

is greater than the execution in the medium. For the conception comes through the actual execution, and before that is blind feeling or sympathetic response. The metaphor of conception is indeed misleading. It omits the impregnating excitement which is supplied by the material in which the artist works when his mind is occupied with a subject matter. Not parthenogenesis but bisexual creation is the true analogy.

The great artist is in fact at once greater and simpler than ordinary men. His simplicity resides in his natural affinity with his subject, so that he lives its life. He is both child and man. He employs his reflective powers and technical expertness, which he shares with the man of science or the craftsman, in order to return out of the man's habit to the intuition of the child, or more strictly, to remain within it and retain its character of preoccupation with the life and even the interior life of the subject matter.

passages need to be read together, and I am sorry that they are too long for me to quote in a note.

CHAPTER VII

SOME ERRORS

IT may be well if I interpolate here some remarks upon certain errors, as I take them to be, in aesthetic theories, either past or now current. Little as I feel inclined to the work of criticism, and wanting as I confess in the gifts required for what is often an illuminating method, yet it argues a certain disrespect for opinion and for the men who are the authors of it, to disregard other views. I prefer to let the data speak for themselves. Yet sparks arise from friction of minds as well as of material things, and as the mistakes of which I shall speak have been implicitly corrected, some mention of them may help to set the conclusions arrived at in the preceding pages in a clearer light.

Tolstoy's doctrine is immediately connected with the end of Chapter V: the doctrine that the aim of art is to provoke in the mind the emotions appropriate to the subject matter which was the artist's stimulus to production and in the end the substance of his work. Such a doctrine on the part of a consummate artist would be strange had he not the precedent of another consummate artist, Plato, in judging the value of art by its supposed utility and approving consequently only those works which have a good educational effect. Tolstoy accordingly censored all art except that which taught religious truth. His censure rests upon a total disregard of the real impulse to art, and degrades it to a mere educational contrivance in the work of satisfying another and quite different impulse, that towards

morality. There is not a word to be said against the
sentimental appreciation of art which grows eloquent
over the passions portrayed in a picture, except that
such appreciation is not aesthetic, and it rests upon a
confusion between the material passions which feed
the constructive one, preconditions of its operation in
the artist's mind, and are reflected in some form, even
if idealised or sublimated, in his finished work, and the
proper artistic impulse. It is impertinent to repeat
after Goethe what is portrayed once for all in his poem
Confession, which was, as I suppose, the origin of the
use of the word philistine to name this habit of judgment. Moreover, some artistic craft is employed to
teach, even if nothing else is done, and it is not necessary to deny its usefulness. Only to treat it as typical
of art is to mistake the accident for the essence. For
nothing prevents the beautiful from being used educa-
tionally, though that is not its purpose.

The real answer to such doctrines has been already
indicated and I do but repeat myself. If the work of art
is beautiful it conveys to us the form of its subject. But it
may suggest also that subject in the manner proper to the
subject and not to the picture. If it does so in a manner
such as to overpower or outweigh the formal nature of
the subject, it ceases to be beautiful and lays itself open
to moral judgment. If the nude is so treated, that is with
such imperfection of art that it raises in the spectator
ideas or desires appropriate to the material subject, it
is false art and bad morals. This is, after all, nothing
but repeating Kant's distinction between beauty and
stimulus, or his insistence on the shareability of beauty.
Now it is clear that the more provocative to the passions
the subject in its own material character is, the harder
will it be for the artist to represent it beautifully. I can
see no limit to the choice of subject provided it be

treated beautifully. Even a pornographic subject might
conceivably be handled by a rare artist so as to be
beautiful and therefore fail to raise the sensuous suggestion. But the difficulties in certain subjects of presenting them without material suggestions may be so
great as practically to preclude them from the artist's
choice. It is here that the Puritan and the Philistine
have their opportunity. They try to judge art by a test
which can be applied only to works which fail of attaining beauty. It is the intrusion into art of an irrelevant
standard. The issue is one not of art but of prudence
in avoidance of subjects beyond the artist's skill to make
purely beautiful.

   The same answer is perhaps sufficient to those who,
like Ruskin, suppose that beauty in the work means
virtue in the worker, and vice in the worker defect in
his work. Everyone may approve his indignation at
the disgusting grotesque above the side door of the
church of S. Maria Formosa in Venice. It is ugly
not so much because the sculptor was foul-minded as
because the sensuous suggestion could only have been
overcome, if at all, by inconceivable artistic skill.
Vice in the artist may affect his work in allowing him
to choose for subject what his art is insufficient to
endow with beautiful form, and can only leave in a
condition where it excites personal and unshareable
pleasure. Otherwise, I take it that weakness of character may affect his work in diminishing his faithfulness to his artistic aims, as Browning implied in his
study of Andrea del Sarto. Doubtless since artistry is
the practical life of the artist, defects of character may
vitiate that part of his business of life. So also a defect
of character may affect a man's gift for science where
hardly anyone would think that the exercise of that
gift has any concern of itself with morality. But this

inquiry is not intended to be a study of practical behaviour.

A common belief about art is that it centres about
emotion, arises from emotion and has for its aim the
expression of emotion. The belief may appeal for authority in part to the great and venerable name of Wordsworth, in the famous dictum that poetry arises from
emotion recollected in tranquillity. What is really vital
in the saying is the reference to tranquillity, in which
emotion loses its sting. It is tempting to think that art
has to do with emotion as science with intellect and
right conduct with will. But it is a commonplace that
this clean-cut separation corresponds to no reality. All
mentality is intelligent and emotional and, it goes without saying, conational. Doubtless the artistic tempera-
ment is specially emotional, but unless all art is lyrical
in its subject, as it plainly is not, the subject of the
artist is not confined to emotional states but plays over
all experience. What divides art from intellect and conduct is that it is conversant with physical materials and
fills them with meaning. That meaning may be derived
from the emotions or any other source, but it is not
emotion which the work of art depicts or expresses.
Music, thought sometimes to be especially the field of
emotion, is emotional rather in its effects than its
nature. Emotion is a poor and improbable way of describing the meaning of a Mass of Bach, the Eroica
or the Fifth Symphony, a concerto, even less a minuet
of Mozart. Fancy and, much more, thought or even
will are equally applicable descriptions, if all of them
were not alike irrelevant, and did not the music mean
only the form of its tones, to which analogies may be
traced probably in virtue of the emotional effects in
various subjects of thought or feeling or will.

K

Feeling enters as material passion into the artist's mind, as has so often been explained, and correspondingly it is reflected in subordination to the dominant purpose in the finished work. But feeling is not the only constituent. In that 'incubation' which in Wallas's happy language precedes the birth of the work, thought enters, and imagination, and all the motives, conscious or hidden, which stir the mind. It is not these material emotions which create art. But there is an emotion which does create it, and that is the artistic emotion, which is reflected into the form of the product.

Usually it is not difficult to discriminate in the work the unity of design which is truly beautiful and the elements corresponding to the material passions or other motives of the situation which have been taken up into the form. Where trained sensibility to artistic form is lacking, it is these material elements which prevail in the appreciation of the spectator, and a picture, for instance, is judged from the attractiveness of the persons depicted or their nobility of character, or, in inferior works, their open appeal to mere sentiment. The old problem of how tragedy pleases while it excites a sympathetic sorrow finds a simple solution. The incidents are painful because they appeal to pity or terror. The whole pleases, in successful art, because it satisfies the aesthetic passion, in the satisfaction of which these material passions are, in both senses of that word, purged, are allowed their vent and purified through their place in the total. Where the feelings excited are most poignant the satisfaction of the aesthetic passion and the material ones are in great art felt in their unity and their discrimination: hopeless sorrow in Lear's lines on the Fool's death, and overpowering tenderness in Hermione's recovery of Perdita:

Thou'lt come no more,
Never, never, never, never, never.

You Gods, look down,
And from your sacred vials pour your graces
Upon my daughter's head.

Where the material and constituent passions tend to
overpower the artistic unity, there is defect in the art.
Of the two great Victorian poets, neither of them, as I
suppose, of the highest rank, the greater artist, Tennyson, secures his end in easier and thinner matter; in
Browning the weight of substance overpowers the
artistry, and even in his finer passages the strength of
the material passion is apt to be unbalanced by due
subordination to the unity of the whole, and the beauty
is consequently felt less than the interest of the situation. It may be worth while adding that while mono-
tony in reading of poetry is tedious, it has in its favour
that it leaves more play for the undisturbed appreciation of beauty, while the lively rendering may obscure that appreciation by over-excitement of the
material passions. Significantly enough, it is said that
Tennyson read his own poems in a monotonous chant
and Browning with the liveliness of experience. The
instructions of Hamlet to the players remain still the
pattern: "In the very torrent, tempest, and—as I may
say—whirlwind of passion, you must acquire and beget
a temperance, that may give it smoothness". In good
reading or recitation no effort is made to throw feeling
into the words, but when the words are spoken with
temperance and full value is given to the sounds of the
words themselves and they are not slurred, they of
themselves carry with them the due proportion of
emotion.

There is a doctrine popular at present which has

deservedly great authority, though it is often current in an indefinite form and is more difficult to deal with because it contains so much truth. This is the doctrine that beauty is essentially expression. As thus loosely described, it is open to much objection. Expression of what? If of the feeling, the doctrine has been considered already. Beauty is the expression not of any and every feeling but specifically of the aesthetic feeling. If expression means only expression of the artist's personality, the description is too wide, for everything we do or make is the expression of our personality. What we desire to know is of what part of our personality.

The importance of Mr. Croce's form of the doctrine is that according to him the images which are beautiful and are translated for purposes of communication into material form are themselves expression; image and expression are one. The spoken word is the most obvious instance of expression of an inward idea, and accordingly linguistics is a department of aesthetics. Ideas and their motor issue or overflow are part and parcel of the one whole. As a fact of psychology I accept this last statement unreservedly, and I may seem to have been saying the same thing as Mr. Croce, and to differ from him might be thought cavilling.

The divergence arises from the different approach I make. I am not writing philosophy and make no assumption or hypothesis, still less start with a proposition which to so many students of philosophy seems self-evident and has seemed so since the days of Berkeley, that physical existence is itself spiritual and has no existence save in the mind. With that belief to say that image and its expression are one offers no difficulty, except that we desire to know and are not told what an image is an image of.

Unless we start with this philosophical prepossession,

the statement of Mr. Croce seems to me to invert the plain order of facts. Assume a physical world and no questions asked, a perception in the mind (for 'image' includes perception) is the condition of mind directed upon that perceived object, and the object is perceived only through the act of mind which is directed upon it and, as we have seen, has been wrung from our minds by the physical compulsion of the external thing itself which is perceived. Images in the strict sense of the word become, then, what is revealed to the mind in the absence of the actual thing imagined. Images are then intelligible. I submit that with a different approach images are taken for granted, and since both the external thing and the image of it are mental existences, at once the intimate connection of image or perception with the physical object is insisted upon (and that intimate connection is true) and the connection left unexplained. The need of explanation of the intimacy of image and expression is slurred, and the image is left a mysterious thing. When, on the other hand, we realise that the image is revealed through the expression, we are left with no mystery except the fundamental one that there is an external world to be revealed. That remains a mystery for the philosopher to treat, but it is only the statement of a fact.

Moreover, I find it impossible to account for or reconcile with his own doctrine Mr. Croce's other characteristic doctrine, that the embodiment in material form of the image is merely the technical process of giving publicity to an expressive image. Here again the order of plain fact appears to be reversed. If speech is typical of the expressive image, nothing is more public than speech, and no literary art seems to be required to make an image common property. So too are the other motions in which images express themselves, move-

ments of the hands with the chisel, or of the feet or
voice. They are only in one degree of publicity removed from the actual modifications of stone or tones
or pigments, in which these motions end and (in the
arts) exist only in that completion. Only in the song
and dance does movement stop with bodily gestures.
In all the other arts the movements mould bodies external to the artist's body, and, as we have seen, the
artist discovers in that completion what the mental
condition, let us say the idea, was with which he began.

In the order of fact and actual existence, accordingly,
we must assert rather that the image, instead of being
a private possession of the artist communicated only
by his technical accomplishment in stone or bronze, is
from the beginning potentially public. What has to be
explained is rather the privacy of mental conditions as
distinct from the public images upon which they are
directed or which they have for their objects.

I am anticipating what belongs properly to a later
stage of the inquiry,[1] but in order to indicate that there
is no valid distinction of technique from artistic expression, and that rather art and its technique are one
and the same thing. Only technique must not be
understood as mere facility of execution, but as including any device of outward expression which is
needed to give complete vent to the complex motions
in the artist's mind. Mere facility or accuracy or perfection of finish may even be detrimental to the larger or
the finer movements of the instrument which secure
the artist's aim; as some artists have discovered to
their cost, as I understand, who have left the finishing
of their conceptions to pupils or experts, who in their
limited technical perfection have made too smooth what
should have been left rough.

_____
[1] Chapter X. on 'The Objectivity of Beauty'.

At any rate the notion that technique is a mere means to publicity seems to me irreconcilable both with the idea that ideas in the mind are themselves of their nature expressions, which is true, and with the truth therein implied that the outward expression in material form is organic to the artistic impulse, whether it takes effect in speech or other medium, which again recurs to the truth that the artistic act is public, or potentially so, from the outset.

There is another meaning of the proposition that beauty is expression which is not an error, and indeed in another place has been indicated before.[1] The beautiful is expression as expressive of its subject matter; that is, it portrays the real or true character of its subject. It deals, in the Aristotelian phrase, with the universal or general as embodied in the particular; it is the universal rendered in concrete form. This doctrine is compatible with the admitted fact that art is always individual, the work of art some individual subject. For it may be that the artist strips off the transitory particularity of an individual thing and gives it, not as the photographer does at some one moment of its existence, but, as the portraitist does, as it is at no one moment of its existence, and yet gives the essential nature of the subject. Such a portrait is. the 'singular universal' of the subject's transitory states and is, as it were, their continuum crystallised into a single view. This notion of expressiveness is that which Sir Joshua used in his treatment of the grand style, but describes more lightly as the typical. It was urged by his later contemporary Goethe under the name of the 'characteristic'. However difficult it may be of application to all art without exception, seeming rather

---

[1] Chapter VI., à propos of music, p. 117.

to derive its force from classical art, or what is called classical, it says something fundamental about the work of art; but it raises questions about the relation of the artistic expressiveness to the truth of things, which makes it convenient to defer such fuller treatment as I can give to it.[1]

---

[1] See, later, Chapter VIII. on 'Beauty and Greatness'.

CHAPTER VIII

BEAUTY AND GREATNESS

THE existence of a subject matter and its distinction from the form of the material accounts for the double valuation of or judgment upon a work of art, its beauty and its greatness.[1] There is a similar distinction in morals and science upon which I trench for a moment because the double judgment is plainer there than in art. Virtue is virtue wherever it is found; it is the action which is done in the right spirit and is appropriate to the circumstances. But it varies in magnitude or splendour. The widow's mite is just as generous as the millionaire's endowment of a hospital; it may even have more merit, but it is not so large or magnificent. A good savage is as good as a good Christian, but his goodness is not so large, because it is appropriate to simpler conditions. The Christian would repudiate much that the primitive does, though apparently, if Mr. W. J. Perry is right,[2] some primitives would repudiate the quarrelsomeness which Christians have not always condemned. Morality has problems to solve which are presented by circumstances: what shall we do which shall satisfy the social sentiment, which shall be fair between us and our fellows; goodness is the quality of the conduct or the person (for in the end these are the same thing, conduct being not mere physical action but action which comes from a mind), which is suitable and solves the problem. What is inappropriate is not good, because it does not

[1] The following chapter is largely reproduced from *Proceedings of the Aristotelian Society*, N.S., vol. xxx., 1929–30, 'Beauty and Greatness in Art'.
[2] W. J. Perry, *The Growth of Civilization*, chapter x. London, 1924.

solve the problem. Aristotle has a happy example of
the virtue of 'magnificence'—giving a small vase to a
child; an expensive gift (as if nowadays I were to give
the child a motor bicycle) might be wanting in virtue.
Thus there is a double standard by which conduct is
measured or judged. It must be virtuous, and if so
there is no difference between conduct in one man or
another, in one age or another. But its scale differs, and
this is a difference which makes progress in morals
possible. For as circumstances change and the minds
of men become susceptible to what they were insensitive
to before, different kinds of conduct are required. There
is an order of actions according to their distance from
virtuous action. But within virtuous action there is an
order of greatness or smallness, an order of perfection.
It is clear that these standards are not separable though
they are distinguishable; for if an action has not the
greatness necessary to its circumstances it is also wanting in virtue.

In science the difference is still more obvious. What
is true is true, but one truth is not so big as another. The
man of science has attained the scientific end if he has
discovered a property of a species of plants as much as
if he has discovered the formula of the law of gravitation.
But the two truths are not comparable in greatness.
Truth varies with its subject matter just as virtue does.
But there is no preference among truths in respect of
their truth.

In art there are these same two standards: there is the
strictly aesthetic standard, Is the work beautiful or not:
has it attained beauty?; and there is the question, Is it
great or small? We are always being told that there is
no sense in asking whether one poem is more beautiful
than another; and there is not. Yet we continue to ask
the question because we mix the two standards. *Queen*

Mab (I mean Mercutio's) is not less or more beautiful than "the baseless fabric of this vision", but the second is a greater poem. The same thing is true when we compare artists, say writers. One artist may be a more perfect artist than another, may never be careless in his art: Jane Austen is a more perfect artist than Dickens or Scott, and Tennyson than Browning. That is a purely artistic comparison. But we should say (at least I should) that Scott or Dickens is a greater writer than Jane Austen because there is larger range of human nature in the subjects they choose and greater penetration into character. The amplitude and variety of their subject, of their world, outweigh in the comparison the imperfection of their artistic skill. They do not write so well, but they are bigger persons and their bigness is reflected in their topics. The balance is often, perhaps always, very difficult to strike: how much imperfection in the one aspect can be atoned for by greatness in the other aspect. We never have a doubt that *Queen Mab*, which is only a delightful fancy, is less great than the speech of Prospero, or *Midsummer Night's Dream* than *Much Ado*. But as between poems of the same poet, and still more as between different poets, the judgment is generally perplexed and hence the endless controversies of preference. Or we may contrast the relief of the girl bending to tie up her sandal with the Hermes of Praxiteles or with the Theseus of the Parthenon; or in painting the 'Source' of Ingres with the 'Birth of Venus' of Botticelli or with Tintoretto's 'Presentation in the Temple' in Venice or Titian's picture of the same subject; or in music Bach's Gavotte with one of his own Masses.

Now this contrast of beauty and greatness is the old contrast of form and subject matter, which is found also in goodness and in truth. But in these last the

contrast offers no difficulty or little, whereas in aesthetics
it is a fruitful source of conflict, and some think vain
conflict. It is worth while, I think, to indicate why the
topic is so important for art. The reason is that in representative art the subject matter is not of the same sort
as the material in which it is embodied. Take science;
that is only, directly or indirectly, remotely or immediately, a rearrangement and organisation of the data
of science. It is full of artifice, but the conceptions used
are all of a piece with the world we live in. The man of
science may carry us off into a world of symbols, but
his symbols stand for features of the external world and
he is bent on verifying them by sensible experience.
He is concerned with measurements; but measurements
are numbers of certain units or standards and these
have reference to the world of things. The physicist
flies off into the empyrean, but he is always access-
ible to signals from the world and sends them in turn
to it.[1]

The subject matter of a work of art, however, is the
meaning the artist himself puts into it, but the material
into which he puts the meaning is a foreign object,
marble or pigments or words or tones. If for a moment
we may consider the moralist or the scientist as an
artificer (which I am sure we can), the meanings they
introduce into their material are characters of the
material itself—of human nature or external nature as
the case may be. But the subject matter of the picture
or the statue is, say, a woman or a god, which have
nothing to do with the proper qualities of paints or
marble. It is not, indeed, the subject as such which the
artist puts into the material of his art. What he does
(and here I am but repeating myself, because of the
importance of the point) is so to fashion his material as

[1] Further discussion later in Chapter XI.

to express the form of the subject matter as he conceives or imagines it. That subject in itself is foreign to his material. The marble block is not really alive but only looks so. But the relations of the material to be correspond to the relations of the subject. What I plead is that it is the material as of a certain form which is judged aesthetically and is strictly beautiful, but the subject matter which is signified by form is not as such beautiful but only important or trivial, great or small, big or little—it belongs to what I should like to call the order of 'perfection' as I said about morals; but the word is too ambiguous and I must say only 'greatness'.

There are thus in works of art a scale of beauty and a scale of greatness. On the first scale a work is more or less beautiful according to its success in achieving beauty. Though there are no degrees of beauty there are approximations to beauty or to ugliness; to be accurate, there are degrees of failure or ugliness. Only, defective beauty is sometimes judged too harshly if described as ugly. Moreover, the word ugly here means unaesthetic and does not apply to those features of a work of art which by themselves would be unattractive or repulsive, like an 'ugly' face, but in the work are subservient to the total effect and may even heighten its beauty.[1] So grotesques may become beautiful by their treatment, or a Gorgon's head, or a devil of Signorelli. Shakespeare in his later period delighted in converting the unattractive into beauty, securing what Bosanquet after, as I believe, Mr. A. C. Bradley calls 'difficult' beauty. Much of Mr. Epstein's sculpture where it is successful is difficult beauty. Correspondingly mere attractiveness in a subject if it stood alone, as Kant said along ago, is different from its

[1] See later the remarks in Chapter IX. on 'Beautiful and Ugly'.

beauty which it receives from the artist. Else our galleries would be filled with beautiful portraits of women, which they are not.

These remarks are enough to show that greatness and beauty are not to be contrasted sharply as if they were quite independent of each other. The difficult beauty which has been mentioned has in it an element of greatness which easy beauty, the beautiful representation of an attractive subject, may not possess.

It belongs to the nature of the case that this is so. For the artist must have some subject, even if, as in the case of music, the subject is not distinguishable from the materials at the limit. Being a man, and himself big or little, he chooses a great subject or a small one and makes of it a thing of beauty. This being so, the problem set for him to solve is different in the two cases. The profounder or larger his subject is, the more difficult it is to achieve beauty in it. Hence, though the beauty of the great work is no greater than that of the small one, the first implies a greater reach of artistic skill. In speaking of great art we are not merely setting two standards and mixing them. We speak naturally of the greater art of the greater man provided he achieves beauty, because he has worked more largely and profoundly to secure his end.

'More largely and profoundly.' The phrase is used advisedly. For when we ask if we can analyse greatness, it is perhaps these characters which make the difference of the great subject and the small. To which we may add 'more complexly' unless we choose to construe largeness in the double sense of extension and detail, or include complexity under the head of profundity. Perhaps the only way of bringing home these criteria of greatness to the mind is by way of illustrations, by comparing for instance the Monna Lisa with

any picture by Andrea of Lucrezia. But such comparisons are endless and may be left to my readers to
supply.

With this I leave awhile the anatomy and biology of
beauty, as I may term them, which I have been for the
most part pursuing hitherto, and proceed to a more
philosophical aspect of the subject. Greatness and smallness depend upon the subject matter, and they suggest
difficult problems about the relation of the beautiful to
the rest of reality which we investigate in science and
the knowledge of which is truth, as well as to the special
department of reality which is occupied by human
affairs and morals. Now the beautiful whether in art
or nature is of course a reality. It is not mere physical
(or human) reality because it mixes the mind with the
physical or, it may be, human topic which suggests it.
But being an amalgam of two real things, the one
physical and the other the mind, the product is also real
and has its own autonomous reality. Yet since the
interpretations of the subject come from the artist, art
makes a new world for itself which, as in a fairy tale,
in Southey's tale, for instance, of the *Three Bears*, may
be very remote from the world of fact. How does this
man-created product we call the beautiful and which
gratifies our constructiveness when it has become contemplative, how far and in what way does it bring us
into contact with the world which is independent of us
(I mean in the common-sense sense of that phrase), and
anyhow is independent of any particular individual? It
cannot give us knowledge, for knowledge or truth is,
as we shall see, but the real world dressed up by man,
who eliminates himself from the result. But the artist's
subjects are drawn from nature physical or human,
and though he does not give us truth, he gives us an

experience which with the prophetic inaccuracy of our careless minds we are in the habit of calling truth.

The artist is himself a part of the real world, and to a certain extent he reflects the world in a mirror of the world's own creation, and his picture is only in degree different from the actual reflection of the sun in the lake which illumes the yellow bees in the ivy-bloom. But the greater he is the more he attests the poet's statement that out of these reflections he creates forms more real than living man, nurslings of immortality. It is an old saying that tragedy (which is the highest form of poetry) is truer than history, because it gives us in an individualised shape the universal. Great poetry at least (but the thing is true of all poetry) selects from or adds to its subject so as to portray the essential features, I mean the characters which count, in the real subjects which are the starting-point of its efforts of creation. If there is such a thing as a 'concrete universal', it is to be found surely in a work of art; and perhaps this is the best evidence that the concrete universal is a misnomer and does not exist except in art. Plans which are universal exist abstractly in the real world, which is not made by man, but concretely in the new reality which is made by man. In that mirror, unlike the lake, the image is distorted into perfection; as if a mirror, instead of blurring as all mirrors do the original, should through the artist's magic smooth out the imperfections of all possible merely real mirrors. The faithful newspaper, and even the faithful scientific history, reproduce what has actually happened; the artist creates for us its essential meaning. Hence it has been maintained that the greatest history blends the artist's vision with the historian's fidelity. The most obvious illustrations of the universality of art and its consequent direct connection with truth, which is utterly conversant about

universals, are to be got where the subject is human
nature itself and its life. But they are to be got no less
from the depiction of nature, from the sunset touch as
well as the chorus ending from Euripides (I apologise
for the inevitable recurrence of these familiar tags—
after all they are the words of artists themselves about
their own affairs).

It is easy enough to see that art embodies in its
proper material of words or other medium the truths
which are recognised by common experience or discovered by science to be true of things or minds. Were
it not so, we could hardly understand why art appeals
to many or even all, and acquires thus the status of
objective value. Nor is there any limit that I can see
to the treatment by art of even the abstrusest doctrines
of science, only in a form suitable to the concrete and
sensuous material of art. Lucretius wrote a great poem
containing the science or philosophy of Epicurus. But
we have to remember that what he wrote was not
science nor philosophy but poetry. He would else have
left the dissemination of his master's teaching to some
craftsman of prose, which is the proper vehicle of
science. And his poem is a great one. Lucretius has his
flats and plains as every long poem has, but quite independently of the magnificent half-lyrical passages
which so obviously come from a poet of the first order,
the work as a whole is saturated with poetry. I quote
a passage from Mr. Santayana's *Three Philosophical
Poets*:[1] "There remains the genius of the poet himself.
The greatest thing about this genius is its power of
losing itself in its object, its impersonality. We seem to
be reading not the poetry of a poet about things, but
the poetry of things themselves. That things have their
poetry, not because of what we make them symbols of,

[1] Harvard, 1910, p. 34.

L

but because of their own movement and life, is what
Lucretius proves once for all to mankind."

The poet has exhibited the atoms not as the physicist
sees them but in their own intrinsic life. Still in doing
so he has taken us away from the atoms as they are
for truth, and yet keeps us in contact with truth. How
is continuity of poetic 'truth' with true knowledge to be
accounted for?

The answer so far as I can see it is twofold, first that
the poet or other artist is a man as well as an artist,
and a highly gifted one. He is excited to his art by the
world about him, and is more sensitive to it than the
majority of persons: in closer rapport with it. At least
that is true of the greatest artists, your Michael Angelo
and Beethoven and Shakespeare and your architect of
Cologne Cathedral. The greatest of them are not only
artists but seers. No doubt the lesser ones are also,
along with that special gift they have of art, interested
in a lively way in the world about them.

Secondly, and here is the main point, the special
constructive gift of the artist is not a luxury in which
he indulges as it were for play, but a serious and strenuous execution of his function in the world. It does not
help him to actual survival in contrast with other men
(the survival it gives him is that of lasting on in the
minds of men), but it belongs to him as a specifically
gifted member (I mean that the degree of his gift is
specific) of the human type which has established itself
in face of the surrounding world. And it is part of our
faith in the coherence of the universe, even if its establishment is no more than the work of natural selection,
that the artist's vision of his subject which colours, as
we have seen, the choice and execution of what his
work declares to us and himself, though it is not scientific, gives insight into reality. If it cannot claim to be

science, as it surely cannot, it may anticipate that comprehensive science which is philosophy. Recur for a moment to the poetic animation of the atoms by Lucretius. Science at the present day smiles more and more upon the philosophic conception that things are all in their measure alive, as propounded by Spinoza before. That is why I said that when we called poetry a higher form of truth it was a prophetic inaccuracy.

I recall here the magnificent (if, to my mind, fantastic) conception of Schopenhauer that art exhibits the Platonic Ideas or Forms as they work and live. In his language art displays the Will which underlies all things, not objectified as it is in physical reality, the surrounding world of things, but in its own intrinsic character. To comment on this conception would carry me outside the limited scope of this essay. And I refer again to Lotze's saying that music in its movement of tones is the reflection of the great movements that go through the universe: Lotze professes no knowledge of music and his dictum is perhaps vague, and even rhetorical. But I, who have far greater unacquaintance with music than Lotze had, can still feel that it conveys a truth however dim the expression. No one who listens to great music and abstains from surrendering himself merely to the emotion which it is apt to excite, who tries to listen to it as music, can help feeling its affinity in obscure ways to the great goings on of nature and of human affairs.

It is far more difficult, I think, to answer the questions which arise out of the place of human nature in the world, the relation of art to morals and to history. I must confess that I have little to offer and do not see my way very clearly. Still if morals means the solution arrived at by man in the problem of living in the world,

himself a part of that world, the great art can hardly in
its subject be isolated from that world when it deals
with humanity. Vaguely we can see that the artist, if he
is a great man, sees the world with penetrating vision,
must represent the world as congenial to the permanent
issues of the forces working in human nature; and the
issue of these forces has been virtue. It should not be
necessary for me to repeat that this does not mean that
the proper subjects of art are virtue. That has been dis-
posed of in its place. On the contrary, evil being one
of the major features of life, I was going to say one of
the major interests of life, evil not only has been but
must be among the subjects of the artist. The question
that properly arises is whether great art can leave evil
unredeemed without indication of its submergence in
the total course of things. In other words, does not
great art handle its subject so as to exhibit the world
upon the side of good?

That the greater art is concerned more extensively,
more profoundly and more subtly with the main tendencies in human nature and in things is illustrated
by the common judgment which sets tragedy above
comedy as the greater art. For tragedy depicts the
conflict within man's history of the larger forces at play
in it. This is marked perhaps most strongly in Greek
tragedy; and Hegel's description of the *Antigone* in
this light remains unchallenged—the clash of two vital
forces, brotherly love and obedience to the gods and
primal law, with loyalty to the will of the ruler: in
which clash Antigone perishes. In comedy there is also
vital truth; only there the conflict is between the extreme and not necessarily and indeed rarely valuable
types of character and the general common sense of
society, the conventional standard of living. That too
is a real force in life which in comedy (say of Molière,

for I am following Meredith) prevails against the
offender, but it has not the truth of loyalty but rather
is a habit than a passion. The conflict with it is consequently less serious, and is covered by laughter.[1]

But that tragedy itself exhibits the world as on the
side of good and not of evil, is a harder proposition to
establish. The best that I can do is to refer the reader
to Mr. Bradley's treatment of the topic in Shakespeare
(ch. i. of his *Shakespearean Tragedy*). He first points
out those features of Shakespeare's tragedy which suggest "a moral order asserting itself against attack or
want of conformity"; how the evil is started not by
what is good, as for example the love of Romeo and
Juliet, but by what is evil, the insensate hatred of the
rival houses; and how the hero's fate is in part at least
the result of his weakness (*e.g.* Hamlet). "The tragic
suffering and death arise from collision not with fate or
blank power, but with a moral power, a power akin to
all we admire and revere in the characters themselves."
On the other hand, the evil in the moral order of the
world is part of that world—and its own creature. "The
whole or order against which the individual part shows
itself powerless seems to be animated by a passion for
perfection: we cannot otherwise explain its behaviour
towards evil. Yet it appears to engender this evil within
itself, and in its effort to overcome and expel it is
agonised with pain." Shakespeare was, however, not
attempting to solve the mystery of life, but as a poet
was writing tragedy. And we are left with the mystery
of a world working for good or perfection and yet only
able to overcome its own evil "by self-torture and self-
waste. And this fact or appearance" (the waste of good
in the expulsion of evil) "is tragedy." Perhaps we may
say, then, that this type of tragedy does embody in

[1] The subject is resumed at greater length in Chapter IX.

some form a faith that the universe works in the direction of goodness.

There cannot be said to be in Shakespeare any metaphysics of the world which would settle the issue between optimism and pessimism. What are we then to say of a world view which like Hardy's appears to be definitely pessimistic? In the *Prometheus Vinctus* we are left with the proud defiance of Zeus and his confidence that under the overruling Fate Zeus will still be dethroned (see also Goethe's *Prometheus*). But *Tess* and *Jude* offer no such consolation. The world as the novelist sees it is not on the side of goodness, or at least does not favour it. I refer here to Mr. Lascelles Abercrombie's *Thomas Hardy*,[1] according to whom we are not left with this hopeless conclusion. "The inevitable agony is not only set forth in these two books—it is judged. If man has his intellect which enables him so to conceive the miseries of his existence, he also has his sense of justice; and it enables him, rather compels him, to see this existence of his as a breach and senseless violation of his profoundest belief—the belief that his sense of justice *ought* to be satisfied" (p. 135). And again, "Throughout these two books the atmosphere is charged with a furious indignation against the fundamental injustice of man's existence" (p. 137). Perhaps the same account may be given of *The Dynasts*, whose Chorus plays the part of Fate in Greek tragedy but depicts it as the relentless destroyer of man's ambitions good and evil alike.

We may say then perhaps, following these two critics, that in tragedy either the world is on the side of goodness or we are made to feel that it ought to be so. In neither case does the artist, because he is a man and must not only make his subject beautiful but

[1] London, 1912.

cannot disinterest himself, and would not, from the vital concerns of man, fail to assert that goodness and not evil is congenial to art. The Puritan and the Philistine may take such consolation to themselves from this as they can. It serves at least to show that something is true which they did not mean to say.

This inquiry will be resumed when we attempt later [1] to consider the contrast between moral greatness and historical greatness, which may be immoral.

[1] Chapter XIV. pp. 263 ff.

CHAPTER IX

THE character of the subject matter accounts for certain distinctions current in aesthetic theory and most familiar in literature. They are the distinctions of tragedy and comedy, of the beautiful and the ugly, of the beautiful and the sublime, of the classical and the romantic. All that I can offer upon them is some slight notes, but it seems undesirable to pass them over without some discussion, the more so that in spite of Mr. Croce's disparagement of aesthetic 'kinds' they seem to me to be real and important distinctions.

Tragedy and Comedy.[1]—The reporter of Plato's symposium says that at cock-crow Socrates and Agathon and Aristophanes were still awake and drinking, and Socrates was discoursing and was compelling the other two to acknowledge that the genius of comedy was the same as that of tragedy, and that the true artist in tragedy was an artist in comedy also. Socrates was not the man to shrink from a paradox, and the assent of the other two must not be pressed, for the reporter says they were drowsy and did not quite follow the argument. It is greatly to be regretted that Plato has not preserved Socrates' arguments in some other form. We may be sure they were delightful and full of good sense and subtlety. Socrates had before him the practice of

---

[1] What follows on this subject is taken from a paper on 'Molière and Life' in the *Bulletin of the John Rylands Library*, Manchester, 1926. Instead of dealing with the subject as a whole, for which I have not competence, I deal with it by way of a particular case.

the tragic poets in winding up the trilogy of tragedies with a satiric play; if he had been living in the seventeenth century he could have pointed to Shakespeare and Racine and Corneille, and to the last with peculiar relevance. For although *Le Menteur* hardly rises above the level of a comedy of incident and errors, Molière himself has said that if it had not been for this comedy he himself might have written his lighter comedies but would not have risen to the height of the serious comedy of *Le Tartuffe* and Alceste. Possibly Socrates was influenced unconsciously by the presence both in the tragedy and the comedy of his time of the chorus which in some fashion represents the grave opinion of the public and of life. For there is reason to believe that the chorus or its equivalent enters implicitly or explicitly (that is, in the person of some character or characters) into the very structure of comedy. At any rate in the comedy of Molière this is always so. On the other hand, the chorus is accidental to tragedy in its structure. From being originally a participant it becomes a commentary on the real participants and then disappears.[1] Now Socrates, impressed by the habit of his time, may have thought that both forms of the drama, sharing in so important a feature, were in essentials the same or had the same genius. His arguments would have been subtler and in appearance more profound. Yet perhaps it is here that the real difference of tragedy and comedy may be found, that in the one the judgment on the persons is absent or falls to the spectator, in the other it is in the structure of the play.

Socrates, while he said that the true tragic writer was also an artist in comedy, did not lay down the converse proposition that the true comic writer is also an artist in

[1] C. E. Vaughan in *Types of Tragic Drama* (London, ed. 2, 1924) sees it represented in later tragedy in the lyric element of the speakers.

tragedy. Molière, at least, if he sometimes seems to skirt the borders of tragedy, is never really tragic. We have to be on our guard against reading into him feelings different from his intention or inspired by situations which are more seriously regarded at times different from his. I know one sensitive person who cannot read *George Dandin* because of sympathy with the hero in his cruel deceptions. Yet he is too undignified in himself to be a tragic character—"vous l'avez voulu, George Dandin": the helpless resignation of a foolish man; and we must confess that Molière and his audience were accustomed to regard conjugal infidelity with levity when it did not touch themselves, and that the heartless wife in the play is meant to and does emerge triumphant. Our sympathy with the nobler side of Alceste's character may incline us to weep with him rather than laugh at him; but there is no doubt of the intention of the play. Molière comes nearest to tragedy in *Le Festin de Pierre*. Yet the fate which overtakes Don Juan may give us a thrill of horror but is too melodramatic to be tragic. In a tragedy the vengeance of insulted right would not be left to the strange machinery of an animated block; the just heavens would have embodied their vital presence in the person of some character of the play; whereas Done Elvira, who warns Juan of his doom, finds no more tragic solution of the conflict than to retire repentant into a convent. True to his comic inspiration, Molière, on the contrary, leaves us with the great exclamation of the valet bewailing the loss of his wages. Once, indeed, Molière tried his hand not at tragedy but at an heroic play, *Don Garcie de Navarre*. But he had the good sense to recognise that he was forcing his natural vein, and made the best use possible of his failure by taking passages from the tediously jealous harangues of Don Garcie before his serious and constant mistress, and inserting them into the worthier setting of Alceste's manlier, if still unreasonable, protests against the levities of Célimène.

In order to test the paradox of Socrates by a concrete instance let us ask why *Le Misanthrope* is a comedy and *Timon of Athens* a tragedy. Of the justice of the designations there is no doubt. Alceste upon the stage is laughable and meant to be so. *Timon*, which as a tragedy is not for a moment comparable in artistic merit with *Le Misanthrope*, and is indeed a poor tragedy and only in part, it is said, the work of Shakespeare, is a tragedy. They are worth comparing because in both the subject matter is the same, the turning of what is essentially a noble nature into misanthropy. In both, the hero is ennobled by passion and disfigured by foolishness; in both, the issue is the rejection of the world. Here the likeness ends. The differences arise with the comic or the tragic development respectively.

The passion of Alceste lies in his sincerity and dislike of shows. The man who prizes the rude lyric 'Si le roi m'avait donné' in spite of its archaic style and its poor rhyme, because it portrays a heartfelt passion, may or may not have been a good literary critic (he was surely a good one);[1] but at least he was a man of noble disposition. Timon is mere good nature, till ingratitude makes him flame up into hatred; adversity brings out the man; he ceases to be the genial fribble,

[1] Si le roi m'avait donné
　　Paris, sa grand' ville,
　Et qu'il me fallût quitter
　　L'amour de ma mie,
　Je dirais au roi Henri:
　　Reprenez votre Paris;
　J'aime mieux ma mie, ô gue
　　J'aime mieux ma mie.

　Le rime n'est pas riche, et le style en est vieux;
　Mais ne voyez-vous pas que cela vaut bien mieux
　Que ces colifichets dont le bon sens murmure,
　Et que la passion parle là toute pure?

under which his real force was disguised. "The old Timon with his noble heart," says Tennyson, "that strongly loathing greatly broke"—though the words are perhaps exaggerated. Alceste has his passion within control. Even when he is most agitated by hatred of conventional lies, he remains of the world which practises them. In the great scene with Oronte he is the perfect gentleman—"Je ne dis pas cela". Only when provoked beyond bearing does he tell Oronte flatly and coarsely that his sonnet is worthless. Timon becomes hatred personified, through revulsion from his own good nature. The difference of their fates flows from the difference in their faults. Alceste is foolish through the extravagance of his expectations. Being a large and not a mean character, he unreasonably asks of human nature more than human nature can bear, and the high pitch and tension of his sincerity pervades him so that, comic as he is, he is one of the really concrete and organic types of personality; like Tartuffe in this respect and unlike Harpagon in *L'Avare* perhaps, and certainly Argan in *Le Malade Imaginaire*. That is why, or one reason why, *Le Misanthrope* is so great a comedy and Alceste a comic hero. His fault is not tragic for it is the basis of his character. Timon's fault is not so much extravagance of judgment as foolish and innocent confidence in men. When the unthinking spendthrift discovers that he has placed his trust in summer friends, he recognises the tragic fault (the ἁμαρτία) and his trust is converted into passionate hatred. Were he a more organic person, were he less a mere prey to the revulsion of feeling and the desire to give it vent, he would be more of a tragic figure than he is.

All the same we can in the indifferent tragedy trace all those elements which have been discovered to lie at the basis of tragedy by Aristotle and Hegel, and by Mr. Andrew Bradley in our day. There is the tragic fault into which he slips out of the blind simplicity of his inexperience of mankind. And the play may be said to exhibit within this noble and serious person, turned nobly serious by the issue of his defect, the conflict in which overweening trustfulness is shattered against the real self-seekingness of mankind, and he perishes in the conflict. And at the end Alcibiades enters to pronounce like Fortinbras in *Hamlet* the words which reconcile his death with overruling providence. These features do not stand out so clearly here as they do in *Lear*, or *Othello*, or *Hamlet*; but they can be discerned in spite of the imperfections of the play.

In *Le Misanthrope*, on the other hand, there is indeed a clash or conflict between the high-strung demands of Alceste and the unbending reasonableness of the social standard. But the clash is not so much a clash as a contrast; and it can be so reduced in scale, and become comic, because the conventional judgment which laughs at Alceste for his extravagance and is embodied in the persons of Philinte and Éliante and even, in her way, of the gay and bewitching and entirely reasonable coquette Célimène who is the author of all Alceste's woes—because this conventional standard is not an elemental force in things and human affairs, but rather a matter of sweet reasonableness and moderate expectation, in which all men can settle down as to a minimum. Thus Timon's trust in human nature comes into conflict not with what we may reasonably expect of men in society but with self-regarding human nature, and the end is the destruction of Timon in the struggle. Alceste's revolt against society is not the simple failing of a sincere and noble nature, but a crude misapprehension on his part of the conditions under which society can be carried on. There wants in such a situation the seriousness of issue which in tragedy is always raised. Of the tragic poet is true what Mr. Yeats says of himself with a different application:

> The elemental beings go
> About my table to and fro.

The public standard against which Alceste rebels has not the high solemnity of a great power like jealousy, or, to take again the Hegelian case of the *Antigone*, loyalty to the state, or as in *Hamlet*, devotion to a father's memory. We are not torn in our sympathies between the sincerity of Alceste's passion for unbridled truth and our acceptance of current opinion. Conventional standards do not seem to us to deserve all that pother, and the gravity of tragedy is consequently replaced by light-hearted observation of how the revolter goes under.

It will be urged that Alceste is passionately in love, and there is tragedy in the sacrifice of his love to his sincerity; and it is true that the conflict betrays a noble nature and excites our sympathy, and, if Alceste were different, contains a tragic possibility. The conditions of real tragedy are, however, wanting, the contention between vital elements in human nature. For Alceste's sincerity is vitiated by its unreasonableness, which it is the very gist of the comedy to expose; it has not the 'high seriousness' of Othello's simple trust and honour, poisoned by a friend with suspicion ("it is the cause, it is the cause"). The sacrifice of his love has not the inevitableness of the tragic calamity, nor is the pity it excites a 'cleansing' pity; it does but make the comedy a greater and higher comedy.

In one of his works on psychology[1] Mr. McDougall

---

[1] W. McDougall, *Outline of Psychology* (New York and London, 1923), p. 168.

has suggested that laughter is a preservative against excess of sympathy which would be exhausting. In this play we take the side of Philinte and Éliante, and even Célimène, and laugh in order not to sympathise with the honest sufferings of Alceste. Those who, feeling so strongly his essential but misguided goodness, weep for him, fail to take the point of view of the comic poet and to laugh at the somewhat trivial defiance of an accepted code or anything firmly enough based on common practice to claim reasonable recognition: much as we laugh at Beatrice and Benedict for their playful refusal to acknowledge the claims of their attraction for each other. Hence Alceste, for all his enthusiastic rebellion against the insincerities of polite society, is no grave champion of virtue but a light challenger of the claims of moderation and reason. Noble as he is, he is surrounded with an aroma of triviality. In the end his indignation hurries him into his rupture with the world:

> Trahi de toutes parts, accablé d'injustices,
> Je vais sortir d'un gouffre où triomphent les vices;
> Et chercher sur la terre un endroit écarté
> Où d'être homme d'honneur on ait la liberté.

The issue is too intense for the occasion. Significantly enough it is suggested that his resolution may not be unshakable. The comedy ends, not like a tragedy with the hero's overwhelming, but with the hope that after all he may acquiesce:

Allons, madame [says Philinte to Éliante], allons employer toute chose
Pour rompre le dessein que son cœur se propose.

I do not say that comedy is in the right to ridicule these generous rebellions against good sense and moderation. Heaven forbid that indignation at the insincerities of our accommodated social intercourse should cease. Rather than that, let our Alcestes claim the liberty of saying no word but unvarnished truth, at whatever risk of hurting the feelings of others; or, if they are unfortunate enough to love in their own despite a Célimène who being young and full of the wine of life declines to abandon all society in order to devote herself to her lover's whims and bury herself in hiding with him from the world whose injustice he cannot endure, let them endure their discomfiture. The spirit of revolt is so precious that these sacrifices may be worth while. Yet comedy may still have something to say in its defence. It ridicules in Alceste not his sincerity but his petulance. It raises no laugh at the revolt against serious evils by the valiant champions of new ideals whose aim is to reform: your Francis of Assisi who, bred in luxury and the life of pleasure, gives his cloak to the beggar and embraces poverty. Comedy laughs at Alceste for rejecting what it is not reasonable or worth while to decline for the sake of something which it is not reasonable or worth while to secure. The standard from which it measures its victims may be itself a low one, may express no more than a minimum of requirement, may take human nature too lightly. But it can at least urge for itself that these standards are a solid achievement of good sense and at least something which it is worth while to conserve till a better is found.

The rights of comedy are more palpable when the sin against public use and wont is not the generous unreasonableness of Alceste, but the exaggerations of valuable elements of life into hyprocrisy. When it ridicules the pretences of the false *dévot* it is still more obviously establishing the claims of moderation and good sense. It includes in its subjects (besides the Alcestes) the Tartuffes, and even as in the *Femmes Savantes* the supposed pretenders to a cultivation be-

lieved to be beyond their sphere, even when they do
not, as in this play, carry their pretensions to the
absurdity of refining their language into a ridiculous
precision.

I cannot speak of comedy in general or the comic
spirit. For that I must send the reader to Meredith's
great *Essay on Comedy and the Uses of the Comic Spirit.*
But of Molière's comedy it is true that always the part
of chorus is played by common sense, or sound sense,
current in the cultivated opinion of the time. The comic
motive lies in the contrast of certain characters which
deviate from this standard with the others which represent it. Such good sense is not merely good taste but
right and goodness as they are conceived at the time in
the general current of healthy life. Accordingly Mr.
Bergson, who founds himself in the main upon Molière,
declares in his book upon Laughter (*Le Rire*) that the
comic character is one-sided and presents the appearance of something mechanical, something which does
not share in the full tide of life. The point is well taken,
for the exaggeration, which takes the hero out of the
region of full good sense, whether as in Alceste it is an
offence against good judgment merely, or as in Tartuffe
against the true and balanced spirit of religious devotion, destroys the equilibrium of life. The criticism is,
however, not perfectly good, if it implies that the comic
personage is not in himself a personality organised
completely by his controlling impulse. Such a view
would not hold of Alceste, who is a very living person;
it may be true of Harpagon or Argan, but it is certainly not of Tartuffe, who is a thorough-paced and
vital rascal, who by a kind of fine art can harmonise his
pretended exaltation of sentiment with very human
sentiments of sensuality and vindictive love of gain.
The great comic characters are in fact comic in propor-

M

tion as they are also whole men, with not so much a mechanised life as a twisted one. Was there ever a more living man than Falstaff himself, who was perhaps beyond the reach even of Molière; whose want of principle is idealised into a new irresponsible kind of life, that is never troubled by current opinion and does not so much defy it as rather is innocent of it; who in no sense is like Satan, who says "evil be thou my good", but rather enjoys a merry and delighted obliteration of moral distinctions? The shock with common sense culminates in his case with his repudiation by the prince turned king, in whom indeed common sense in its harder and more brutal form is represented.

Meredith has dwelt on the equality of the sexes in Molière's plays, not equality of privilege but equal opportunity as members of society in their respective spheres. He even regards such equality as the true soil for the growth of pure comedy. "Where women are on the road to an equal footing with men, in attainments and in liberty—in what they have won for themselves, and what has been granted them by a fair civilisation —there, and only, waiting to be translated from life to the stage, or the novel, or the poem, pure Comedy flourishes, and is, as it would help them to be, the sweetest of diversions, the wisest of delightful companions." Such an audience Molière found not so much in the society of the Court of Louis XIV. as in the bourgeoisie of Paris, "sufficiently quick-witted and enlightened by education to welcome great works like *Le Tartuffe*, *Les Femmes Savantes* and *Le Misanthrope*, works that were perilous ventures on the popular intelligence, big vessels to launch on streams running to shallows". And again, "Cultivated men and women, who do not skim the cream of life, and are attached to the duties, yet escape the harsher blows, make acute

and balanced observers. Molière is their poet." Meredith is doubtless right in the part which he assigns to
women in the world comedy. "The man seeks freedom," says the princess in Goethe's *Tasso*, "the woman
observance"—*Nach Freiheit strebt der Mann, das
Weib nach Sitte*. Whatever may be thought of that
antithesis, it is at least true that the equal participation
of women with men secures the atmosphere of ordered
custom, which supplies the standard of well-regulated
judgment against which comedy in its Molièresque
example sets out the laughable follies or extravagances
of mankind.

Beautiful and Ugly.—'Beautiful' (and also 'ugly')
and 'beauty' are used ambiguously.[1] As I have used
the word here, 'beautiful' is that which is aesthetically
approved, the full significance of which statement shall
be set forth in a later chapter.[2] Its opposite should be
the aesthetically disapproved or indifferent. 'Ugly' is
not, however, very often used in this sense, but rather
we speak in such a case of bad art or the non-aesthetic.
'Ugly' generally means something which displeases,
like an ugly face, or an ugly field disfigured by refuse
dumps, without aesthetic reference. But 'beautiful' is
used and perhaps oftenest in a special sense, and 'ugly'
may also be so used, and in that special sense both the
beautiful and the ugly are departments of the beautiful
in its sense of the aesthetically approved. The beautiful,
then, whether in art or nature, is in its general sense
something which is attractive or pleasing in itself or by
itself apart from its aesthetic treatment. Usually, however, the word suggests that besides being attractive in
itself it is also aesthetically right. Consequently a merely

---

[1] See on this subject A. C. Bradley, *Oxford Lectures on Poetry* (London, 1909),
pp. 40 ff. Also W. T. Stace, *The Meaning of Beauty* (London, 1929), pp. 67 ff.
[2] See Chapter X. on 'The Objectivity of Beauty'.

pretty picture or pretty face is one which, though
attractive, fails to excite aesthetic pleasure. Correspond-
ingly, in natural objects, the toad displeases the eye in
itself, but it may be painted beautifully and, ugly and
venomous as it is, may enter into beautiful verse. Otherwise expressed, and the distinction has been mentioned
before, the beautiful is easy aesthetic beauty and the
ugly difficult beauty. Some artists find their very
triumphs in making the ugly or unattractive aesthetically beautiful. Shakespeare's earlier manner, as in
Midsummer Night's Dream, delighted in easy beauty,
and his later manner in the difficult beauty of many
passages, say of *Winter's Tale* or *Coriolanus*.[1]

A subject attractive in itself lends itself more easily
to the artist, and hence the beautiful, as said above,
suggests aesthetic approval as well. When such suggestion is absent we dislike applying the epithet beautiful, as with many genre pictures like Greuze's, which
when they are not good prose tend to be merely illustrative or even sentimental. It is the absence of the
aesthetic refinement or sublimation which allows them
to be set lower than beauty in the special sense, as
dainty or merely pretty.

Ugliness as unattractive is an ingredient in aesthetic
beauty, as the discords in music or the horrors of
tragedy. When it becomes ugly as a kind of beauty it
has been transmuted. Such ugliness is difficult beauty.
For the contrast of the ugliness which is a form of
beauty and mere ugliness, take on the one hand the
actual reputed treatment of the old Walter Savage
Landor by his daughter and the behaviour of Regan
and Goneril in the play to their father, where their

[1] I take as an illustration of difficult beauty the speech of Leontes in which
words unpleasing in themselves and conveying unpleasing, and so far ugly,
images are transformed into beautiful expression. The passage ("Dost think I
am so muddy", etc.) has been quoted before on p. 40.

repulsiveness is lost in the artist's achievement but only just prevented from retaining its hideousness.

Thus nothing is beautiful, whether in itself unattractive or attractive, save so far as it is aesthetically good; and accordingly the ugly and the beautiful as kinds of beauty owe their beauty to their treatment (whether in nature or art) and the distinction of the beautiful and the ugly is seen to be one of subject matter.

The Sublime and the Beautiful.—The sublime and the beautiful, like the ugly and the beautiful, are different kinds of the beautiful in the special sense of aesthetically approved, a difference founded upon the subject matter. For beauty is one and the same character everywhere, but it belongs to different kinds of the beautiful or appears in them in different garb— even if, to hark back to a previous observation, the subject matter be the mere form. After the example of Burke and Kant, and Schopenhauer as well, it has been too much the fashion to look to the subjective processes in the two cases, and thus it has come to appear that these two were not merely different manifestations of beauty but had a different aesthetic foundation. Thus Burke spoke of beauty as based on tenderness for small things and the sublime on fear of overpowering ones, looking to what I have called the material passions in the artist's mind, rather than the formal one. And Kant himself gave a different version of the mental processes engaged in the two cases.   In beauty it was the harmonious action of the understanding with the imagination, the vital truth of which doctrine we have already noted. In the sublime the object which abased the imagination also excited the reason (not the understanding) to feel the superiority of the self to the storm or to the immensity of the heavens. The

truth is that in both cases there is the same harmonisa-
tion of elements, only that in the sublime the supplementing imagination draws its elements from features
in the subject matter which surpass ordinary experience and yet are in keeping with it.

There are two well-marked species of the sublime,
the natural and the moral sublime, the first illustrated
by the familiar storm, the second by the sublime
fidelity of the dog in Wordsworth's poem (an instance
from Mr. A. C. Bradley's chapter[1]), whose master had
perished among the crags of Helvellyn, and who was
found three months after by his master's body.

> How nourished here through such long time
> He knows who gave that love sublime,
> And gave that strength of feeling, great
> Above all human estimate.

In neither case do we feel our human personality excited to the consciousness of its own greatness. In both
cases, when we look at the subject matter we find something exceeding whether in magnitude or in power (I
am here again borrowing from Mr. Bradley, whom
further I accept when he says that the immensity in
question, whether of the starry heavens or the dog's
fidelity, is not felt as infinite but simply as unmeasured).
Yet in both cases the largeness is something with
which we ourselves can sympathise. Though beyond
our attainment it is not unattainable; the dog's fidelity
beyond average human nature yet is attainable and
actually exemplified by maternal love. When that sympathy is not felt, when the largeness of the sublime is
not apprehended as in the scheme of things and an
expression in its naked form of something at the heart
of nature and of ourselves, the effect of sublimity dis-

---

[1] *Oxford Lectures on Poetry*, 'The Sublime' (London, 1909), to which I am
extremely indebted for this section.

appears; as when Carlyle being taken out into a night of stars declared it "a sair sicht" or Hegel regarded Kant's starry heavens as boring. These perverse judgments are good enough to show that those who find these objects sublime do so because they apprehend the vastness of the sublime object as true to the nature of things. When Lotze, as I have quoted him on a previous page, found the beauty of music to lie in its suggestion of the pervading rhythms of the universe, he was perhaps feeling not so much the beauty of music in general as the sublimity of certain kinds of it.

The difference of the sublime and the beautiful seems to be closely akin to that of difficult and easy beauty. Schopenhauer observes that in the apprehension of the sublime there is a check to the free play of our minds. This check is followed by recovery. Without such check we may say we have easy beauty; the subject and the supplementing images settle smoothly into equilibrium and harmony. But with the sublime, equilibrium and harmony (in the object be it observed as well as in the contemplating mind) are recovered after disturbance; the fearful or paralysing object is blended with the thought of the abiding normality of the object which at first seemed abnormal. The storm would be only terrifying to the person who feared it. It becomes sublime to the person who loves it, and feels it to be a vital thing. Just so in difficult beauty the artist, recoiling from the repulsiveness or at least unattractiveness of his object, transforms it into beauty by surrounding it with other images, and in thus harmonising it makes it beauty. In the same way the sublime is a harmony effected in a disturbing situation which becomes a reconciling one on a larger view of itself. The sublime is therefore a special kind of difficult beauty, for not all difficult beauty is sublime, and is consequently another form of beauty.

Classical and Romantic.—The distinction has fallen into discredit and is received with impatience because of the various uses of the two words, and because hardly any definition or description can be proposed which is workable. In the first place classical is often taken to be equivalent to Greek, and yet forms of art usually called romantic may be found in classical literature. There is love of nature in the *Odyssey* and psychology in Euripides, and recently [1] Mr. Abercrombie has, with doubtful success, been proclaiming Empedocles as a romantic because of his introspective vein. Shakespeare seems romantic compared with his not so far distant successor Racine, and classical compared with Byron or Shelley. Further different periods have been called romantic, and it is difficult if not impossible to fix anything in which they all agree: thus Rousseau as contrasted with the general eighteenth century, and the baroque painting of the seventeenth century as compared with that of the Renaissance and the sixteenth century. Gothic architecture of the great period, say Chartres or York Minster, might be called romantic when compared with the Pantheon or with Romanesque or with Italian Gothic, but classical in contrast to flamboyant or to Spanish Gothic.

In this confusion it has seemed to some best to abandon the antithesis. Yet a contrast which has impressed people for so long is not likely to be unfounded, and it is worth while to ask whether there is not some substantial basis for it. Certainly it is not the distinction of form and the formless; for the romantic has

[1] *Romanticism.* London, 1926.

its own form without which indeed it would not be beautiful.[1] Its wildest flights have a unity suitable to their material. It is probable that the truth lies with those who, like Mr. Abercrombie, maintain that romantic and classical designate not periods of art but rather varieties of art which occur in every period, only that in so-called classical or romantic periods the classical or the romantic habit predominates. What are the respective habits of mind which can be thus distinguished, or the corresponding choice of subject matter or handling of the material? A critical judgment may differ as to particular artists. Thus in calling Empedocles a romantic because of his introspection, Mr. Abercrombie seems to forget that the mind is conceived by that poet materialistically, as we should say; that love, for instance, is not so much a mental function as a physical power, and that if Burnet was right the soul as such was not discovered in Greece till Socrates came. Or again when he calls Wordsworth a classical writer in a romantic age, while he appears to me in one sense to be right, because Wordsworth's method was relatively impersonal, yet in another way Wordsworth was eminently romantic because of his suffusing nature with mind as much as Rousseau, and the right reason for deeming him classical is hardly given.

Perhaps an artist friend of my own is right when he says that in the classical the artist goes to meet nature, that is, the subject matter, in the romantic he anticipates nature and imposes himself upon the subject. The difference, then, according to this would be of the proportion of the given and added elements; the given elements being weightier in the classical and the added

---

[1] In comparing Baroque and Renaissance, Mr. H. Wölfflin (*Principles of Art History*, Eng. transl., London, 1932) leaves no doubt upon this point and describes in detail the differences of the respective forms.

elements in the romantic. Thus the romantic is the more personal, the classical the more impersonal. This would be equivalent roughly to the objective and subjective character commonly assigned to the two kinds respectively. Thus adventure and novelty would be more inclined to romance, and mystery would be another source of romance, as in the 'horrid' tales which Catherine Morland in *Northanger Abbey* filled her mind with. Jane Austen, on the contrary, would be classical because her matter is for the most part given and closely observed. Shakespeare on this view is classical because, even when his subject is introspective as in *Hamlet*, the picture drawn is objective. Perhaps the greatest part of Greek literature in its prime shared this objective, semi-scientific character. One of the forms romance assumes from its over-proportion of the personal is restlessness of movement whether in the mind or the body. Movement, whether in Greek art or in that of the Renaissance, has a certain firmness of direction or even repose. The famous words of Wordsworth's *Laodamia*, "the Gods approve the depth and not the tumult of the soul", express this general attitude, classical in both senses of that term, that is, both perfect and Greek. One form of the romantic satisfies the unrepose in human nature: tumultuousness of passion is highly personal. On the other hand, such tumult may be depicted classically or objectively, as the communion with nature may be romantic in *Childe Harold* or classical in *Tintern Abbey*. In the Laocoon or the Pergamenian frieze the romantic is creeping in as the true classical habit is fading away.

I submit therefore for consideration the notion that the classical and the romantic represent a real distinction in the subject matter of art, or of course in its handling, which is another way of choosing the sub-

ject matter or modifying it;[1] that in the main the difference lies in the relative weight of the given and its
supplement, and that periods of art are justly called by
one or the other name according to the predominance
of one or the other proportion, so that there may be
romantic affinities in a work which yet leaves the
artist a classical one, or classical ones in a work whose
general character is romantic, and accordingly Wordsworth remains a romantic and even Empedocles
classical. Just so, to take a parallel not from art but
from philosophy, Kant, for all his rationalism of the
eighteenth century, belongs to a romantic period and is
in part romantic[2] (*e.g.* in his conception of the moral law,
or of the part played by reason, in distinction from
understanding), and Goethe's *Faust* a romantic poem
while Marlowe's *Dr. Faustus* is not.

[1] The problem has been handled afresh by Mr. Herbert Read in *Form in Modern Poetry*. London, 1932.

[2] See an article 'Kant' in *Holborn Review*, October 1924.

CHAPTER X

THERE remains a series of philosophical or semi-philosophical questions to discuss, the first of which concerns the objectivity of beauty.

Beauty, or rather the beautiful, is objective, first, in the sense that it is communicable or shareable. Its communicability or publicity arises from its physical character.

The belief that beauty is a private experience comes from supposing it to be a mere state of mind. A man's sensations or imaginations or even his thoughts may be regarded as his private possessions, like his feelings or his organic sensations, such as hunger or thirst or general well-being. I cannot feel your pleasure or your hunger or your toothache. Nor can I possess your images. Knowledge is public but mental states are private. Now, declining as I declined in Chapter I., to enter upon general philosophy, I must still hold that images and even external, as distinct from internal, sensations have at least an external reference. The mental process is private but the total experience is potentially public. Though we cannot share with one another the sight of yellow, we can be aware of the same quality of things, and yellow is clearly not a property of our sight but its object, however in the end the objects of our mind are philosophically interpreted. I cannot have exactly the same image as you, only because the object imagined may, and probably does, vary from individual to individual. But our images are always images of certain objects which are physical, however differently each person modifies the object. The organic sensations are indeed not shareable, but that arises from the nature of their object, which is the individual's own body as apprehended in this particular way. The depletion of my body cannot be sensed by you, because only I have the necessary organs of apprehension. What I feel as hunger you apprehend in me as physiological depletion. But even my organic sensations are apprehensions of the thing called my body, and do not differ in kind from external sensations, except in the privileged and private character of the object. It would seem that the only private objects of our experience are the feelings, pleasure and pain and emotions, and it is at least arguable that these are in the end reducible to experiences of the nature of organic sensations. What is purely private appears to be our awareness of our mental processes as such, as processes; our sensings and imaginings and thinkings and the like ; not the objects corresponding to these processes.

But with beauty this general philosophical problem does not arise. For the experience of beauty is embodied in the physical material used by the artist or contemplated by the spectator, or provided for us by nature herself. What needs to be noted in the beautiful is not so much that it is public and potentially shareable, but rather that it contains an element of mind, because half its contents are suggested from the artist himself, and without a mind, accordingly, to interpret the work, the art and its beauty do not exist. This is the only privacy that beauty can be held to possess. If it be asked, How, then, can we know the interpretation to be placed upon the work, and is not therefore beauty completely private? the answer has been already supplied. To the

susceptible mind the interpretation is embodied by the
artist in the form he has given to his material which
suggests the necessary interpretation. The suggestible
mind is needed to notice the nuances of the material
work, as was indicated even in the most difficult case
of all, that of musical beauty. Just because the material
formed contains all that is necessary to evoke the
aesthetic response by inducing in the observing mind
the supplements involved in the work, we are apt to
suppose that the physical work of art is altogether
independent of any mind. But as a mere physical object
it is a curious conformation which leaves the unsym-
pathetic observer, or an animal, cold.

The communicability of beauty is, however, only a
condition of its objectivity in the more important sense
of that term, that dependent though it is upon a mind,
it is not dependent on an individual mind, but is a
common possession of many minds. Beauty must be
said to have a social character, provided that word is
not taken to imply that the minds which possess it in
common are necessarily a society in the strict sense.

It has sometimes been asserted that the artist creates
with an eye to other persons, and this is of course
implied as at least a counsel of perfection upon such a
theory as Tolstoy's. The truth of the assertion is extremely questionable as a statement of fact. What the
artist thinks about is not the effect he is going to have
upon other people. He need not disdain popularity or
the approval of fellow-artists. But he does not work for
that end, so long as he is a faithful artist. What he cares
about is how to render his subject in his materials to the
limit of his endeavour and skill. Alas! that short time
and the weakness of the flesh and perhaps the inexor-
able cares for a livelihood may lead him astray, and he
then becomes what is called (in one kind of the material)

a journalist. With injustice to the journalist, who, being for the most part a skilled craftsman, may yet often be an admirable artist.

Beauty, being essentially public, excites the constructive interest of many persons. What pleases or satisfies the aesthetic or constructive sentiment of one may fail to satisfy that of another. The conflict or balance of such differing judgments, expressing themselves in judgments of aesthetic pleasure or displeasure, leads to modification of the artistic production till it satisfies many persons. Hence arises the difference of subjective and objective valuation. It is only so far as one person dissents from the common judgment that he can say *he* thinks a work of art beautiful or it is beautiful for *him*. The objective judgment, the satisfaction afforded to a company of minds, is prior to the subjective one, contrary to what might be supposed to be the case. When a man modestly claims that something is beautiful for *him*, he is either making a tentative claim to objective beauty, or expressing dissent. It might be thought that the common or standard judgment is derivative from the many individual judgments. In fact it is only so far as he claims to represent the objective standard that an individual claims to find value, in his own art or in anything which he judges or feels to be beautiful.[1]

We may put a difficult situation thus, that the work *pleases* the individual or satisfies him, but has *value* only in so far as it satisfies a standard mind. The value of beauty lies in its satisfying objectively. The standardised impulse to construction, whose satisfaction is real

[1] I regret to find myself here differing from Mr. Perry, who treats value as interest, and in fact reproaches me gently that in my earlier treatment of value I dealt only with objective value. I regard value as being, as such, objective, but I must leave the defence of this proposition to what I say here and in the sequel (see especially Part III. Chapter XVI.).

beauty and constitutes the value of beauty, corresponds in aesthetics to the 'impartial spectator' in morals. Short of satisfying in this standardised fashion, beauty is not real but only apparent beauty. Beauty in that case pleases the individual much in the same way as the nightingale is pleased with his song. The individual artist is interested in his work, and his work has for him, as we shall see, a value in the general sense of that term. It gives him pleasure after a certain manner. But it has value in the strict sense in the same way as wholesome food, besides pleasing, is nutritious.

Thus personal value is a misnomer. Value itself is impersonal, and when an individual claims to be the standard of value he is leaving something personal in his art, and failing so far of perfect beauty. On the other hand, the person or standard of aesthetic judgment is the man to whom what seems beautiful is really beautiful.

Who, then, are the judges ? The answer appears to be circular, and yet is not. *Solvitur ambulando*. The judges of aesthetic value are those whom beauty satisfies in their aesthetic impulse or sentiment; and the beautiful is what satisfies these judges. The standard aesthetic sentiment is that of qualified persons, and those persons are qualified who possess the standard aesthetic sentiment. The standard is embodied in no one person, except so far as he is taken as representative of it. The situation is the same as in the Aristotelian conception of 'the wise man' by whose judgment goodness is determined, while it is his goodness which makes us count him wise. The judges, as in virtue so in beauty, select themselves. The impartial tribunal is a conspiracy of the qualified against the unqualified, whose judgment they reject, and treat the work which satisfies them as ugly, that is, unaesthetic.

The recognition of value as being primarily objective will be seen to be of importance in the subsequent attempt to trace value in the shapes which it takes in the subhuman world.

It follows that there is no fixed or eternal standard of the beautiful but that it is relative to age and people. This is a direct consequence of the fact that value implies a relation to the appreciating mind, whether the appreciator is the creator of the beauty or only its spectator. There is nothing that can be said of beauty wherever it appears except that it satisfies objectively the aesthetic sentiment of those who find it beautiful, and that it possesses the character of unity amid variety of its parts, and this we have seen to correspond to the unity of the aesthetic act.

On the other hand, beauty admits progress, or at least change, because of its changing subject matter. At any one time there are no degrees of beauty, and what are called degrees of beauty are degrees of approximation to beauty; there is a scale of less or greater defect of beauty. Beauty is beauty and is itself perfect. There is, however, a scale, which I called the scale of greatness, in beautiful works according to the subject matter of the work. Similarly what is beautiful once is beauty always in relation to its appreciators. But since the subjects which occupy the minds of men and move them to artistic creation vary from age to age, development and progress are possible and the beautiful has a history. Auguste Rodin is reported to have denied in a conversation the existence of progress in art and pointed to the perfection of Greek sculpture. Beautiful it remains, but he would be a bold man who should maintain that Greek sculpture has closed the history of sculpture; and in fact no sculptor of our time limits

N

himself to the Greek type, or perhaps could succeed if he tried. Quite apart from the addition of colour and even of ornament, of gold or ivory, which the Greek statues originally possessed, the repose of classical art, not in sculpture alone, is gone from our ideals, and with it that limitation of idea which Hegel described as characteristic of Greek culture, in art and religion, and elsewhere. There is beauty attained in negro sculpture, but it does not in its native form appeal to ourselves, not because it is deficient in beauty, but because it solves the problem of beauty within a different range of interests. It remains to be seen how far the negro type of subject can secure the franchise of beauty in our later artistic civilisation. The problem which the innovators have to solve is of so much greater difficulty because the form of the human body has to express a much wider and perhaps higher set of suggestions—a proposition compatible with the intrinsic formality of beauty at all times and whatever it represents. Not to go so far afield, a comparison of the David of Michael Angelo, or his Slaves, with Greek statues is enough to point the difference of form which beauty assumes at different times, and to raise the question of the conditions which underlie development in the beautiful.

They are partly the growth in men's conception of things and partly the discovery of new forms of technique, such as the discovery referred to on an earlier page of the arch and shaft and vault and buttress in building to replace the pillar and flat roof. It was also pointed out there that the new ideas expressed in the use made of these discoveries, though they described rightly the effects of the new structures, did not describe the formal and therefore aesthetic differences between the newer and the older works; but that at the

same time newer ideas seek forms consonant with themselves. *Hamlet* is not more beautiful than the *Oedipus
at Colonus*, but it is different in form because of the
difference in the subject. Not being an expert in criticism of art, I have not been able to do more than suggest[1] wherein lies the difference of classical and romantic
which nobody yet has described to the satisfaction of
all. It does not seem to me to be true that classical
means greater attention to form and romantic to substance. Romantic art has its form as much as classical.
The difference lies in the difference of two forms corresponding to different sets of material passions or ideas
or thoughts in the artist.

Whether such changes are to be called progress or
not depends on how far the later passions embodied
in art are to be called greater or not. So far as they are
wider or subtler they are greater. The doctrine of relativity need not imply greater genius in its discoverer
than Newton's, but the later discovery replaces the
earlier because of the greater exactness of its subject
to the actual nature of things. So it is with development in art. The naïveté of primitive music is less
developed than the complexity of Beethoven or even
than such naïveté as is exhibited in Mozart. And we
must add by way of caution that just as in reckoning
greatness in art of any one time, subject and skill in
the art are allowed to compensate each other, so in
assessing beauty as progressive or not, a relative
failure in the attainment of beauty may be compensated
by the difficulty presented by the enlarged range or
subtlety of interest.

Beauty, accordingly, is that which satisfies objectively the aesthetic impulse or sentiment, that is, the

---

[1] See preceding chapter.

constructive impulse used contemplatively, and is beautiful or has value because it pleases us after the manner so described. There remains the strictly philosophical question, What, then, is the status of beauty: is it a quality, like what we usually call qualities; and if not, what sort of a character is it? The answer I shall give is that it is not strictly a quality at all, but a value, which we may if we please erect into a quality by calling it a tertiary quality.

It is not a primary quality like figure, for there is on beauty except through the co-operation of mind in its constitution, and this conflicts with the accepted Lockian definition of primary qualities. Beauty does not belong to the merely physical beautiful object, for the object as beautiful contains elements imported from the mind and exists only on that condition. Some there are who believe beauty to be a character which belongs intrinsically to the beautiful object and is merely observed or discovered by us. They forget that the physical object, so far as physical (and of course 'physical' here would include states of mind as described, say, in a lyrical poem), is not the whole beautiful object. When I said on an earlier page (p. 73), following Michael Angelo, that the artist discovers his creation in his materials, I was thinking only of the physical object to which in his discovery he imputes himself or which is so formed that it contains modifications of form which embody himself, that is to say, are initiated from himself. Therein lies the art of the sculptor, that by chipping away the marble he discovers such a physical vehicle of beauty when the contemplating mind is by.

It is not always easy to know in what sense beauty is believed to belong as a quality to the beautiful object. Probably it is not thought of as a primary quality but rather after the pattern of secondary qualities, like yellow or soft or sour, when such secondary qualities are believed to be as much independent of the mind as primary ones, a doctrine which for my part I accept, though it is contrary to the accepted one inherited from Locke. The difference would, on such a supposition, be merely a convenience of description.

It is sometimes held that there may be impersonal values. If our previous treatment is correct, beauty at any rate is not an impersonal value in the sense of being independent of persons. It is impersonal in the sense of being objective, not dependent on a particular person, but, dependent as it is on the personality of artist or spectator for the mental constituents embodied in its form, it is in that sense eminently personal. It is not like knowledge, as we shall see, depersonalised.

Is beauty, then, a quality like the secondary qualities which are described as effects produced upon the mind by things which possess of themselves only primary qualities? Assume that this description is correct, as it is certainly traditional. Is beauty, then, a character of the physical beautiful object which produces in the mind the aesthetic experience? The answer is, no. For the object which produces or elicits the aesthetic experience is already infected with that experience. The beautiful is never a mere physical thing which elicits aesthetic sentiment, but that thing interpreted as containing elements imported into it, or imputed to it, from the aesthetic experience. Now a secondary quality like yellow is supposed to be a mere affection of the mind when the eye is stimulated by light of a certain wave-length from the 'yellow' object. It is a passive response to a certain stimulation, and the mind has no further part than to be passively affected thus. In fact it is the incredibility of this doctrine, the mystery of

finding in the mind itself yellow or hard, which has led
others to reject the 'mentalistic' doctrine of secondary
qualities and to attribute yellow to the external 'yellow'
thing itself. Now there is no organ of beauty in the mind,
so that it should attribute beauty to an external thing as
it attributes yellow. There is only an aesthetic impulse,
which makes no new quality, but sets the mind going
in certain conative directions, which give unity to the
object in its variety and construct the object so as to
contain qualities not inherent in it; to find movement in
the arabesque, or in the series of tones, or likeness in
the lines of a neck to a stately tower.

Beauty is in fact not of the order of secondary
qualities; its effects upon the mind are not of the order
of colour or taste but of pleasure. It is a form of
pleasantness. The so-called beautiful object has of
course primary and secondary qualities, colour and
shape and tone and the like, which belong to the
materials. But there is no quality of beauty in the objects comparable to the sweetness of the sugar, to be
cognised (as it were, sensed) by some organ of beauty.
No such organ exists. What underlies the beauty is the
parts and their relations, which might be compared
to the underlying chemical constitution of the sugar,
were it not for two reasons. The first is that the parts
and relations of the beautiful object are experienced in
the experience of beauty, while it is not the chemical
constitution of sugar which is experienced in the apprehension of the sugar, but its sweetness. The second and
more important reason is that the beautiful object
having been selected or created so as to satisfy the
aesthetic impulse, and containing elements supplied
from the mind's initiative, the beautiful object involves
essentially a reference to the mind whose aesthetic impulse it satisfies.

CH. X THE OBJECTIVITY OF BEAUTY 183

In experiencing sugar as pleasant, the pleasure belongs to the mind but does not belong to the sugar. In the experience of beauty, and beauty in a beautiful object does not exist except so far as it satisfies the mind which is actually contemplating it, the pleasure in like manner belongs to the contemplating mind. Pleasure is not an ingredient in the words of a poem or the formed marble of a statue or the tones of a sonata. The difference between the work of art and the sugar is that sugar happens by its nature to please, while the beautiful is constructed so as to please. It contains a reference or relation to the mind which is to appreciate it. Its beauty is founded upon a relation to the mind, a relation which is already implied in the choice of its elements in their internal relations. It is intrinsically pleasant, so far as such language can be used intelligibly. It is satisfactory to the aesthetic impulse. And we may add now that it is objectively satisfactory.

Now the word 'value' of ordinary speech, and the phrase 'tertiary quality', invented I believe by Bosanquet and specially adopted by certain philosophers, expresses this complicated situation. The beauty of a beautiful object is not a quality of it, but is a character it possesses of satisfying in its material form a certain impulse of the mind. Its relation to the mind is its value and is experienced as a pleasure. As Hume said of virtue that we do not apprehend an action as virtuous as if virtue were a quality of action but we feel it to be virtuous in feeling it to please after a particular manner, so there is no quality of beauty in the beautiful object, but in feeling it to please the aesthetic impulse we apprehend it as beauty. We can do so because it has been chosen to satisfy that impulse.

In the total experience of the beautiful, in its re-

lation to the appreciating mind, the pleasure belongs
to the mind, the beauty is referred to the object which
is said to have value in virtue of its relation to the mind,
which relation is already embodied in its own form.
Value is thus experienced as pleasure, as marking in
the mind the satisfaction of the aesthetic impulse. The
beautiful is said to possess value or to be a value, but
value is not a quality of the beautiful but its relation to
the mind, which is a partner in the total experience of
beauty. Satisfactoriness in the object, satisfaction in
the subject: this is the distribution of parts in the whole
complicated situation.

If it is answered or objected that there is surely a
feel about beauty which is comparable to the feel of
sweetness or fragrance or of pitch in a tone, I can only
appeal to the objector to ask himself whether, in his
experience of beauty apart from the particular features
of the formed material, he finds anything in his mind
but a certain pleasure. His pleasure has its peculiar feel
because it is the pleasure of satisfaction of the aesthetic
impulse and attaches, as the pleasure of sugar attaches,
to an object of a certain kind.

In describing beauty in the object as satisfactoriness
to the impulse which it satisfies, I am but indicating its
relational character, and not attempting to ride off
upon a vague quality of satisfactoriness. Complex as
the experience is, it is perfectly intelligible. The pleasure
in which beauty is experienced is the pleasure of constructive exercise (such as may be observed or presumed in a bird busy in bringing together the materials
to make its nest). The object is that about which the
impulse is exercised, and it is accordingly described as
satisfactory. The impulse and its object are correlative
and imply each other. There is no pleasure of construction unless something is constructed; there is no satis-

factoriness unless that which is constructed satisfies. Satisfactoriness is attributed to the object as it were by a projection on to the object of the satisfaction it gives, just as food is naturally described as pleasant because it satisfies the impulse to eat. Nor would any difficulty be felt were it not that the elements in the work of art, the actual materials used and the ideas they mean, have their own distinctive material pleasures as well.

The characters of the beautiful which make it satisfactory have been described already in Chapter III. For our immediate purpose the most important is the harmonious arrangement of its elements. Harmony pleases, and possibly might be imagined to supply a pleasure distinct from the pleasure of the constructive exercise. In fact the unity in variety, which since the Greeks has been seen to be the obvious feature of beauty, is the immediate correlate of the unifying constructive act. There is no pleasure of harmony added to the pleasure of the constructive act which effects the harmony. We are not to suppose, either that beauty is some pleasure apart from the impulse which is satisfied or pleased, or that beauty is a character in the material object which makes it beautiful independently of the mind. The beautiful is a certain arrangement of material elements which is beautiful in so far as it satisfies, and that it does satisfy is implied in the choice of this particular arrangement.

The pleasure of the exercise of the aesthetic impulse is the satisfaction of that impulse as it proceeds towards its end. It must, however, be distinguished from the excitements which attend that exercise —some pleasurable, others which arise through difficulty and frustration and are in themselves painful, and may intensify and add a passionate character to attainment when the tension is overcome. These last attend the aesthetic exercise, not in so far as it is satisfied, but in so far as it fails of satisfaction, and are doubtless never absent. But they are subsidiary to the attaining of satisfaction itself. Moreover, it is to be remembered that that process of attainment is rarely of short duration, and yet at any stage in so far as success is attained the pleasure of attainment is the pleasure of beauty as attained at that stage. As Aristotle observed, the building of a temple is not complete only when the temple is finished, but has its partial completion at each stage of the work.

If these statements are faithful to the facts, then, at any rate in the case of beauty, value is not something mysterious of which no further account can be given, but is the satisfactoriness of the value, or the valuable, to a human impulse and is experienced as a certain manner of being pleased. What that manner is I have, with whatever imperfection in the exposition, or circuitousness for which the complexity of the situation is in part responsible, endeavoured to set forth.

I have but to add, in order to guard against possible misapprehension, that in my constant use of the statement that beauty is what satisfies the aesthetic sentiment I am guilty of no circularity. I do not mean the tautology that beauty is what satisfies the sense of beauty. I am following once more the precedent of what Hume said about virtue, that it pleases because of some motive distinct from the sense of its virtue. The artist does not aim at beauty; he aims at making an expressive object, and what drives him to do it is the constructive impulse. It is only by anticipation that such an impulse or sentiment can be called the impulse or sentiment of beauty. Morality is not directed upon morality itself, but is the result of the moral impulse. Beauty is the result and not the motive or aim of an impulse, which is called aesthetic merely in order to avoid this very confusion with beauty itself (which is its fulfilment) that would ensue if it were called the impulse to beauty.

PART II
TRUTH AND GOODNESS

CHAPTER XI

SCIENCE

"No action", said Hume in a passage already quoted which cannot be repeated too often, "can be virtuous or morally good, unless there is in human nature some motive to produce it distinct from the sense of its morality." In the preceding chapters I have attempted to apply the general principle which underlies this proposition to aesthetics, and to show what motive it is in human nature (distinct from any sense of beauty) which leads to the production or discovery of beauty. I have suggested for consideration the thesis that beauty is the satisfaction (the objective satisfaction) of the impulse to or motive of material constructiveness when that impulse is diverted from practice and treats the materials of its construction for their own sake. The modification of the constructive motive which is needed for such diversion we found to be accounted for by the admixture with the sensuous material of elements embodied in the form and initiated from the mind itself. Those elements lifted also the sensuous materials given for the artist to work upon into the condition of being contemplated for themselves.

In the pursuit of truth, which is science, the impulse distinct from any original sense of truth which leads to the discovery of truth is the impulse of curiosity, when it is diverted from practical ends; and the identification of the motive for science is much easier and more unquestionable than that of the motive for fine

art. The curiosity of the animal is exercised for practical purposes, as exhibited by the dog to gratify his
sense of smell and his impulse to sex. But how the
practical impulse becomes directed upon the objects
of curiosity for their own sake, and generates not mere
cognition or knowledge in the loosest and most general
sense of that word, but in the strict sense of knowledge
or truth, needs explanation here as much as the constructive use of materials for their own sake needed explanation, and could not be passed over with a phrase.
The explanation here is a different one.

Practical curiosity becomes contemplative and ex-
amines things for their own sake when such an animal
as man (for I leave unraised the question whether
other animals do not in some measure share with us
this privilege), having arrived at the stage of ideas and
thought, applies them to the data presented by sensible
experience. Those partly supplement each other, and
partly they contradict each other. Such situations the
animal also experiences and confronts them practically,
as when, for instance, the same sort of object, say a
trouser, fails to smell of a dog's master, or smells of
an unfamiliar other dog. What the dog treats by a variation of conduct, Isaac expressed in a proposition, when
the feel of a hand conflicted with the sound of a voice
from the same person. With the entry of ideas[1] and
comparison, conflicts and corroborations in experience
become objects of contemplation for their own sakes.
Conflict is perhaps the more important of the two. The
Greeks said that philosophy began with wonder, but
wonder is a somewhat later stage in the process which

---

[1] I say 'with the entry of ideas' in order to avoid an inquiry which does not
concern me here. I believe that ideas come into being with the desire (originally
practical) to end conflicts in practice, and ideas do not so much solve conflicts
because the mind already has ideas, as that ideas come into existence as a part
of the process of reducing the conflict. See the paper already referred to on p. 12).

leads to knowledge. Science arises from disappointment, hesitation and doubt.

By the use of ideas the mind, under the spur of curiosity, produces unification of the information and experiences which are thus considered for its own sake. All the contrivances that the logician or 'epistemologist' speaks of as synthesis and analysis, comparison and distinction, arise out of the unrest of the mind in face of the disconnection among the objects it is curious about. Out of these elements it constructs a unity of knowledge. And here it is well for me to say that when I spoke of a constructive impulse at the basis of art I meant by construction the putting together of physical materials. In a wider sense of construction (of which no doubt material constructiveness is a special form), construction is a feature of any process of unification. Now this tendency of our mind to get rid of unrest in the data of its experiences and to connect them where they reinforce each other, produces at the level of ideas in the mental life contemplation of objects for their own sake, and not merely a satisfaction of practical curiosity, and leads on to the building up of science.

The modification of the practical impulse to construction into contemplative use of materials was due to the mind's habit of intruding into its materials with elements initiated from itself. With science the practical curiosity is modified by a simpler tendency in the mind towards unification of its objects. There is no ultimate difference between these two modifying processes whereby the mind is deflected from practice into contemplation. They are both methods of interpretation possible to a mind which has reached the stage of ideas; and the issue in both cases is unity or organisation of the materials. But in neither case would the interpretation be effected, nor the tendency of the mind

o

to interpret and unify be of any use, were it not for the drive of the original impulse, in the one case to material construction, in the other towards finding out more about the object, which I have called constructiveness and curiosity. Except for this initial drive, the tendency to unify would not exist. Unification and organisation is not itself an impulse in the mind, though philosophers may have referred it to reason, inventing an unverifiable power in the mind to account for the effects of perfectly verifiable powers when those powers are modified by the existence of materials derived from memory and ideas. The data before the mind in constructiveness are the material elements used in construction, in curiosity they are the objects presented in sense,[1] and the initial impulses of the two cases are deflected from practice.

But there is a difference in this deflection from practice into contemplation in art and science arising from the difference in the two situations. In fine art, in the pursuit of a constructiveness set going by the topic, the subject interferes with its object, the materials, by introducing features 'foreign' to that material; whereas in science the object about which the mind satisfies its curiosity is the actual world given to it without admixture from the personality: any such interference would be distortion. This remark is, however, subject to a reservation to be made presently. For the mind does enter into science, but instrumentally and not as in fine art constitutively.

Truth, then, or true knowledge or, simply, knowledge is that which satisfies, and satisfies objectively, the impulse of curiosity when that impulse has become contemplative. It can only be fitly described by reference to the mind which it satisfies. It is therefore a

---

[1] Or, as in mathematics, in thought. See later, pp. 213, 220 ff.

work of art, though not of fine art. For knowledge is
not the actual world of things, but that world as used
to satisfy the impulse to science. The objects of the
actual world recur in science but held in relation to the
mind. Accordingly, in order to make science, the mind
selects from the world, as in each of the separate departments of science, according as science is of inani-
mate things or of life or mind or the like; separating
these departments of the world from their surroundings, and considering even different aspects of things
separately. Moreover, in the work of co-ordinating and
unifying things of the world, it introduces conceptions
of its own, as will be verified at greater length, even
going so far as to use conceptions which are at first
blush arbitrary, in order to pursue its work, using
them thus instrumentally, and never pretending to put
into the world what is not there or is uncongenial to
the world. I am speaking in terms of a common-sense
or realistic philosophy when I say that knowledge is
real things over again and taken up by and held or
possessed by the mind. But on a different philosophy
corresponding language must still be used; there is still
the same difference between the real if mental world
and that world as selected and otherwise manipulated
without distortion by the mind.

Because truth is held by the mind and is truth (as
distinct from brute reality) as thus held, truth or knowledge is a work of art.[1] I began this inquiry with fine
art because fine art is the more complex and exhibits
the factors in their doubleness. In fine art the two elements of physical material and mind are displayed in
their commixture and interference. They are found
again in truth, but mind though vital to truth is con-

[1] See on this subject 'Truth, Goodness and Beauty', *Hibbert Journal*, vol. 28,
1929–30.

trolled by reality, and science is a faithful representation of reality within the limits set by the art of science.
In fine art mind and material have joint control, and
if there is question of higher rank, it belongs perhaps to
the mind. But in science the mind humbles itself to the
lordship of reality. Hence in fine art personality enters
into the product though in impersonal form, while in
science the mind depersonalises itself, and science is
impersonal in a sense different from the impersonality
of art, that is from the mere sense of objectivity. The
attainment of the impersonality of science, in which
mind leaves itself out from the product while it main-
tains possession of it, does not, however, mean passivity of the mind as if the mind were a mere mirror to
nature. On the contrary, the treatment of the world by
the mind so as to leave out its own personality is so far
from passivity that it involves the highest exercise of
personality. I need hardly say that the nature of personality or any other character of the mind may itself
become an object of science, but here too the inquiring
mind leaves itself out of the picture.

It is not strange, therefore, that in the history of the
race science should be much later than fine art. It
needs a greater fetch of abnegation to keep oneself
from interference than to interfere, however imperson-
ally, as the artist does.

In the remainder of this chapter I shall, by reference
to the separate sciences themselves, try to develop these
two features of science: its artificiality on the one hand,
and on the other hand its control by reality. The first
feature is so generally recognised that there is some
danger of losing sight of the second. We are tending to
suppose that science is a pure construction of the mind.

It will suit my purpose best to begin by tracing in

general outline how science grows, through the inter-
action of the two elements in it which I have called the
material and the mind. It grows out of what used to be
called history, as by Bacon, that is a collection of
facts; and is most easily illustrated from what we call
history. We may see the first approaches to scientific
history in our newspapers, which consist of two parts,
the bare facts collected as news and the comments on
the facts in the leaders. The leaders are reflections upon
or interpretations of the news in the light of the policy
or principles professed by its editor, in politics or literature or economics or music and the like, according to
the journal's interest. But it fails of being science for
two reasons: first that its principles, if it is an ordinary
newspaper, are practical and concerned with affecting
public action; and secondly, that news and leaders are
strung together and are not organically connected.
However, in a great newspaper like *The Times* or the
Manchester Guardian there is a pervading spirit which,
to a certain extent, approximates the paper to a work of
science.

Such a newspaper is a great deal more than a mere
chronicle, for it reviews facts in the light of ideas. We
get history proper, when the ideas which the writer
brings to his news or facts are no longer purely practical but theoretical. This at least is the first element in
the transition from the journal to history. The facts are
co-ordinated not so as to serve as the text for policies of
practice, but so as to bring out the meaning of the
events of the period under consideration. The meaning
of the facts is gathered by the historian's mind, using
its appropriate ideas—which are suggested by the facts
themselves but acquire distinctness as he goes on—
because he starts hypotheses as to the significance of his
subject, and is helped therein by all kinds of knowledge

or imagination that he brings with him from his knowledge of life or from his acquaintance with other periods
of history. All these helps or *adminicula* he uses as the
leader-writer uses his practical principles, and there
would be no history proper except for his intervention.
But we note at the same time that however fertile he
may be in his resources of interpretation, he is bound,
on pain of being unhistorical, to keep strictly to the
facts, or as I put it, he is, for all his artistry or manipulation, controlled by his material. To arrive at their
meaning he must select, and he may illustrate or interpret so as to co-ordinate the facts, to make the essentials stand out and the trifling or inessential data slip
out of the focus, to get a consistent picture if he can,
or so far as he can. But he is a scientific historian only
if in organising his material he does not distort. He
would not naturally falsify, but falsification may come
about in effect, not in intention, if he selects, say, to
heighten the picturesqueness of his narrative or to over-
emphasise salient features of a character or of a party.

In this process from the chronicle to the history we
can see thus both science and art, as fine art, playing
their part, and always because of the mind's intervention. Various histories illustrate these features in
differing degrees. Gardiner's history of the Civil War
betrays very little of the artist, but is an admirable
example of scientific history, which, far away as it is
from the chronicle, and bringing out the great movements in men's minds during that period, and even
full of luminous ideas of statesmanship which the
author brings to the understanding of human things,
is, as far as a layman can judge, rigidly faithful to his
data, impartial and even austere, so much so as perhaps
to repel. On the other hand, Macaulay is far more of an
artist, and sometimes forsakes the duty of the historian

to use the freedom of the artist, by onesidedness, and what must be called, however agreeable is its effect, abstractness, heightening the colours or the shadows, and sometimes not free from prejudice. In judging the greatness of a historian both scales have doubtless to be used.

The co-ordination of facts by ideas supplied from the mind, or at least through the mind's action, and yet moulded to the facts, is, however, not the whole of the difference between history and chronicle. Along with the work of organising there goes the process of testing the facts themselves, so as to secure precision. Thus the facts which control are themselves in part the outcome of the effort to create the work itself which embodies them. This demands in the historian expertness in description, and has led to technical sciences like palaeography or chronology, the first example of which last science was, I believe, the elder Scaliger's work; and it requires skill in estimating the value of evidence, the skill of the scientific judge, so as to sort out the data which are worthy of belief. So intimately then is the scientific treatment of facts dependent on the historian's mind, not only for collating ideas but for establishment of the facts themselves.

When history takes its higher flights, as in recording the whole life of a nation, or still more when it becomes comparative, as it unavoidably does, and includes many nations; or when it traces a department of civilisation (*e.g.* Lecky's two famous works), or reaches to what has been attempted as the philosophy of history— it exhibits more and more the use of hypothesis to supply connecting clues, the larger sweep of mind which can make a conspectus of great tracts of time and human motives at work therein, and betrays more and more the controlled art, and therefore not fine art, which is exhibited at its lower level in any historical work that can be called scientific.

It has sometimes been denied that history can ever be a science, except so far as scientific methods are used in the technical ascertainment of facts. It should be clear by now that this is only partially true and misses the essential. It is only true in the sense that history is not physical science, for when it begins to furnish laws of human nature or generalisations, it tends to lose its character of history and to become the science of sociology. Even within its proper range it is scientific, like the biological sciences, because of its control by its material.

But it does in another respect resemble rather fine art than science. For it is concerned with individuals and series of individuals, and individualisation as contrasted with generalisation is a distinctive mark of art. Hence the close affinity of history with the drama. Even so, a contrast of real history with one of Shakespeare's Histories, or with what closely resembles these in our own time, Strachey's *Elizabeth and Essex*, is enough to mark off history from fine art. For these dramas claim the freedom of art from control by the facts, and use the narrative not as history but as material to exhibit play of character under historical names, and they have thus the universality which Aristotle made the characteristic of drama. History is, in fact, a connecting and transitional link between science and fine art, sharing with the one its subjection to things and with the other its limitation to individual existence.

Although history is the form of science which is the least developed in the sense that it is more like literature than other sciences, our description of it has brought out the two features which it shares with every science. The first is the freedom which it owes to the movement of the mind amongst the facts, organising them so as to make them significant, much in the same way as the astronomer groups his stars into constellations (an example used so often by Sir A. Eddington). The second is the restriction of the mind in this process by the facts themselves, much as if the stars compelled the astronomer, by virtue of their special relations to each other independently of their mere spatial proximity, so to group them, as the parts of an animal body compel us to consider them as more intimately connected with each other than with things outside them.

Now it is this second feature of control of the mind by the material which is so palpable in history when we compare it with the other sciences or with fine art. What distinguishes the natural sciences, and above all the physical sciences and mathematics, is the increasing entry into them of the mind's freedom of construction.

The biological sciences mark the transition to physical science; they are more like history and less like mathematics, and there is consequently less artifice in them than in physics. Between them and physics comes chemistry, which is fast approaching the condition of a branch of physics.

Botany and zoology begin as natural history, and they retain to the end the qualitative character, which increasingly disappears from science to be replaced by the metrical or quantitative character. 'History' or the collection of facts in biology, as it becomes more methodical and systematic and precise, becomes dignified with the name of morphology. But as these sciences grow and become more scientific, that is approach to the ideas of the physical sciences, not only does generalisation enter, but measurement; and again, introducing experiment, they become physiological and admit of the statement of laws. Darwinism illustrates excellently both these aspects. It is a qualitative theory, and not a metrical one. At the same time it is an immense historical comprehension, and indeed it strikes the note of the historical method in science, which came to be so marked a feature in thought as men's minds swung back from the rationalism of the eighteenth century and from the so-called mechanical philosophy. It may be noted, by the way, that Mr. Whitehead's introduction of the idea of organism into physics and philosophy is avowedly a reaction from the mechanistic philosophy of physics in our own day, after the triumphs which that philosophy had won in actual physical investigations right on to the end of the nineteenth century. Moreover, Darwinism, besides being a great historical synthesis, offered in the notion of natural selection a physical law regulating the historical procession. With Mendelism we have introduced into historical biology the method of statistics, and something in biology approaching the atomic theory in physics and chemistry, in the search after units, still qualitative and far removed from the units of chemistry, underlying the genealogy of living forms.

Perhaps the best illustration of the effect of experiment on the lifting of biology from history to science or artifice is to be seen in the growth of scientific medicine. Medicine, which in its beginnings is purely empirical (for I need not go back to its kinship with religion), owes its scientific standing to physiology, which does not merely observe, or even employ experiment as a help to observation as in statistical inquiries, but relies from the beginning on experimental interference with the course of life, and is able to establish laws. At the same time, if any one needed convincing of the artificial character of science, he has only to observe how completely this master science of life is a creation of the mind by observing that, for a large part, in his experiments the physiologist isolates the separate portions of the body, as for instance in a nerve preparation, and observes the laws or regularities of their separate workings. He has consequently to correct this artificiality by precautions to interfere as little as possible with the organic connections of the part under experiment, as for instance in careful vivisectional experiments. I may instance the knowledge acquired by experiment of the co-ordination or integration of nervous impulses and of the paths which nerve impulses travel. Sometimes by events, which are disastrous for the patient but fortunate for science, nervous lesions from disease or war may take the place of experiment, as in the well-known observations of Sir Henry Head.

At the same time, in pointing out how science grows away from history through artifice, and the increasing share of the mind in its creations, I am intending no depreciation of history as such. It will, in fact, be one of my main contentions that science, even at its acme in physics and mathematics, never frees itself completely of history, and, artificial as it is, this dependence on history prevents it from being artistic.

Chemistry, which comes next in the series, is so interesting from our point of view because almost under our eyes it has been changing from a historical to a semi-physical science. Qualitative it remains: the elements are distinct in quality as much as the species of animals and plants. But there have been two processes going on, which are not altogether distinct from each other. One is the mitigation of the qualitative distinctness of chemical substances by uniting the elements into one great synthesis comparable to the Darwinian synthesis in biology; the other the way in which the conception of the molecules and the atoms has become geometrical, a process described so excellently by Émile Meyerson in his book *La Déduction Relativiste*.[1] Already chemistry had learned to shed fictitious qualitative conceptions like those of caloric and phlogiston, which were in fact the qualities of heat and combustibility, made into substances very much in the same way as the early Greek physicists thought of love and strife, which were causes of mixture and separation, as being physical things or elements like the four elements of earth, air, fire and water. Meyerson happily recalls (ch. xxii) the 'dormitive virtue' of opium, by which Molière's candidate for a degree in medicine declares that opium makes us sleep. These virtues became actual substances. But when once these fictions were banished by Lavoisier at the end of the eighteenth century, there began the attempts to relate the different elements to one another which culminated in Mendeléef's great synthesis. According to this the elements, when arranged in the order of their atomic weights, fell into groups or constellations, which repeated each other in their chemical and physical properties. The presumption underlying the synthesis is that the elements are connected together genealogically, and are ultimately derived from some one substance by descent. This has, of course, been confirmed by the discoveries made about radium, certain elements being experimentally produced from others through loss of the constituent electrons. So far the movement has been comparable to the Darwinian synthesis, but more penetrating.

But along with this, and in fact part of the same movement, there has gone the spatialising of which Meyerson speaks, by which molecules are exhibited as

[1] Paris, 1925.

containing their atoms in a certain spatial arrangement, the atoms holding hands as it were in a kind of
dance. Many years ago W. K. Clifford compared the
molecule of benzene to a game of 'here we go round the
mulberry tree' played by a ring of children. Moreover
not only is the molecule spatialised in this physical
chemistry, but in recent times the atom itself has been
spatialised into the conception of a central nucleus
made up of units of positive and negative electricity,
with electrons or units of negative electricity revolving
around it in orbits like those of the planets. This conception has already broken down under the difficulties
presented by the quantum theory. Those difficulties,
however, concern the notion that the electrons can be
treated as if they were small pieces of matter. It still
remains true that in the advance of chemistry, as the
science is handed over more and more to the physicists,
the qualitative character of the science is replaced by a
metrical character.

For us, what is chiefly to be noted is that chemistry,
in ceasing to be purely qualitative, has become more
abstract, for it is more abstract to identify a colour by
the wave-length of its light than by its sensible property. More science, if it means greater power to the
mind in comprehension of its material, means also
greater assertion of the mental element in the science
and greater intrusion of artifice.

In the exact sciences of physics and mathematics I
shall, again, be concerned to exhibit the two features
we have found in the quasi-historical sciences, their
artificiality and their control by the facts. That it is an
art is more obvious of physics than its control by a non-
mental reality. For at an early stage physics becomes
metrical and ceases to aim at merely qualitative pro-

positions, such as that heat expands bodies. In doing so, in abstracting from the sensible characters of things, it is plainly the work of the mind. And in its later stages in its efforts at explanation it has long passed the ideal of a collection of empirical laws so carefully stated as to be called causal laws. Even the principle stated by Kelvin, that explanation is only satisfactory when it is possible to construct a mechanical model, has ceased to be accepted. At the present time, owing to two theories, that of relativity and the quantum theory, the ultimate formulation of physical laws involves a mass of constructions by the mind which aim at any rate at making physics purely a mental work, corresponding, no doubt, in some sense to the objects of perception, and yet hardly to be described as dealing, however indirectly, with those objects. It will be convenient to take Sir A. Eddington's work[1] as a text for my remarks, because with him the artistic or artificial character of physics comes out so strongly, and the element of what I have called control drops apparently into the background, which is the very point I am wishing to question.

Physics itself, on this view, is a closed circle into which the study of consciousness does not enter, but physical objects are metrical constructions which imply the action of the mind, much as the shape of the statue implies the artist's chisel. The objects of physics are groups of metrical characters which are not perceptual objects, but only symbolic of them. In a striking passage Sir A. Eddington writes:[2] "Our knowledge of the external world cannot be divorced from the nature of the appliances with which we have obtained the knowledge". I add the following sentence because of

---

[1] In particular *The Nature of the Physical World*. Cambridge, 1928.
[2] *Loc. cit.* p. 154.

its bearing on what comes later. "The truth of the law of gravitation cannot be regarded as subsisting apart from the experimental procedure by which we have ascertained its truth". The symbols in question are, in fact, 'pointer-readings' from various instruments of measurement. Physics attends only to these readings of weight, temperature, speed and the like; so that in his familiar illustration of the elephant rolling down a grassy slope, we have one set of pointer-readings 'moving' according to another set down a slope also recorded by a reading of its angle. All this is perfectly clear. What is not so clear is that these readings are purely symbolic of the perceptual object, and not merely an abstraction from that object of its metrical characters; in which case the 'physical object' would really belong to the perceptual object, in a sense in which the life inspired by the sculptor into the marble does not belong to the material, though of course the physical notation might be very indirect.

How much Sir A. Eddington emphasises the part played by mental construction in the making of physical, science is best seen by following as far as possible his account of what he calls world-building; how by starting with elements described in the most abstract way possible as relata and the relations between them, and assigning to each relatum four numbers constituting a monomark (an abstract idea used to avoid calling the numbers co-ordinates which imply space and time), we can exhibit the structure of the world in a formula in which the coefficients correspond to certain concrete concepts like space, time and gravitation, electricity and magnetism. In this way we, as it were, build up the familiar world out of abstract numbers and their combinations, and can derive certain of the laws of experimental physics. But the way in which mind enters can only be understood when we follow him in the division which he makes of the laws of nature into three types.

He distinguishes[1] (1) identical laws, (2) statistical laws, (3) transcendental laws. The identities are the laws of conservation of energy, and momentum, and even the law of gravitation, the inclusion of which is one of the most remarkable of his results, the one which most provokes reflection. They are "the laws obeyed as mathematical identities in virtue of the ways in which the quantities obeying them are built". They cannot be regarded as genuine laws of control by the basal material of the world. More than once he calls these fundamental laws a 'put-up job',[2] or truisms, though he adds: "not truisms when approached in the way mind looks out on the world, but truisms when we encounter them in a building up of the world from a basal structure". We find them in nature because we have 'ordered' nature as it were in this form. We have a passion for permanence, or an interest in it, the same interest which underlies our idea of substance. "The law of conservation is a truism for the things which satisfy it; but its prominence in the scheme of law of the physical world is due to the mind having demanded permanence".[3] It is as if the bursar of a college should think that he has discovered something in the real life of the college by finding that the accounts balance; he has but arranged that incomings are plus and outgoings minus. In the same way as the different aspects in which the realities of the college overlap in the world of accounts, so the law of conservation represents "the overlapping of the different aspects in which the 'non-emptiness of space' presents itself to our practical experience. . . . We can measure certain forms of energy with a thermometer,

---

[1] *Loc. cit.* p. 244.   [2] P. 238.   [3] P. 241.

momentum with a ballistic pendulum, stress with a manometer. Commonly we picture these as separate physical entities whose behaviour towards each other is controlled by a law. But now the theory is that the three instruments measure different but slightly over-lapping aspects of a single physical condition, and a law connecting their measurements is of the same tauto-logical type as a 'law' connecting measurements with a metre-rule and a foot-rule." He adds, however, that "the proviso must be remembered, granting that the identification [of their subject matter]", *i.e.* of energy, momentum and stress, with certain 'principal curva-tures' of the world, "is correct. . . . From a practical point of view the law would be upset if it turned out that the thing conserved was not that which we are accustomed to measure with the above-mentioned in-struments, but something slightly different."[1]

I will quote another paragraph because of its bearing upon what follows. Though consciousness is not itself included in the cycle of physics, yet according to Sir A. Eddington it exercises "a selective influence on the laws of Nature by choosing the patterns which suit itself".[2] And this is to say "that *values* are created by the mind. All the 'light and shade' in our conception of the world of physics comes in this way from the mind, and cannot be explained without reference to the char-acteristics of consciousness." That value, at any rate the highest value, such as truth, is created by mind seems to me eminently true. But the question still re-mains whether the creation depends on the character-istics of consciousness, as I have urged beauty does, where, for instance, the mind inserts into the marble characters which do not belong to the marble; or whether the mind in science is not rather truly selective,

---

[1] *Loc. cit.* p. 239.   [2] P. 243.

P

taking from nature by selection what is really already
in nature.

I shall return to this later. Meantime I resume the
enumeration of the types of natural law. Besides the
identical laws, there are secondly statistical laws, of
which the chief is the second law of thermodynamics,
that is the law of the running down of energy in the
world into the form of heat unavailable for work (the
loss of available energy being known as entropy).
"Statistical laws", to quote further, "relate to the behaviour of crowds, and depend on the fact that although
the behaviour of each individual may be extremely un-
certain, average results can be predicted with confidence. Much of the apparent uniformity of nature is a
uniformity of averages." These statistical laws, however, he does not regard as laws of control for they
involve a notion of probability for which there is as
yet no place in the current conceptions of the world
substratum [*i.e.* the basal structure].[1]

It is in the third group of the transcendental laws
that we must seek, according to Sir A. Eddington, for
the genuine laws of control, if there are any. They
"comprise all those which have not become obvious
identities implied in the scheme of world-building. They
are concerned with the particular behaviour of atoms,
electrons and quanta—that is to say, the laws of atomicity of matter, electricity and action. We seem to be
making some progress towards formulating them, but
it is clear that the mind is having a much harder
struggle to gain a rational conception of them than it
had with the classical field-laws. We have seen that the
field-laws, especially the laws of conservation, are indirectly imposed by the mind, which has, so to speak,
commanded a plan of world-building to satisfy them.

[1] P. 244.

It is a natural suggestion that the greater difficulty in elucidating the transcendental laws is due to the fact that we are no longer engaged in recovering from nature what we have ourselves put into nature, but are at last confronted with its own intrinsic system of government. But I scarcely know what to think. . . . It may be that the laws of atomicity, like the laws of conservation, arise only in the presentation of the world to us, and can be recognised as identities by some extension of the argument we have followed. But it is perhaps as likely that after we have cleared away all the superadded laws which arise solely in our mode of apprehension of the world about us, there will be left an external world developing under genuine laws of control."[1]

It would seem to follow from this that though the external world may be in the end recalcitrant to mind, the ideal of physics is a system of identical laws representing the mind's own will with nature. "Where science has progressed the farthest," he says elsewhere,[2] "the mind has but regained from nature that which the mind has put into nature." Such science is, of course, only "knowledge of structural form and not knowledge of content". The philosophical suggestion is that in the end the content itself is the stuff of our consciousness. This last suggestion, however, it is not necessary to consider. If the ideal of physics is the one described, physics would be completely an art, conforming to forms of structure chosen by the mind, as the sculptor imposes on his marble the form he chooses, and no part of the material but obeys this form. This would make science at its highest, in physics and mathematics, akin to fine art to a greater degree than seems, as I hope to indicate, to be the truth.

[1] *Loc. cit.* p. 245.
[2] *Space, Time, and Gravitation* (Cambridge, 1920), p. 201.

Accepting from Sir A. Eddington his picture of world-building as practised by science, I would ask whence the mind derives the idea of permanence which justifies us in saying that the laws of conservation are identities. So far as the statement goes, it would seem to be a creation of the mind itself. But there is something like a miracle in this supposed capacity of the mind, unprompted by experience of things themselves, to originate the notion of permanence. Precedent for affirming such capacity might be found in the Kantian doctrine of the categories, such as substance and the others, which the mind introduces into the material supplied by sense; to which, however, of course, Sir A. Eddington does not appeal. But at any rate, even in the Kantian doctrine, though the categories may be *thought* by themselves (how, Kant never explains), they cannot be *used* by themselves. If we suggest that we experience substance in the permanence of ourselves, the answer must be made that if by ourselves we mean our bodies, these are a part of the external world already, and we derive the idea of permanence from what is non-mental. If we answer we have it in the experience of our minds alone, the answer is that we never do have experience of our minds (in what Kant called the inner sense) except in and through the experience of some external thing—say our own body as the most familiar case or any other external body, but some external body there must be. This consideration, which is so distinctive of Kant, does not receive, I think, its due consideration from Sir A. Eddington. The mind may act wilfully in ordering its physical world, but if it does so according to ideas, those ideas seem themselves to have come from physical experience, and to be in the end empirical or experimental notions suggested by external experience, and by the self as the most familiar instance of that experience. We might go on to urge, not by way of criticism of the notion of world-building from relata and their relations, that the ideas of relata and relations themselves cannot be regarded as creations of the mind, but are nothing but abstractions of the most general aspects of concrete experience. Even the numbers which are used for monomarks of relata are supplied to the mind, not made by it. Sir A. Eddington himself quotes with approval the famous saying of Kronecker about pure mathematics, that God made the integers, all else is made by the mind. In general it is safe to say that no idea attributed to the mind's own creation but is derived by it from some experience of what is not mind, or at least not without such experience. The ideas which even in a work of fine art are imported into the product by the mind are ideas not created by the mind itself, but supplied from its experience of things not minds (unless, indeed, the artist is portraying mind itself as in a lyric poem). Doubtless these reflections do not appeal to those who, like Sir A. Eddington, regard the mind's experience of itself as direct and of external things as indirect, whence he is able to speak of physical things as mere symbols of perceptions. But it seems to me as true as to Kant that it is only in and through the experience of external things that we can have experience of the mind itself, and if it is a question of which of the two is rather to be called direct, that claim must be assigned to external experience. The mind of which we have direct experience without experience of physical things, and except through that experience, is a ghost, or, to quote a phrase of Lotze's, it is as unreal as grinding without grist.

I write on these matters with some timidity, partly lest I should appear to be questioning Sir A. Eddington's exposition, and partly lest I should be really failing to understand him. What I question is merely the authority ascribed to the mind. As I read the case, the ground of the law of conservation is the experimental fact that the different measurements are merely different aspects of the same reality. If we then build up the world from a basal structure, we choose forms which embody the permanence we have found in nature; we find in nature the forms of our choosing because we have chosen them after first finding them in nature.

Perhaps the caveat I am making will be clearer if I go on to his much more startling proposition that the law of gravitation is a truism or a 'put-up job'. The way in which he shows this is as follows. It is well known that, according to the Einsteinian doctrine, matter is present where there is a hummock or curvature in space-time; that is to say, this wrinkling of space-time is not merely due to the presence of matter, but actually *is* matter. Sir A. Eddington in two masterly chapters first of all expounds the law of gravitation, and then 'explains' it, the explanation being that it is a truism. For what the formula in the doctrine of relativity states is that the ten principal coefficients in it vanish in empty space, or, what is the same thing in another form, that "the radius of spherical curvature of every three-dimensional section of the world, cut in any direction at any point of empty space, is always the same constant length". I must be content to ask my readers to accept this statement from Sir A. Eddington even if they do not understand it entirely, remembering that, as he says,[1] "the absolute curvature at any point is measured by a single quantity called the radius of spherical curvature". This condition limits the possibility that the curvature of space-time should be quite

[1] *Loc. cit.* p. 120.

arbitrary. Now we need to explain this regularity, and
the explanation is this: To say that this 'directed radius'
is constant in length means that it contains the same
number of metrical units, metres, or feet, etc. All length
is of course relative to some unit. Thus, if the directed
radius is of constant length, that must mean that the
standard metre is the same fraction of the radius no
matter what new position or direction the standard is
moved to. But what else could it do, seeing that the
radius is distinctive of the region in which the measur-
ing-rod comes to be placed? It makes itself the same
fraction of this directed length as it did before in its
previous position.[1]

But is this convincing? It is well known that if a rod
is moving relatively to a stationary observer, and is
placed in the direction of the movement, it shrinks for
the stationary observer. For an observer moving with
it there is no change, for his standard length shrinks in
the same proportion. But in the case supposed of trans-
ference of the standard from one position to another we
have the standard applied not to its old radius under
the new conditions, but to a new radius under new conditions. Why should we be unable to see how it can do
anything else but adapt itself to the new radius? Does
not the law of gravitation assert that as a matter of
fact it does so, and is it not this which is the import of
the law? Directly you make this assumption, which is
verified in various ways, you construct your world
scientifically in accordance with it. But that choice does
not, so far as I can see, depend on our inability to
imagine anything else, but on this character which has
been discovered of the world. Once more, if this reflection be well founded, it is not our mind which settles
the matter, but something inherent in the external

[1] *Loc. cit.* pp. 140-43.

world which is formulated in the statement of the law given above. Were it not that I do not wish to digress into philosophy, I should say it is the truth that universals are an item in the world.

I have dwelt at such length on Sir A. Eddington's statements because he seems to me to exaggerate and even misplace the action of the mind. But before continuing this subject and indicating an alternative view, it may be as well if I digress for a moment to speak of a common misunderstanding of relativity, not irrelevant to our inquiry, but not chargeable to Sir A. Eddington. It is the notion that relativity reasserts the Kantian doctrine that space and time are merely forms of the mind and are thus subjective. What relativity asserts is not that space and time are forms of the mind, but that to separate them is an error, and that the objects of experience are events. But granted that our seeing the world in space and time is a habit due to our weakness and so far subjective, relativity does not mean that therefore our views of the world are relative to us and purely subjective. On the contrary, it means the world is such that from whatever point of view we split space-time in our measurements so as to get different actual measurements, the laws of physics remain the same for all observers or for every point of view. The problem, for instance, in finding a formula for gravitation is to get something true not for me or you, but true for all. 'Relativity' is in fact an unfortunate word. It might be replaced, were it not for the cumbrousness of the phrase, by absoluteness in spite of relativity. Meyerson has made clear[1] that what the theory aims at is the objective. This is relevant for us, because it means that the universe is such as allowing our minds to use the numbers appropriate to the relative positions

[1] *La Déduction Relativiste*, pp. 212 ff.

and motions of the mind requires them to conform to
laws dictated to them and not by them.

Thus, while it is true, as Sir A. Eddington says in a
passage I have quoted above, that our knowledge of
the external world is bound up with our instruments
for attaining it, that knowledge, if it is to be true knowledge, that is knowledge at all, is limited by the com-
mands of the universe itself. This may be otherwise expressed by pointing out that the instruments we use in
obtaining knowledge are devised by us, in the same
way as our instincts and other human capacities are
acquired in the course of animal history, in the process
of adapting ourselves, in order to live in the world, to
the nature of the world itself, as indeed is indicated by
Sir A. Eddington himself in a later passage.

The suggestion, then, is that it is not as expressing
itself that the mind makes the work of art or artifice
called physics, but that it creates the work through its
instrumentality, not importing into nature ideas of its
own or due primarily to itself, but using its tools so as
to fashion out the form of nature by obedience to her.
Perhaps we might find an analogy which is not too far-
fetched in the unfinished Slaves of Michael Angelo,
where the figure appears to emerge from the marble
block. Overpowering as the impression is that we receive from these works, because they show how the
great man worked,[1] the adherence of the shapeless
block is an accident. In physics it is as if what is an
accident in art is part of the essence; as if the form of
the slave which is due to Michael Angelo were accidental and the marble to whose nature the workman
has to conform were essential.

If this be so, it would remain true that in the highest
and most abstract science control is not as Sir A.

[1] See above, p. 73.

Eddington uses the word, from laws of the basal structure chosen by the mind, but ultimately, sooner or
later, the control is from the external world, which is
primarily presented to our minds in perception, just as
it is admitted to be in the verification by which ordinary
experimental laws are established; or for the matter of
that in the theory of relativity itself, which was established because it was found to work. According to this
there is no discontinuity between the crude stuff of perception and the most abstract thoughts, it is only that
thought comes from selection of certain aspects of perceptual matter. Physical objects would not then be
mere symbols of perceptual objects, but arrived at by
this selective process, which makes science artificial or
artistic; to which is superadded the extreme freedom of
the mind in manipulating its thoughts by the help of
instrumental methods which it chooses. It does not
seem true that the elements of the basal structure,
relata and relations, have no analogue in familiar experience; on the contrary, they are the extremest abstractions or selections from that experience. But it is
true that in handling these concepts the mind goes beyond anything found in perception, not inventing new
material, but combining its store of material in ways
suited to its own purposes. In the end it seems that the
physical reconstruction of things from above, if understood as a pure creation of the mind, implies that old
contrast of familiar experience and things in themselves which has been so profound a difficulty in philosophy since it was formulated by Kant. It is, however,
beyond my scope to discuss the attempts made since
his time to remove those difficulties and banish the
spectre now apparently revived. On the other hand,
the difficulties do not arise, and the spectre remains
laid, so long as the new way of approaching the world

from its most abstract characters is regarded as a method of rewriting the objective or given world, of which experimental physics writes the record approaching it from the concrete side. The alleged truisms then take their place as the record of the highest abstractions which we can make in our selection from nature. Whether the atomicity of nature, supposed to be as yet recalcitrant to mind, shall remain so or be regarded as fundamental fact of basic structure, will depend on whether it is found possible, as in the case of number or constant curvature, to find concepts from which certain and unavoidable consequences follow so long as these concepts remain integral to the world.

This being so, it is illegitimate to suppose a chasm between the brute facts of physical nature as presented in sensible experience of particulars and the most abstract principles; and data of sense are a part of the body of physical science, just as they are in the historical sciences. Facts and principles make up a single system, the facts being massed together for the most part in the form of empirical laws. The rationalised and consequently deductive portion of the sciences is never completely detached from the irrational element, which may always contain surprises. The slave never rises completely out of the block. If it did, science would be a fine art, as I have already said. Accordingly it is not so much intrusion of the mind which characterises science at its highest remove as the rationalisation of the subject matter more and more by means of the mind.

The physical sciences have exhibited not only the freedom of the mind in selection from its material and in invention of constructions such as those illustrated

from world-building, but also the limitation or control
of the mind by its subject matter. The first feature
likens physics to an art, the second unlikens it to fine
art. When we come to mathematics we find the mind's
freedom at its highest, and particularly in pure mathematics, where, starting from the integers, the mind has,
by successive stages, constructed whole creations of its
own in which there seems to be complete emancipation
from any control by reality of a non-mental character.
No one would subscribe at present to the Kantian doctrine, that mathematics derive their validity from their
applicability to sensible experience. Here in these constructions the mind claims for itself complete freedom
to follow its own will; and this science might claim for
itself to be wholly an art. Examples are the arithmetic
which includes not only zero and fractions but negative
numbers, the real numbers and imaginary numbers; the
idea of systems of fewer or more than three dimensions,
or to describe them generally n-dimensional systems;
the mathematical theories of infinity and continuity;
the transfinite numbers. The constructions thus made
seem to be self-contained, and they have upon the
mind an effect very like the aesthetic impression. And
yet even these works differ from works of art, though
for a different reason. We denied to the other sciences
the claim of being fine art because they were controlled by their subject matter from the outside. Here,
while the outside element seems to be wanting, the
product fails to be fine art, because the material is itself
the mind's own creation, whereas fine art is always the
informing by the mind of a material of sense or imagery
given to the mind.

Even so the extent of the mind's creativeness in
the unbounded freedom of pure mathematics is to be
qualified. The products it creates are extensions or

generalisations of ideas like integral numbers given
to the mind, or arrived at by combinations of such ideas,
as, for example, the notion of five-dimensional systems.
It may be doubted if the mind invents a single new
quality or kind of object, as it would, if it could, acting
upon its own idea of permanence, invent, *e.g.* the idea
of another self distinct from its own. However complex
the thought may be, it is, if not suggested by sense, yet
derived from elements suggested in the end by sense,
or like integers given otherwise to the mind, not made
by it. The point may be illustrated from a famous passage of Hume, who, after denying that we could have
ideas without preceding impressions, admitted that
this was possible in the rare case where we imagined a
quality in a scale, say of colours or tones, intermediate
between two given colours or tones without any previous impression of the intermediate. Hume is probably
mistaken[1] and confuses the *thought* of an intermediate
colour which we can well create on the ground of
analogy and the actual image of such a colour, to be
acquainted with which we should need to experiment,
as the painter doubtless does, mixing his paints until
he finds the satisfying shade.

Perhaps the best way to understand the unlimited
freedom of the mind to follow its own bent in these
creations of whole regions of scientific thought, in the
creation, for instance, of a calculus, is to remember that
all science is but practice become disinterested. In practical curiosity the end is sometimes interrupted by the
need of finding means to secure the end. Now the
sciences, in working out the implications of ideas which
mind itself creates in the qualified sense just explained,
may be properly regarded as departments of mental

[1] I have, however, to observe that Mr. Whitehead in *Process and Reality* not
only accepts Hume's admission as true, but takes it as an instance of a fundamental principle.

technique. The mind follows in such elaboration its own laws of implication or inference.

And yet even in these regions there is not complete liberation of the mind from what is non-mental. For pure arithmetic coheres with its basal elements given in whole numbers, created, Kronecker said, by God, and so, I add, constraining man. It takes us away from integers, but never loses touch of them completely. This is true even when arithmetic is submitted to a still further process of sublimation and becomes a piece of logic, when an integer is treated as a class of classes. For though a class is a mental conception, and there are no classes in actual reality, yet reality does contain individuals which, though not mental, suffer themselves to be so grouped because they possess the same qualities. The connection of mathematics with sensible reality, though we cannot speak of control from that side, is plain in geometry, which cannot now be treated as pure mathematics, but since the supersession of space and time by space-time has become a kind of physical science. And though the validity of mathematics does not depend on verification in sense-experience as Kant thought, yet the signal triumphs won in physics, as recently in the doctrine of gravitation, through application of mathematical techniques devised without any ulterior purpose than the deduction of implications from the premises with which they start, are enough to show that the minds of mathematicians in their extreme cult of the useless are guided by some divination of the useful. This is not so strange. We are back again at the fact that minds are themselves a part of nature and made by adaptation to the rest; and if in following their nature they devise thoughts to which nothing in nature directly corresponds, their freedom or wildness has its roots in nature itself. It would seem then that, though free from limitation by the non-mental, even pure mathematics is remotely correspondent to nature, and still less remotely connected with the whole numbers, which, if not sensible things, are at any rate not made by mind.

This may seem, and is, a long circuit to have fetched in order to establish what is at first sight a fairly obvious and simple result: that in science the work of the mind, however free, is controlled by what it sets out to investigate. It was, however, necessary, because it had against it a tendency to attribute an overpowering and constitutive part in science to the mind. The real upshot of the discussion is to show first that science is dependent on the mind, so that without mind there would be no science, but we should be confronted by a real world which we did not understand. So far as this is so, as science proceeds by selection from its subject and elaboration by its own tools, which may be of the greatest abstractness, it creates a body of truth which is more than reality, is reality as elaborated by the mind and become its possession. So far science is an art. But in this elaboration of its material, the mind introduces no ideas of its own in the sense of being its own creation. The function of the mind in science is instrumental, to construct its work in obedience to and, as I have so often phrased it, under the control of the non-mental material. The mind does, of course, introduce ideas from itself into the body of the science, in so far as it brings the riches of its experience of the subject or kindred subjects to bear upon the interpretation, or invents hypotheses. But all such introduced ideas are congenial to the subject, and not, like the life introduced by the sculptor into the marble, uncongenial to the material on which the artist operates. Consequently, directly or indirectly, immediately or remotely, the ideas which the scientific material admits are found in it and verified by it. So that there enters into every science, as there entered into historical and quasi-historical science, the mass of particular facts with which the science begins and which it retains to the end. The mind establishes coherence amongst the facts of perception by means of laws obtained through selection and reflection. The mere laws of the science, except so far as empirical laws sum up the experience of particulars, do not themselves constitute a self-contained and harmonious whole. The raw material, whether presented in perception or in thought (as in the facts of quanta), is carried into the product, only organised and rearranged. It is true that in various branches of mathematics the science itself forms a self-contained whole, but then the material is itself supplied by the mind itself and simply worked up by logical methods; though even here, as indicated before, these creations are constrained in the end by ideas, like integers, given to the mind from without.

It has been my object at once to point out the artistry of science and to indicate where science differs from fine art. It may be useful in conclusion to add to this impression of artistry produced by science by comparing the mind's own use of its logical methods, inference and the like, to the technique of the artist. Logic in the ordinary sense is then the science of scientific technique, and the special logical methods of different sciences are comparable to the special technique of the artist according as he works in stone, or words, or paints and the like. I do not quite see what corresponds in science to what is called style in a fine art, which is a function of technique. Such comparisons are perhaps apt to mislead. For the difference of artistic technique and logical technique is fundamental. The technique of the artist gives meaning to the artistic product. The technique of the scientist does not enter into the very constitution of the work, but remains purely instrumental.

CHAPTER XII

TRUTH

THE true which satisfies curiosity shares with the beautiful which satisfies constructiveness certain features the discussion of which can, accordingly, be shortened to avoid repetition. It is disinterested and communicable. It exhibits variety of its parts but unity within that variety, because it is the satisfaction of an impulse which in its contemplative form is single in itself and seeks to remove the unrest of mere difference in its facts and to bring together data which reinforce each other as, to recur to a Baconian metaphor, the separate bristles of desultory information are tied together in a broom. Whether the subjects of separate sciences can be unified into a single science is a question which belongs to philosophy; it may be that the world is a plurality to the end. But within the ring fence which any one science, and still more any one department of it, sets up in its artificial procedure the result displays and must display unity in its variety, or at least the science aims thereat and does not rest satisfied so long as the unity is not secured. Physics, for instance, at the present is confronted by the seeming disconnectedness of data which can be explained on mechanical principles and those which require a different set, but the science is puzzled and seeks to remove this disparity.

But because the reality which controls the pursuit of science lies outside the mind, there is a difference between science and fine art, which is an amalgam of real matter and the mind which transforms that matter.

Science exhibits two features one of which, coherence, it shares with art; the other is peculiar to science, its correspondence with fact. Each of these two features has been claimed by various writers to be the test of truth. The criterion of correspondence is the more obvious one, but rightly understood the two tests are identical. For coherence within the science involves correspondence with fact, and correspondence with fact involves coherence within the science. To take the second first, correspondence does not mean that science is a mere repetition of facts; that would be chronicle and not science. It means the verification of the science by the facts. What 'corresponds' to facts is their orderly, co-ordinated selection in the form of generalisations and laws. Now a single law is itself the coherence of the facts which exemplify it, and a multitude of laws corresponds to facts only in so far as the laws accord with each other and with the facts. They must accord with each other otherwise the facts in which they share would be separate for each law.

On the other hand, the coherence of laws implies correspondence to the facts, and the contrary opinion only arises from forgetting that the facts themselves enter into the body of the science in the form of judgments made by the mind as contrasted with the brute existences which we understand by facts with which correspondence has to be attained. Facts are particular, and brute facts test the truth of a law because they may bring the inquirer plumb up against something which contradicts or confirms it. As we proceed in an inquiry we adjust our laws to the brute facts and the brute facts are received into the science in a form which may be altered by the adjustment itself. So that the particulars which appear in a science are not necessarily exact copies of the brute facts but the inter-

pretations of them which are discovered in the course
of the inquiry. This situation accounts for the extremely
loose language of some writers who insist that facts
themselves are values, which only means that every
so-called fact is not merely like a stone wall which stops
advance but is an interpretation of that brute existence.

The particulars, then, are part of the science itself,
though they are replaced by the generalisation or law
which implies them or is verified by them. *Per contra*
laws or universals have always a latent reference to the
particulars which embody them. They have no habitat
of their own apart from their functioning in things, and
the separation of them from the things or particulars
to which they belong is an abstraction for the purposes
of scientific art. They are in fact the patterns of particulars which are fashioned in their likeness.   If this
were an inquiry in philosophy proper, it would be
maintained that the particulars themselves and the
patterns are made of the same stuff. At any rate, when
once it is seen that particulars themselves (of course
as transformed in the mutual adjustment of brute fact
and proposed law) are included in the body of science,
either directly or by delegation to their deputies which
are laws, the test of correspondence and that of coherence coincide, the second expressing the artificiality of
science, the first its submission to control from reality.

Truth is objective like beauty, and for the same
reasons. It deals in the sciences of nature with public
matter, and when, as in psychology, its object is mental
states which are private to the individual, it treats them
as typical, not for their own private sakes, but as conditions which are verifiable in their degree in the private
experience of other persons. In the more important
sense of objectivity, the true appeals to the scientific

impulse in many persons, and is not specific to any
one person. These persons are the qualified persons,
and as before the qualified persons constitute themselves the arbiters of true and false, and truth is a conspiracy of experts who condemn what fails to satisfy
their scientific sentiment as false. Herein lies the social
character of true knowledge. Not only is what is put
forward by one person as true open to the judgment
of others, but it solicits and compels such judgment,
partly by contradiction and partly by reinforcement of
what satisfies them, but partly also because each person
sees his own portion of the subject and makes his
special contribution to the common stock of knowledge. Out of the process of adjustment between the
deliverance of many individuals results the true, or
science. It is that which satisfies the standard curiosity.
The scientific man is the man who represents in his
person the standard judgment. Only there is this difference from the case of the beautiful. Since in beauty
the mind is always mixed with its material but in
science the mind is detached and instrumental though
always presupposed and present, the individual artists
are always unlike one another though as good artists
they embody a common standard, but the individuals
who have truth are all alike, or differ only in dealing
with distinct portions of their subject. The artist has
his tastes and passions which qualify his work of art.
The man of science has no material passions to disturb
his contemplation, so far as he is man of science. This
does not prevent the personality of the man of science
from entering into his work and particularly into its
exposition. But then so far his work is fine art, with an
architectural or even poetic character which could be
illustrated from many works of science. Truth is not
incompatible with beauty but seeks its aid, witness

Plato or, at a considerable remove, Huxley. And just because science shares with fine art its attainment of unity in variety, science may and does, quite apart from explicit artistry in the exposition, produce upon the mind the same kind of effect as beauty and is called beautiful. In reality it is satisfying a different impulse in much the same way.

Truth as objective is prior to truth as subjective, what seems to any individual to be true. I can only claim a proposition to be true, or say *I* think it true, so far as I have before me the idea of a standard truth. Objective truth does not arise, therefore, out of the competition of personal truths, my truth and your truth. I make a proposition not claiming it to be true for me but putting it forward as a statement of how things are as I see them. Such propositions lead on to the notion of truth because of the competition between them as put forward by different individuals; and the competition is possible between theoretical propositions, which at first blush would seem to be indifferent to one another (how can my opinion compete with yours?) because of the social nature in the first place which induces us to desire community of views, and second, because propositions are the beginnings of action.

When the idea of truth has been established, the opinions of persons may then claim to be truth, but any such truth-claims (to use a phrase used to good effect by pragmatism) are pretenders to objective truth. Subjective truth is thus a later derivative from objective truth. We should not call our opinions true did we not claim for them objective truth.

In the true as in the beautiful we can distinguish the formal truth from the greatness of the work. There are no degrees of truth, but only degrees of failing to reach it or succeeding in its attainment. But one piece of

truth or knowledge may be greater than another, from
the largeness or importance of its topic, its greater com-
prehensiveness (like the theory of gravitation in its
time), or its profundity or its subtlety and complexity.
The greatest truths are perhaps those which being
simple in themselves illuminate a large and complex
body of knowledge. The two standards of judgment
interlock with each other, and a certain want of unity,
for instance, may be condoned and compensated by
mass of detail. The birth of the greatest truths is for the
most part an event in which some simple statement of
the widest generality emerges out of a great mass of
more or less separate pieces of knowledge to which it
suddenly supplies a clue or enables it to be taken in at
once in a flash.

Knowledge or science is accordingly relative to
men's minds and the extent of this experience. What is
true at one time, as establishing coherence within ideas
and correspondence to fact, remains true for that range
of experience, but is displaced for fresh truth to suit a
larger experience of the world of things and minds.
More plainly than beauty truth has a history, which is
possible by the attainment of formal truth within a
varying greatness of the materials, that is, the data of
the world, which are to be taken up into the scientific
artefact.

The true, or knowledge, or truth in the concrete, is a
complex of propositions, universal and particular, that
is, of facts and laws about any department of things. Its
truth is no quality of knowledge in the ordinary sense,
but a tertiary quality, a property founded on the relation of the true to the contemplating mind which it
satisfies objectively, *i.e.* to contemplative, or, in a word,
scientific, curiosity, or the scientific sentiment, some-

times called the logical sentiment. The value of the true lies in its thus satisfying the scientific sentiment, and that value is experienced in the pleasure which this satisfaction gives to the mind, in its pleasing us 'after this manner.' Truth belongs to that artificial arrangement of things in the world, and the manipulation implied in this arrangement, which is knowledge, and the true and the truth of it exist only so far as the world known is possessed by the mind. Mind does not interfere with the things it contemplates but makes them over again in a certain manner which, as exhibited in the previous chapter, may imply the use of instrumental helps from the mind. The intrinsic relation to mind is implied in the coherence of knowledge and its equivalent correspondence with reality.

But this property of satisfying the mind in its scientific impulse and sentiment, though exhibited in the organisation of knowledge, is not, as happened with beauty, reflected in the constitution of the things themselves which are the subject matter of science. In fine art the mind supplied the form of the material and the form was embodied in the material itself. The life of a figure or the flowing outline of an arabesque means a definite modification of the materials employed in the art. But science does not alter what it studies. It unpieces nature and repieces it again, and in doing so acts always at the bidding of the things themselves, following in the organisation of its propositions, as Plato said long ago, the real articulation of things. But the coherences and implications that exist between propositions though they are founded in nature do not themselves belong to nature. Reality does not cohere nor imply. The organisation among the elements of knowledge which constitutes a satisfaction of the mind, is based upon reality, but merely indicates that the world has been rearranged under the control of reality so as to satisfy the mind. The method of science at once obeys the material and rearranges it, using such help of its own invention as it needs for the purpose of co-ordination. The mind, as in fine art, supplies the form, but the form does not alter the material, but renders it intelligible.

There is indeed coherence in the world in a certain and different sense. It has been repeatedly observed by Mr. Bergson that our separation of the world into departments is to some extent arbitrary and a matter of our varying interest. Plato said before him that a hand was either one thing or several things according as it was treated. But there are organisms in nature in which the parts are coherent in the sense that they operate upon one another. Some parts of the world compel us to consider them as made of elements which affect each other; and the present-day extension of the idea of organism downwards to inorganic matter means that there is greater closeness and intimacy in the internal constitution of things than we have been supposing hitherto, up to our present epoch. But this organic connection and mutual interplay of parts is not the coherence between laws and other laws, or between laws and their examples, and implications, that is meant by scientific coherence, which is the co-ordination introduced into facts by the mind.

All this follows from the situation that mind though vital to knowledge is instrumental to it and not constitutive of it. The coherence of propositions in knowledge is the reflection of the mind's need for arranging the objects of its theoretical experience so as to secure the smooth working of its own conations.

Truth, then, or true knowledge is true and has value because it satisfies us after a particular manner. Like the beauty of the beautiful, the truth of the true is a relational character, a tertiary quality or value, referred as a quality to the object itself as being a species of satisfactoriness, and experienced as the pleasure of satisfaction of disinterested curiosity. That pleasure is sometimes felt passionately, most often it is a calm delight in contemplating the harmonies of knowledge. It may be attended by subsidiary excitements in the work of investigation, some of which are pleasurable in so far as the labour tends to success; others involve pain or suspense. The release from such tension, when disappointment and frustration are replaced by discovery, adds a glow to the exercise of the search. As with art, the proper pleasure of the exercise is to be distinguished from these attendant features, however much blended with them in fact. Truth is the satisfaction of disinterested curiosity, not of the labour incidental to and for the most part inseparable from it.

CHAPTER XIII

MORALITY

MORALITY, like truth, is a work of art, but not of fine art. In claiming it to be an art I do not merely mean [1] that there is a fine art of conduct, of which good manners are an obvious instance: the delicate adjustment of behaviour to small or subtle changes in our circumstances, the variation of our responses with differences in the age, standing, consideration of the persons with whom we talk. That there is such an art of good life is true, but it only means that in the instruments of life, as with our microscopes and telescopes, there are fine as well as coarse adjustments. Nor do I mean merely that, as Plato said, living is a craft, like weaving or carpentering, and that virtue is its technique. I mean something more than an analogy; and that the best way to understand morality is to see what it has in common with fine art, and at the same time the differences which, leaving it still an art, separate it from fine art.

In fine art we mix ourselves with the material, filling it with our personality; in science we so behave towards the material as to depersonalise ourselves. In truth, of the two factors implied in art and in truth, the personal element gives way to the material one, the facts of the real world. In morals, on the other hand, we are concerned with the passions of men, with their desires for material (or it may be immaterial) objects, and the

---

[1] This chapter, down to p. 253, is largely reproduced from *Journal of Philosophical Studies* (1928), 'Morality as an Art'.

problem which morality has to solve is the fitting satisfaction of these passions, both as within the individual himself, and as between individual and individual. Now, our desires and wills are directed to some object external to us, in the sense that it is not yet ours, and in general, as with food, clothing, sex, office, riches and the like, the objects are physical material foreign to us which we make our own. And morality may from one point of view be treated as adjustment in practice to our surroundings. Yet these surroundings, when they are external nature, are but secondary to the desires, or rather to the wills, which are bent on attaining them. Goodness is an affair of motives or wills. External nature is material in respect of which we realise our moral nature. Goodness consists not in the good things we get, but in the good directions of our wills which good things satisfy. The foreign material is secondary to virtue; what is primary is our practical human nature. Virtue is not so much adjustment to our natural surroundings as it is adjustment to one another in the face of these surroundings. All humans desire objects, and will their attainment. Virtue lies in a certain distribution of our wills for objects among the humans who practise virtue, or it may be in a certain distribution within the one person of his various capacities for satisfaction by natural goods. The foreign material is secondary. What is primary is the direction of personality itself.

Thus in art the two elements of personality and material clearly mark their presence in the product, and that is why art is easier to begin with. Neither of the two elements is in single control. The artist needs, indeed, to study his material and adapt himself to its ways of going on. He needs a different technique for stone and wood and pigments and words and musical tones. And he blends himself with his material freely and imprints himself upon it. But in science or truth reality itself controls, and the personality, though essential, follows the object. In morality it is personality which controls; the external material is ancillary to the direction of our wills. We could have no wills unless we willed things and learnt their ways, but they are the stepping-stones to reaching our real selves as practical agents. Thus in science the personality, and in morals the external material, seem each in turn to vanish in favour of the other ingredient. In art both ingredients are palpable. Science and morality are, as it were, limiting cases of art, when the control ceases to be divided and is handed over to one or the other element; just as in the limiting case, an oval or ellipse turns into a straight line when the minor axis is diminished to zero, or into another line at right angles to the first, when the ellipse is flattened along the direction of the major axis.

Morality is wholly concerned with practice; and it might seem extravagant to describe the moral judgment which assigns goodness or badness to character and conduct as contemplative like the predicates of the scientific and the aesthetic judgment. But the case is so, and practice is in morals considered as practice still, but at a higher remove. Our acts are judged for their own sakes, for their bearing upon character and irrespectively of their results, though not independently of them. This is the foundation of the feeling which says, 'right is right', 'justice though the heavens fall'. These sayings are exaggerated and mistaken only if they are intended to shut off inquiry into the nature of right or goodness.

How, then, do we come to judge practice contemplatively, and at this higher remove from ordinary practice? The question asked about the contemplative nature of aesthetic and scientific judgment has to be asked about the moral judgment; and I need not quote again the famous passage of Hume to make sure that there is some impulse in human nature distinct from the sense of its virtue which accounts for our judging action to be virtuous. Now the direct impulses of action are palpable; they are the ordinary desires for various objects, from food up to knowledge or beauty, or even to virtue itself or duty when we aim at ideals. These practical desires become organised through memory and imagination and expectation and all sorts of syntheses; but this systematic manipulation of our passions would not give us the contemplation of practice for itself. They merely minister to prudence, a useful quality which it may be a virtue to cultivate but is not in itself practice for its own sake, but on the contrary only a more enlightened practice. The co-ordination of our bits of experience explained how curiosity became sublimated into pursuit of knowledge, when experience from many quarters conflicted with or reinforced itself, given the initial impulse of curiosity. But a similar tendency which is of course implied in the growth of moral judgments does not help us to understand how practice, however much enlightened practically, be- comes lifted, as it were, above mere practice.

Action comes to be considered as a matter of char- acter when individuals compare themselves together in respect of their actions. According to the famous saying of the Herbartians, we get to know the 'I' by experi- ence of the 'We'. It is through experience of one another, through intercourse of all sorts including speech, that we come to know that each of us has a self at all, and does not merely act as a self or feel as one, which the animals do or even the plants. The impulse, then, which lifts practice into a subject of contemplation is the social impulse, which we inherit indeed from our animal origin. But with animals, at least with most animals, the social impulse takes the merely practical form of gregarious action, helped out by devices of collective action such as signalling an enemy, as when rabbits scurry off turning up the white under-surface of their tails. In its lowest form such gregariousness is seen in the wild stampede of a herd of bulls; in its higher form in the societies of bees, where there is no reason to suppose anything which anticipates scientific construct-iveness as in a craftsman, where, however, there is anticipation of something which forms a stage in the history of morality, to which I am presently to call attention.

It is thus the social impulse which directs our atten-tion in animals such as we are, with ideas, to one another's actions, so that we become interested in them and consequently also in our own actions for their own sakes. Its place in morality corresponds to that of curiosity in science and constructiveness in fine art. In both those cases we traced the ways in which funda-mental impulse was modified so as to make the impulse contemplative, and divert it from practice. Here, in morality, we are dealing all the time with practice, and we have only to account for its becoming regarded as a piece of character for its own sake. The social in-terest we take in the acts of others, that is to say, gre-gariousness developed into conscious social interest, effects this diversion and is the foundation of our moral judgments. The ordinary passions are directed by an-other passion, that of sociality. Social passion on this view of the matter takes the place of reason on that view which regards moral distinctions and laws as determined by reason. Now reason can be found at work calculating means to the satisfaction of the passions and also, as Hume had the fairness to add, when he said reason is and ought to be only the slave of the passions, coolly comparing different ends with one another and balancing their attractions. But no such thing as a reason which claims to settle moral laws can be detected as a verifiable process in our minds, and indeed reason is hardly anything more than a name for the fact that there are moral laws and a system of interrelated moral judgments, to account for which a faculty of reason, or rather this capacity of reason, was invented.[1] Conscience is a verifiable mental function, but reason in the alleged capacity is not verifiable.

But the full genealogy of morals is not yet told. Besides, or rather as an incident of, the gregarious impulse, there exists in the animals the impulse to retort upon offenders, and there can be traced, less easily, a corresponding impulse of kindliness to helpers.[2] In its cruder form, below the gregarious life, it is the individual animal's response with beak and claw, to an offending individual. But it may assume a collective form, as when dogs turn upon and kill weak members of the pack or administer rough animal justice to offenders against custom.[3] Now both in morals and amongst the animals, vengeance upon the criminal

[1] See before, Chapter XI. p. 194.
[2] I quote from Mr. E. Westermarck's recent book *Ethical Relativity* (London, 1932): "Among a gregarious species of animals the members of a herd are at ease in each other's company, suffer when they are separated, rejoice when they are united. And, as has been pointed out before, with the pleasure they take in each other's company is intimately connected kindliness towards its true cause, the companion himself. Associated animals very frequently display affection for each other—defend each other, help each other in distress and danger, perform various services for each other." And he refers to Darwin's *Descent of Man* (p. 100) and other authorities.
[3] In the charming *Paradise of Birds* of W. J. Courthope (Edinburgh, 1870), the chorus of birds says about the rooks:

When they build, if one steal, so great is their zeal for justice that all at a pinch
Without legal test will demolish his nest, and hence is the trial by Lynch.

The chorus speaks in human terms in trying to show that the birds are the authors of human institutions.

bulks more largely than benevolence to the orderly member of the group. And here in distinctive retribution we have the forerunner of moral disapprobation. What in the animals is retribution is with men called resentment, with its corresponding gratitude. When these two are socialised, they are disapprobation and approbation.

In his latest work, which has just been cited, as indeed in his previous work on *Moral Ideas*,[1] Mr. Westermarck has surveyed the evidence on the strength of which he claims that resentment and gratitude (which he calls emotions) are the foundation of moral judgments. He has rendered to ethics an incontestable service, and it is only with diffidence that I differ from him as to the proper place to be assigned to these reactions in the history of morals. He himself allows and declares that these two reactions of resentment and gratitude (for I do not enter into the question whether they are properly called emotions or not) need, for morals, to be socialised, that is, transformed and made disinterested by the social sentiment. I regard them accordingly rather as anticipations of moral judgment than as the foundations of it. The pleasure of approbation and the pain of disapprobation take at a lower level the shape of these animal responses, which stand to moral response much in the same relation as craft stands to fine art. They are part of the practical life, but the distinctiveness of morality lies in its disinterestedness. In moral approval or disapproval, I should say, the true emotional element, over and above the element of judgment, is that which belongs to the social sentiment; while in it we can trace, as subordinate material elements distinct from that formal emotion, the animal vindictiveness which defends the herd, and

---

[1] *The Origin and Development of the Moral Ideas.* London, 1908.

is itself rooted in mere individual defence, which it transcends. These animal passions are felt most vividly when the community is animated with anger against some heinous offence, but always a flavour of the animal passion may cling to the moral sentiment. Thus animal resentment among gregarious animals is found where the society has not yet reached a higher condition than that of common or collective impulse, an infection which spreads through the members of the group; and is thus not the foundation of the true moral emotion which is social sentiment proper, but does anticipate it as being the way in which a simpler and undeveloped form of society defends itself.

The problem of morality being to secure among the members of a society, or within any individual, a certain approved distribution of gratifications, why, it may be asked, appeal to any sentiment or impulse of sociality any more than to reason in order to account for moral precepts? The same question was raised in aesthetics,[1] where it was urged that the beautiful was an equilibrium among ordinary experiences and this equilibrium established itself. In one respect the case of morals is different from that of beauty. For the equilibrium secured in morals is an equilibrium of practical passions, and these, it may be said, interfere with each other whether in the society or within the individual. Leave the passions to themselves, and they will fall into an adjustment which will satisfy. In fact, however, the problem is left unsolved and hardly approached. In the animals, adjustment within the individual is already secured through the periodicity of the animal's wants, and within groups of animals there is no balancing of the wants of individuals, one against another, but the mere response, illustrated already, to what disturbs the

---

[1] See before, Chapter III. p. 48 f.

collective custom. To reach equilibrium among humans, we need to attend to each other's wants, and this is secured, and at the same time the balance adjusted, through the social sentiment or passion acting through sympathy. A specific passion is needed both to set the problem and to solve it.

To convince ourselves of the part played by this controlling passion in the generation of morality, let us watch the actual growth of morality, that is, of judgments of right and wrong. It is a safe rule: if you want to know what a thing is, watch it as it comes into existence. Now the beginnings of the broad rules of virtue are hidden in the past. But moral rules gather around moral institutions, and we can observe the small or great modifications which occur in them. Such modifications may occur in any age, and the present age seems peculiarly favourable for observation, because of the unsettlement in men's minds, not about the broad lines of virtue, but about its special obligations, in particular in relation to property and marriage and the status of women. The simplest procedure is to take action in which moral questions hardly begin to be involved, where the question is rather one of wise policy than of right and wrong. Take the work of a committee determining a policy even of inconsiderable importance. The members of the committee are guided not by what they think is right, but by what they want. Before the committee decides, there is no right or wrong course to take. Each person advances his claim or his opinion as to what is advisable. The decision is the adjustment of these different claims to one another. It represents what the body as a whole agree to as satisfying the claims of the whole or of most; and if the matter is determined by a vote, normally the minority accept the result as something in which they can acquiesce. Their desires are thus attuned to one another. It may sometimes happen that what is adopted after discussion differs from the proposal of any member, and emerges from the discussion itself as a kind of discovery of what all come to desire.

Or take a more serious conflict such as a strike which is settled by agreement. Before that agreement is made, what is economically right is not known. There are the employers desiring one thing and the workers another. The peaceful settlement of the strike means that employers and workers have entered into each other's wishes. When the adjustment of wishes fails, the issue is left to force, to poverty, and starvation, which means that the way of economic justice has not been found.

The main feature, then, of such an experiment in practical politics or in economics is that there are contending parties who advance different claims. They do not mean this or that is *right*, though they often say so, but I wish this or that, or I mean to have this or that. What is desirable does not exist in advance of the decision, but is determined by the capacity to sympathise with one another's claims, a sympathy which is a means of carrying out the social impulse. But this simple and bare outline of the procedure must be supplemented and qualified. In the first place all sorts of actual judgments of right and wrong may enter, in so far as a problem is a complex one and as certain principles may be taken as accepted. Moreover, the parties, instead of making claims, do often urge their claims as rights; a misnomer, since the only rights are claims which have been recognised. As in war each party holds that God is upon his side, anticipating the issue of the war, so in the settlement of practical affairs we anticipate, and having claims describe them as rights. Sometimes to proclaim belief in your own forecast of

how an experiment of a social sort is to end may sway
the judgment of the social body in your direction.
Those who proclaimed the rights of man were strictly
guilty of a misdescription: there is no right to freedom
or life. But each man does claim such freedom. And
forecasting success in establishing his claim he helps to
win assent for it.

In the next place, besides considering the desires of
persons in the committee or the conference, the parties
may at any moment and throughout be considering the
actual consequences which may follow in the way of
good, that is, happiness or unhappiness, from the adoption of any proposed course. That may modify action,
because the wishes and claims of parties may vary as
the consequences of any course become better known
and are better realised. But the primary determinant is
the claims of the parties, their desires and wills.

Further, in this play of claims and wishes ending in
a decision, there may. be some who refuse to accept the
collective decision, and are excluded from its benefits
as recalcitrants. On the other hand, there may be a few
(or even one) who, advancing at the beginning a claim
which is contrary to the general views of the rest, so
work upon their sympathies that they impose their
desires upon the whole. These are the successful reformers, the prophets of wise change. And observe
that, putting forward a view opposed to the general one,
they, in virtue of their solidarity with the general,
advance it as a claim to be adopted by the general. A
man may stand alone in what he desires, but if he has
the committee-spirit, or the spirit of industrial co-operation, he sees what he alone claims as something to be
adopted by the whole to which he belongs.

These examples have been taken from ordinary conduct of affairs and from economics. But it is only a step

from economics to morals. The day has long passed when economics could be regarded as a mere matter of material advantage. It is a commonplace that they are permeated with morals, and if anyone needs convincing on this head he may be referred to the writings of Mr. R. H. Tawney, especially his work on *Religion and Capitalism*.[1] If we take the changes that are proposed experimentally in such institutions as marriage which are admittedly moral, we find the same state of things. Proposals to ease the conditions of divorce, or to control the number of births, are met at first, as is natural, by a storm of moral indignation. But gradually these proposals are submitted to the test of whether people want them or not, sympathise or not with those who propose or practise them. Considerations of the consequences enter indeed at every stage, and so does such a properly moral question as whether more harm will be done to morality by weakening or subverting established usage than good by the satisfaction demanded by some; but in the main the answer is determined, if it is determined at all, by the sensitivity of the community. We ourselves also desire or think it reasonable to gratify what certain persons desire. There is and can be no rule for settling beforehand what is right and wrong in such cases as if right and wrong were fixed for all time. There is justifiable prejudice in favour of what is already accepted, but if the new is found on trial to excite the sympathy of the whole with the impulses of some, the new enters into the changed code of moral conduct.

Thus in changes of morals which we can observe we have found that the new or modified precepts are established experimentally by a successful attempt to excite the sympathy of others who share in the impulses or desires of which new rules are the expression. The

[1] London, 2nd ed., 1932.

process is abbreviated in all manner of ways by reflection and consideration of consequences and of the dependencies of the suggested reform upon other desires. Yet in these complex and special cases the procedure is fairly clear. We may with this result in mind properly apply the same principle to those more fundamental relations whose regulation is the rules of goodness and badness; and we see that virtuous action is the outcome of sympathetic consideration for the wishes or desires or claims of men in society. The members of society desire ends claimed as good in the attainment of which they are confronted with claims, mostly similar, sometimes diverse, on the part of others. Goodness is the mutual adjustment of these claims, and is founded on the interplay of the impulses from which men act. It embodies thus the harmonising of the wills of individuals, and is discovered experimentally in the effort to obey the gregarious impulse and effect solidarity. As there is no beauty till it is made through the artistic passion, neither are there rules of right and wrong till they are made through the slow but persistent push of the social instinct in its human form. Even elementary rules such as those of respect for human life or of temperance are discovered through the wrath excited by the transgressor; as the stories of Cain and Noah illustrate. Concerned as these discoveries are with the simplest relations of life, they assume the character of invariable rules, for the impulses which they reconcile are universal; and this identity in the solution of the great moral problems has often been mistaken for some peculiar and *a priori* and even God-given character of moral laws. Whereas even these suffer small variations from place to place and from time to time. Witness the changes in the institutions of marriage and domestic life, in the right to personal liberty, in the widening of the sphere of application of moral principles from fellow-citizens to all mankind, which T. H. Green noted as distinguishing Christian from Greek morals of the Socratic age, in the change made famous by the formula 'from status to contract' and the later change, which seems to be supervening, from contract back to status again, but a status founded not upon mere usage but upon reflection.

These illustrations might be multiplied indefinitely. They do but confirm the main proposition that morality is matter of discovery under the guidance of sociality. Hardly, therefore, can any law be pointed to which is invariable absolutely. Even the golden rule, which might best put forward a claim to be so considered, is not so much a moral law as the definition of morality itself. For the satisfaction of the social instinct means that nothing can be good which another might not do in my place or I in the place of another. The categorical imperative is so empty for the same reason, that it rather defines the social instinct than offers a key to the actual details of virtue.

Further pursuing the example of the committee, we learn that while goodness is the claims which effect harmony between individual wills, badness is the recalcitrant will which is excluded and ostracised, *pro tanto*, as impracticable. And lastly, while goodness is the artistry of the gregarious instinct, there is room for the revolutionary moralist, the man who, putting forward a scheme of goodness new and paradoxical, like Jesus, is in fact forecasting a social scheme, who is in truth a genius of a social life which has yet to be and which, if sound, wins its way from derision to acceptance.

It is no new doctrine of ethics which I have been suggesting, but in a different form that which was put forward by Adam Smith. Hume had declared that moral distinctions are founded on a moral sense; our approval of certain characters or certain conduct is the feeling that they please after a certain manner. If morality is the satisfaction of the gregarious instinct as I have pleaded, the doctrine of a moral sense is on the lines of the truth. Hume's further account of the moral sense was that it arose from sympathy with the general effects of actions or character, "their tendency to the happiness of mankind or of particular persons". Like the utilitarians who came after him, he looked ultimately to the effects of action in the way of giving pleasure or pain. Adam Smith, with a surer eye, declared the sympathy which determines our approbation or disapprobation, not so much to be directed towards the effects of action as to the impulses from which action proceeds. He considered our actions in their origin rather than in their outcome. The good action is one to which other persons can attune their impulses. We approve benevolence because we ourselves are kindly, and should disapprove the weak benevolence which helps others merely because they are others, because we do not want to be kind beyond a certain point. We disapprove theft because we wish to keep our property and sympathise with the similar desire of the person robbed, and have no sympathy with the robber because we do not ourselves want to rob. The 'impartial spectator' represents in an ideally imagined person the 'pitch' to which the wants and impulses of all can be tuned; the word is Adam Smith's own. Not that utility is of no account. On the contrary, actions which harmonise persons are in the main identical with those prescribed by utility. But utility is not the first or principal source of our approbation or disapprobation. I have no doubt that Adam Smith has touched the matter on the quick, as anyone may verify for himself who asks why stealing is wrong. Does he first think of the uncertainty and pain produced by that conduct, or does he not disapprove because he himself feels the resentment of others at being disturbed in the exercise of their determination to retain their possessions? Is it the pain of the victim which makes him hate the murderer, and not rather his sympathy with the victim's claim to life and horror at the attempt to disturb his claim? To hold this is quite compatible with the recourse to considerations of utility which may and do crop up at every turn. In every moral decision the two kinds of sympathy may be involved with one another. But he who goes to the impulses from which action proceeds goes to the roots of action, and not merely to its issues. And if the impartial spectator has lost for us its eighteenth-century attraction, that is because we are now accustomed to trace things historically to their instinctive sources. That is why for the impartial spectator I have substituted here the play of the gregarious impulse as it makes members of society settle down into a harmonious satisfaction of their primary impulses. This formal impulse is the harmoniser, not reason, nor even moral sense. Moral sense is only a name for something otherwise recognisable, considered as the determining formal factor in the discrimination and establishment of right and wrong, of virtue and vice.

The impartial spectator of Adam Smith leads naturally on to the perennial question of the relation between 'ought' and 'is', of obligation and fact. What the impartial spectator approves is right; his is the judgment of the good man, 'the wise man ($\phi\rho\acute{o}\nu\iota\mu\acute{o}s$) as Aristotle said. But this judgment is itself a work of art or craft, a new fact established or created or discovered by an experiment which is directed to discover what passions may be satisfied, in what degree, at what time and place, in what circumstances (as Aristotle put it), so as to establish a social harmony among wills. Such a fact is a value. Still it is a new order of fact, just as the beautiful is a new order of facts. Even as there beauty is a blending of mind with material so as to satisfy disinterestedly the constructive impulse, so here moral value is the blending of the will under the impulse of sociality with the passions which are its material. Ought is therefore, we may strictly say, but a new sort of reality, made creatively out of natural impulses by the introduction amongst them of another natural impulse, which dominates, regulates and harmonises them. Ought is not the prescription set to the natural passions by some supposed non-natural element in our natures, not even by reason, but the arrangement or order established amongst them by another natural passion, and obligation is but the relation of any single element to the whole system. We ought to be virtuous, because any single act of virtue is what is needed to maintain the system of sociality.

In that process of discovery the wills which fail to join harmoniously with the other members of society are ostracised and declared bad. The vicious are cast out, or rather they are cast out in so far as they are vicious. For while their acts are condemned, they are as persons retained within the society for reformation. Virtue is thus maintained by the tyranny of the majority which wants to be good over the minority which desires courses of conduct that cannot be adjusted to the social whole. And so the virtuous cast out the vicious and seek to redeem them.

Further, in this experimental movement, there may arise someone who desires a scheme of life which his fellows do not understand and have no sympathy for.

He appears directly to contradict the view that virtue is the artificial work of gregariousness. For his will opposes that of society. But his ideal is still a forecast of a new social ideal, and he propounds it in the hope of attracting the rest of his fellows, by discovering to them feelings to which they have not yet awakened. The prophet of a new order is rejected by the men of the old one, but maybe he wins his way to the acceptance of his ideal hereafter. His singularity is thereby attested to be the truly universal.

Accordingly morality is a work of art, in which as in fine art we can trace the blending of a formal element with a material one. The difference being that there the artist is not separated from his materials, and is replaced by the members of society themselves acting in virtue of their sociality or gregarious instinct, which impels them to form a group, and in virtue of their sympathy with each other's impulses to avoid conflict and to secure co-operation, and establish an harmonious system of willing whose technique is the laws of morality. Sharing each other's tastes for good things, and therefore competing with one another, we have devised a system of distribution of our activities, which the good accept, and the bad reject or disregard. In the end the good differ from the bad by a difference of tastes, and the distinction is established by the operation of a formal taste, which is disinterested, and is equivalent to the practice of putting oneself in the place of another. Disinterestedness is a feature present in art as well as in virtue, taking there the form of choosing such products for beautiful as can be shared with others. Fine art unites men into society in respect of production, virtue unites them so in respect of practice.

Morality or the morally good is that system of will or conduct or of willed ends, for these phrases are all equivalent, which satisfies, and we may evidently add, satisfies objectively, the impulse of sociality. The pleasure which the good man feels in such satisfaction is the feeling of approbation, and his displeasure at that which fails to satisfy it is disapprobation. It pleases after a particular manner because it appeals to what we have called the social impulse or sentiment, or what may be called the moral sentiment. As in the phrases aesthetic sentiment or sense of beauty, or the scientific sentiment or sense of truth, there is the appearance of circularity, but only the appearance. For these names are given because the objects which satisfy them respectively are beauty and science and morals. They do not imply any sentiment which is directed upon beauty or truth or goodness as such and prescribes originally what falls under those names. On the contrary, it is because there is no such original sentiment that I have tried to trace its origin to some independent passion in human nature. The passion is merely called, without fear of confusion, after the result it produces. Accordingly the notion of a moral sense is retained but it is given a different meaning from its eighteenth-century meaning.

When, on the other hand, conscience is erected as by Butler into a faculty which pronounces with authority (though not always with power) upon what is right or wrong, this is the setting up of an authority which does not exist. The conscience which can be verified as operative in our minds is, as Mill described it, nothing but the mass of loyalties which gather round ends which have been found experimentally in the course of time to satisfy the passions of men as adjusted to one another in submission to the social sense, and which is accordingly consulted as occasions arise as a short compendium and convenient vade-mecum of conduct.

Moral goodness may be accordingly described as that which is approved by the social or moral sentiment. Certain comments of a more or less desultory character seem to need making here which may serve as answers to possible objections.

In the first place I have spoken indifferently of right and good as if these two conceptions were interchangeable. That is because I am dealing with moral goodness, and I am assuming that what is right is also morally good. There may be a larger sense, a more extensive and less intensive valuation, in which 'good' extends further than morals, and in this extension of 'good' it is possible that right is a distinguishable notion.[1] But these matters belong to a later inquiry into value below the level of the intrinsic values. At present I am content to treat right action as good action, at least so far as such action can be taken externally as a particular form of outward behaviour.

Second, it has been urged by Mr. de Burgh, in the first of a recent series of papers,[2] that two standards of judgment about conduct are used, right and good: one where ends are chosen from the sense of their rightness, and the other where objects are chosen because they are good, where action is spontaneous or natural and a man eats and drinks because he is hungry or paints because of a passion for painting. This distinction leads on to a refusal to admit the specifically social character of moral goodness.

Now here we have partly the situation mentioned just now that not all valuation of conduct is moral valuation. On the other hand, to insist on this duality of standard leads to certain difficulties. It implies, what contradicts common sense in morals, that a man who

[1] See later, Chapter XVI. p. 283.
[2] *Journal of Philosophical Studies*, vol. v., 1931, 'On Right and Good', Preliminary Survey.

by force of habit has come to behave morally with a
positive inclination for it, or from some original happy
disposition, such as Wordsworth speaks of in an oft-
quoted stanza of the *Ode to Duty*, seems to desire naturally what others desire by an acquired taste, is not
properly good in the moral sense. This is dangerously
near the doctrine that it is a higher state when the
machine acts with friction than when it acts smoothly,
which is so directly contradictory to the Greek conception of virtue. It puts the notion of duty performed
with struggle over that of free service.

The notion I have adopted in the above sketch of
morality allows its place for duty as the function of a
part of society in the whole organic life of society, and
consequently obligation is felt by the good man,
whereas the bad one feels constraint. Kant's magnificent conception of a kingdom of ends is far more vital
to the nature of morality than the categorical imperative, which always carries a flavour of antagonism to
the sensible impulses. Duty is but sense socialised, not
sense restrained. The merit of the conception of morals
as natural impulses organised in the service of society
is that it gives a proper importance to the sensible
impulses themselves, without whose satisfaction no
society and no morals could exist for a day; and at the
same time exhibits morality as due to another and
formal passion adjusting these material passions.

Accordingly, the distinction drawn above is not, I
think, in this form well taken. The real contrast is not
between ends pursued and acts done naturally and
automatically and ends chosen because they are right,
but between ends pursued spontaneously or unreflectingly and ends willed for their own sakes or intrinsically. But all that is required to make the choice of an
end intrinsic is that the object should be lifted out of

routine pursuit into contemplation, as it is by sociality.
Duty as the satisfaction of sociality is itself a passion
to which we are naturally inclined. At the same time
morality does include the performance of the natural
impulses and takes them for granted as underlying the
moral system. It includes them explicitly in moral
valuation only where there is possibility of maladjust-
ment to society or within the individual, as is of course
made clear by Mr. de Burgh.[1] Eating and drinking are
not judged morally as such, but only their moderate or
excessive indulgence, which are under the control of the
will. Moral valuation intervenes in intemperance; and
not primarily because of the evil consequences of that
excess, but because I do not want to drink too much
and have no sympathy with you when you do; when
there is such sympathy, the three-bottle man is half
virtuous. There may also be occasions when it becomes
a positive duty to eat and drink, as in cases of indispos-
ing illness.

The same thing is true when it is proposed to deny
the foundation of morals upon society by pointing to
the artist or man of science. It is not necessary directly
to approve a painter for painting well. He will do so
because he likes it above all things. But it is the social
system itself which allows a place to the artist because
his art is his proper work which he is to do for society.
In the adjustment which is morality, different men have
different offices, and moral laws are only universal, as
said before, in so far as anyone must do the same as a
particular individual if he were in that individual's
place. Secondly, in any fair-minded judgment of the
artist's or the scientist's life, his faithfulness to his
special job is rightly set off against his possible trans-
gressions in other respects in making up his account;

---

[1] *Loc. cit.* p. 254—an admirable passage.

just as in estimating a man's place in the scale of perfection (to anticipate for a moment) the moral judgment, not withholding condemnation of a particular lapse, may not condemn the man wholly for it.[1]

Some have understood the alleged social character of morality as meaning that all duty consists in promoting the good of others, and point to the love of truth or intellectual integrity as an undoubted element in a good moral character.[2] But to say that morality is socialised conduct is not to say that good conduct is altruism. The individual is as much a member of society as his fellows, and part of his job is to develop himself. There is great truth in Butler's saying that enlightened selfishness is on the whole a better road to happiness than any other. But it would be accepted by the social theory of morality with cordiality and without inconsistency, in the sense in which it is intended.

This objection rests on complete misunderstanding. A different and weighty doubt is raised by Mr. Bergson's recent contention[3] that there are two sources of morality, one social and the other the teaching of specially gifted individuals, who may be prophets or even mystics, men who propose new ideals of life founded not upon social experience but upon deeper insight into man's nature. It has been implicitly answered already. Such teachers reveal to man new passions which had not been suspected before, or not in this simplicity and fulness. They enlarge the contents of human nature or alter the spirit of men's actions. Still, like other reformers, they propose an ideal which is fitted for use among men, and their ideal is a social one—"that ye love one another". They do not supersede society but propose a new form of it.

---

[1] Compare Browning's *Rabbi Ben Ezra*.
[2] W. D. Ross, *The Right and the Good* (Oxford, 1930), p. 153.
[3] *Les deux sources de la morale et de la religion* (Paris, 1932), ch. i.

When their teaching has been accepted society has been transformed. They are teachers of morality by setting new problems to society for social adjustment. We have seen a smaller instance in the moral ideas introduced through sensitiveness to the claims of labour.

Mr. Bergson draws a striking distinction between 'closed' societies whose structure is defined and 'open' societies of which the boundaries are fluid or indefinite, such as humanity or even the League of Nations. In the first, social rules arise out of the structure of the society itself and the obligation to them is the 'pressure' exerted by the whole mass of observance on any part of it. In the second, the precepts draw men to them by 'aspiration'. I cannot, however, help thinking that he has erected into distinct stages of moral life what are only two features of every society that can be called moral, any society in which ends are pursued for their own sake and in which individuals take an interest in one another and are not merely creatures of instinctive imitation or infection. Mr. Bergson is comparing a fixed morality with a morality in the making, whereas, if I am right in the picture I have drawn, morality always is in the making, and great changes are but conspicuous instances of what occurs or may occur on a smaller scale at every stage; and indeed Mr. Bergson is the first to insist that the two kinds of morals overlap. It is true that there is discovery in morals as well as in science, and it is true that the greater part of our element-ary rules of good life are deeply founded in the nature of human society. But even these have their fluent edges, and even these were adopted as moral rules by the same process as new ways of life are established. What is now pressure was at one time aspiration.

CHAPTER XIV

GOODNESS

FROM these desultory comments I may return to the exposition. If I am to avoid a repetition which may now be left to the reader, it remains only to state briefly certain propositions which apply to the moral good as they have applied to the beautiful and the true.

Moral good is shareable and objective from the nature of the case. This not only leaves room for variations in good conduct as between different members of society, but requires such differences according to the different functions which persons perform in society. Some passions and impulses are common to all, and so far as these are concerned the same or similar conduct befits all. Hence the elementary rules of morals, truthfulness, respect for life and the like. The elementary rules of virtue correspond to the identity in the situations which call them forth. It is only in this sense that the same observances are required from all alike. The universality of moral rules means only that a law which holds for one person holds for another under the same circumstances. But there is no moral rule which does not admit exceptions. The rule only, as Kant said, admits no exception in favour of the individual. But it is not true that precisely the same conduct is required from all alike. On the contrary, the existence of society means that functions are demanded from each person according to his place in the society and his special capacity of service. What makes specific service universal is the sanction of it by the society. A man must not lie, but it may be legitimate for a doctor to lie to save his patient. The one rule which allows such variations from an elementary law is the security against its abuse by individuals in their own favour.

Morality is objective just because it is determined by the adjustment of individuals, and it has therefore authority over any one individual. The right distribution of service is settled experimentally in the way which has been described, though except in very few cases the experiment has been tried ages ago, and any one society takes over most of its morals from its predecessors by education of the young and other forms of tradition.

The judges of what is right or wrong, good or bad, are self-selected and impose their approbations or disapprobations on the remainder. Those who do not conform are condemned as wrongdoers or immoral. The standard of right or good is embodied ideally in the good man, and conscience in any individual is the vicegerent of this impartial judgment.

The objectivity of morals implies the relativity of morals to the conditions which call for a satisfactory distribution of services and satisfactions. There is no such thing as an absolute and eternal law of goodness. The absoluteness of a law lies in its being the satisfactory solution of the problem of distribution.

Men's passions and wants may vary from age to age and according to the society in which they are to be satisfied. Accordingly progress is possible in morality, though the formal character of morality does not change. There are accordingly no degrees of goodness at any one time nor as between different times. The widow's mite, to take the stock example, is as good and generous

as the endowment of a hospital. A good Greek or
Fijian is as good as a good Christian, though their ap-
provals may and do vary. But though goodness does
not differ in degree it may differ in largeness or greatness, or, to use the Aristotelian language, in splendour.
Aristotle's example[1] was the little vase which a generous
man would give to a child, while he would give a more
splendid gift to an older person; and Christianity added
the widow's mite, because of the new passion to recognise the equal worth of individuals.

One form which the variation of goodness in respect
of greatness takes is the recognition of merit and of
heroism. In both cases the double valuation is seen in
operation. Merit is the extra admiration which belongs
to a greater act, though, as the saying of Pippa runs,
"all service ranks the same with God". Merit marks
the difference between the largeness of an act and the
average which is expected from the average man. It
may be deserved for two kinds of reasons. The good
conduct may be of an amplitude rarely possible to the
ordinary individual. The man who performs it has
merit but not greater goodness, for he does but rise to
the level of his opportunities. Or he may do the good
act in the face of the strongest distraction or tempta-
tion, and his merit lies in a strength of character, above
the average, which enables him to persist. Common
duties are devised for the average capacity, and we do
not expect from a man sacrifices which the ordinary
man cannot bear. When he performs such sacrifices he
is meritorious though he has not greater goodness.
Merit is thus awarded on two different grounds.

Heroism is the same thing over again. A hero is not
a hero to himself; he does what society speaking
through his person requires of him. But his action,

[1] Quoted before, Chapter VIII. p. 138.

whether from the larger scope offered to him or from his own greater gifts of character, is larger or more splendid. Approval is not affected, but admiration attends him.

The greatness of which the moral judgment takes account is moral greatness, greatness within morality itself. There is, however, another greatness, historical greatness, which is not judged great on moral grounds. The relation of morals to this greatness raises a difficult question to which Mr. de Burgh has called attention.[1] It arises from the place of morals in reality.

Goodness is an artificial product into which mind and nature both enter, but the control is in the hands of the mind itself. The product is entirely mental, a system of relations between the wills of individuals in society. But the element of physical reality is present though in the background. For all passions or volitions are directed upon nature (which includes psychological as well as physical nature). We desire objects and nature stimulates us to our impulses. Morals are thus a disposition of actions within society which takes place under the conditions set by external reality. Because of these conditions morality has been and is properly described as an adjustment of man to his environment, and the rules of morality are contrivances which secure the persistence of society. A system of morals, if it were thinkable, which disregarded these conditions would perish. It is only loosely, however, that morality can be treated as adjustment to the environment. The adjustment distinctive of it is to the human environment set by society, under the conditions supplied by nature. So indirect does nature become when the

[1] *Proceedings of the Aristotelian Society*, vol. xxxii., 1932, 'Goodness and Greatness' (Presidential Address).

control in the artefact of nature and mind passes to mind.

Now this artefact of human society, which is a possession of mind like the other supreme artefacts, and doubly so because it is entirely mind working under its physical conditions, is itself a reality in the midst of other reality, and depends not as art did on interpretation supplied by mind, but is penetrated with mind.

What, then, is the relation of this artificial construction of man to historical greatness? For historical greatness is not always goodness. On the contrary, it may belong to men who may be thought immoral, for example, Napoleon, and, as some would say, Bismarck, who have played an important part in history and have worked great changes. The world admits two kinds of greatness, moral and historical, and they are apparently independent of each other.

A similar problem arose in aesthetics,[1] for the artificial thing beauty, though it depended upon interpretations, introduced by mind, claimed insight into the real world of human nature and even of things. We had to ask how we could feel assured that what the artist said in poetry or in music or elsewhere could be verifiable in the real world independent of the arts. Our answer there was a very incomplete one. We pointed to the place which the artist held in the scheme of things, his work the issue of an impulse in which he responded to the real world as other men do, and because of his gifts with deeper penetration than less gifted men; but we had to fall back upon faith to support us in believing that the interpretations given to the world of things by such persons whom the world of things itself produced were likely to be true and well-

[1] See before, Chapter VIII. pp. 147 ff.

founded. Something similar is all that I can offer towards the present problem.

Historical greatness is not the same as moral greatness. Is moral greatness likely to give more of a clue to the tendencies of things than historical greatness? Has it any primacy over historical greatness which is attributed not only to the authors of important events or movements, but to individuals marked out by superior efficiency or skill, even to a Borgia or a Catiline? In a way the problem is easier here than in the case of great art, for moral greatness is the achievement of society advancing under the conditions set by reality itself, and in turn producing a species which is part of nature. There is a fascinating passage of Green's writings [1] in which he claims that great men have not been determinative of the course of things by their evil, if they were evil, but in so far as their work was the vehicle of larger forces. His instance is Napoleon, whose evil was the undoing of his schemes for the overweening power of his country, but led to the unity of Germany through the War of Liberation. The same note is struck by Carlyle: what was wicked in the French Revolution recoiled upon itself; what was morally great was its gift to France and all Europe. Reflections of this sort may help us to believe that the world which produces moral good is itself upon the side of good, and that it is the goodness of great men which counts in the end and not their badness, or, what better describes them, their independence or carelessness of the moral judgment. Bismarck, for instance, is without doubt a great man, but some of his great acts were not so much immoral as unmoral or a-moral, as Mr. de Burgh has said. In the end we are left to faith

---

[1] T. H. Green, *Principles of Political Obligation*, Works, vol. ii., London, 1886 (also published separately, London, 1895), secs. 127 ff.

that the quest of virtue under the circumstances always arising in history afresh to set problems to statesmen who may occupy themselves with quite other considerations than public and private virtue is somehow in the line of what the world is likely to produce. And if, to some, such a faith seems to be too optimistic and easy-going, we have to reinforce their unfaith by remembering the convulsions which physical nature has always in reserve to destroy the good works of men, earthquakes of Lisbon, eruptions of Mont Pelée, though even these the eye of faith may regard as fresh incentives to repair the destruction of men's hopes. Even if man were destined by some later convulsion to be wiped out entirely, he will still have done his part, and through his moral rather than his historical greatness. No need to ask if these things are part of Heaven's design. The question rather is what place is to be found for heaven, and for a heaven of what sort, in a world in which man is so liable to the overpowering force of nature.

What remains to be said of goodness, its status and value, is hardly more than repetition. Goodness is not a quality in the accepted sense of the term, but a tertiary quality or value. It is the character which good conduct possesses of satisfying the social impulse, and of being approved, while its contrary is disapproved. Its value lies in its capacity of this satisfaction, and such value enters constitutively into the structure of morals. The pleasure and pain of approval and disapproval are the experience we have in which goodness reacts upon acts which are conformable or non-conformable to its requirements, and are, as we have seen, anticipated in the semi-animal responses of resentment and gratitude.

There is, however, a certain difference in the pleasure of goodness and that of beauty and of truth, though it does not affect the nature of the values in the three cases. In truth and beauty we can distinguish the subject judging from the object judged: in the case of truth the object was nature itself arranged indeed in a certain way by the mind; in art it is a material object, though altered so as to embody elements contributed from the mind. Whereas, in goodness, subject judging and object judged are of the same order, are *in pari materia*. It is mind judging mind, either the minds of others or the mind of the judge himself. We have conduct judged by the subject of conduct. The true and the beautiful are set over against us and it is natural to impute these qualities to the object and the pleasure they give us to the contemplating subject. It is not so easy or natural to do so in morals; and accordingly our social sentiment is rarely called into evidence, except when some particularly flagitious or heroic act has been performed or when we wince under the stings of our conscience, which is the vicegerent of the social sentiment.

I may gather up the results of the inquiry into the three highest values in a brief summary. By asking how these values or valuable things come to be regarded for their own sakes, as plainly they are regarded, we have found also the answer to the question what the motives are in human nature, which in the spirit of the passage I have quoted from Hume,[1] distinct from any sense of beauty or truth or goodness, lead to the exist-

---

[1] I say in the spirit of Hume's saying—for as to the substance of Hume's conclusions I have in respect of morals followed not Hume, but Adam Smith. I find myself in complete agreement with Mr. Westermarck (*Ethical Relativity*, p. 71) when he calls Adam Smith's *Theory of Moral Sentiments* "the most important contribution to moral psychology made by any British thinker". And in respect of beauty I have not found Hume enlightening.

ence of these values. Those motives have been found
to be respectively material constructiveness, curiosity
and sociality, and in us men, with our advance beyond
sense into the full use of memory and imagination, it
is the deflection of these impulses from mere practice
which lifts the objects of pursuit into contemplation
and makes them desired for their own sakes. The distinguishing features in the process in the three cases
arise from the relative parts played by the mind and
external nature, both of which are factors in all three.
In art the control is divided between mind and the
material, in truth control rests with the external
material and the mind's part in the result which as
truth or science is not so much constitutive as instrumental. In goodness control rests with the mind itself,
though always the external nature in which men live
their lives and practise the art of living remains as the
background of life. The values are not the creation of
any so-called reason but of the motives which have
been assigned. Reason is but a name for the unified and
organised character of the products. I know indeed that
to some it will seem that it is this character of unity and
organisation which is of importance, and its importance
has not only been exhibited but implicitly insisted upon
here. If it is urged that little is gained by tracing these
values to their ultimate source, I can but plead that,
if the result is established, it may be, like any addition
to truth, worth knowing. The effect has been to re-
instate three conceptions, now demoded but familiar
once, the moral, the aesthetic and the logical sentiment, shorn of the mystery which may have seemed
to surround them.

It has been explained that these characters of beauty,
truth and goodness are not qualities in the proper
sense of the objects which possess them, but relations

between those objects and the other ingredient, which is mind itself; that in this relation the satisfaction which is felt belongs to the mind and is experienced as being pleased after a particular manner, and the characters in question are referred to the objects as qualities. In reality they are relations. Finally the mind which enters into the relation with an object in virtue of which the object is valuable and the mind is satisfied in respect of a certain capacity, is a standard or objective mind; and these values are objective, and nothing is good, or true or beautiful, for a particular mind, or has subjective value, except in a derivative fashion, only intelligible as a claim to objective value.

PART III

COMPARATIVE—VALUE IN GENERAL

CHAPTER XV

THE HIGHEST VALUES COMPARED

IT is not easy, and not very important, to say where science ends and philosophy begins in the study of the values. So far I should prefer to say I have been pursuing the science of values, describing them as the different species of things that they are. In the remaining chapters I shall be, however, quite clearly engaged in philosophy, considering the relation of the three values to each other and then going on to consider under what forms value may be traced below the level of the highest values, and what its place is in the whole scheme of things. Philosophy or metaphysics always enters with such comparative inquiries. I should add, however, that I shall largely be repeating in what follows what I have already written in a previous work, and the present chapter will be mostly quoted from that work.[1]

First we have to trace the relation. Each value in turn seems to include the others, and this is at first sight puzzling and contradictory. But it is not difficult upon reflection to see that they include and are included in the others in different senses. Thus practice includes both truth and beauty, for each of these is a good or human satisfaction and enters into the Good as a whole, where the expression, 'good', is used in the wider sense, though the Good as a whole is made the end of the specifically moral life, and each of its parts, though

---

[1] *Space, Time and Deity*, London, 1920, vol. ii. bk. iii. ch. ix. E, F. The present chapter is, with some changes, quoted from E.

not primarily the end of a virtue, becomes upon occasion the end of a virtue (see before, p. 255 f.). Intellectual and aesthetic satisfactions are as much part of the Good as material satisfactions, such as those whose virtue is temperance. Moreover, there is a virtue of truth or beauty as well as of ordinary practical life. For the pursuit of knowledge or of beauty is a practical endeavour and is acknowledged as a matter of moral approval; partly as a general duty to cultivate these powers, but partly also, in the case of persons specially gifted in these respects, as one principal part of their contribution to the social good. The artist or the scientist or the philosopher are not, as some Greek philosophers tended to think them, set apart from society because of their special qualifications, but are on the contrary included in the society, whose interest or good it is that its members should do the work for which they are best fitted. The philosopher is morally no different from the blacksmith or weaver, but his business is very different, and maybe it is a higher or more perfect business. The pursuit of truth or beauty is good in so far as it is carried on industriously and to the full measure of the individual's skill, and with due regard for other duties which fall to him as a man. He is to do his special work well, as the weaver his.

Now it is clear that science and the pursuit of it are not good in the same sense as they are true or scientific. A man is not a bad man because he is in error, unless the error is avoidable with due care. The moral defects of the thinker are such as make him unfaithful to his work, *e.g.* laziness or prejudice. His defects as a thinker are his idiosyncrasies which make him an uneven mirror to things. No doubt the two sets of defects (and correspondingly of merits) may slide over into each other: defects of temper or character may mean (as where there is prejudice or prepossession) defects of insight. Thus truth is a good, as the satisfaction of a human impulse according to the measure of its claims when considered along with the claims of other human impulses; it is true, in so far as it achieves its own purpose. Compared with the moral end, truth as truth is technical, just as being a skilful blacksmith or surgeon is technical. Truth is involved in goodness in yet another and more obvious way, not as a department of the moral end but as a means of guiding action, which needs knowledge of human nature and of the conditions of action. Here plainly truth is technical; it is the element of wisdom or insight which has always been acknowledged as an ingredient in goodness and sometimes has been treated as a virtue. Whether truth is a special part of the moral end, or in the shape of wisdom an ingredient in moral action of all kinds, truth as truth is technical for morality, which is concerned with the value of human character and with truth only as part of it or a means to it.

In the same way, just as beauty is one part of the Good and to pursue it is a virtue, so goodness and truth are species of the beautiful, or they have their aesthetic side. Some parts of mathematics have been described as poetry and certain methods in science are, to indicate an exceptional excellence, justly called beautiful; and good actions may have beauty or grace or sublimity, or a life may be a true poem. The aesthetic feeling in these cases is distinguishable from the mere 'logical' sentiment for truth or the moral sentiment of approval. What is true or good is treated much as we treat a piece of natural beauty, such as a beautiful face or the beautiful figure of a man, where as it happens no selection or supplementation from the spectator is necessary, though

T

the spectator still needs to recognise it with his aes-
thetical appreciation or approval. Thus the beautiful
theory seems to us animated by a purpose or appears to
be the creation of some constructive mind. Or the noble
life is for us a work of art, the outcome of some imagined
exaltation of mind or refinement, like the life of Pom-
pilia as the Pope fancies it in Browning's poem.[1] It is
not the goodness of the life as judged by mere morality
that is beautiful; the spectator does not so much sympathise with it morally as blend himself with it into a
new unity. Thus as before what is true is not beautiful
in the same sense as it is true. To be true it follows the
tests of science. It is for beauty technical, just as the
material which is to be the Hermes observes the technical limitations of marble. And in like manner of the
beauty of goodness. Consequently badness may (like
Iago's) be beautiful, but not for the same reason as it is
bad; and even error, like a well-wrought but fallacious
theory, but not because it is fallacious.

The case of truth is somewhat more complicated.
There is a goodness of truth-seeking and a beauty of
truth. But also goodness and beauty are each of them a
department of truth. This must be understood in a
double sense. In the first place goodness has its truth,
much as truth has its goodness; goodness (or beauty) is
technical for truth. That is, goodness is the truth of
human nature, and badness the error of it, and in the
same way beauty is true and the ugly erroneous. And
even as truth prevails over error and excludes the
erroneous proposition from the realm of reality, so
goodness tends to supersede badness and beauty ugliness. The unvalues are morally false or aesthetically

---

[1] The marvel of a life like thine, Earth's flower
She holds up to the softened gaze of God.
    The Ring and the Book, X. ll. 1018-19.

false, just as the erroneous proposition is false. Yet, goodness and beauty, though they thus share in the nature of truth, follow each its characteristic nature. They are not true for the same reason as they are good or beautiful. Consequently a murderer may possess profound knowledge of anatomy, and a learned historian of poetry be a poor poet. In this respect, then, goodness and beauty are technical for truth.

But there is a different sense in which these considerations do not arise and in which goodness and beauty are not technical but merely parts of truth or reality. For goodness and badness, and beauty and ugliness, are, like truth and error, themselves new realities and take their place in the whole of reality, alongside realities of a lower order.

Moreover, not only are the moral and aesthetic judgments realities, but also the good or bad acts or good or bad volitions (the constituents of the moral situation) and likewise the objects, which are beautiful or ugly, taken apart from the aesthetic judgment of them, are real. Thus truth and error, goodness and badness, beauty and ugliness, are all realities among the sum total of reality. Now truth we have seen is reality as possessed by mind, and hence in this sense the other values are parts of truth and truth is all-inclusive, because its object is reality. True knowledge therefore comprehends the whole of existence, including truth and error itself.

Thus all things of whatever grade of reality enter into truth or true knowledge, because truth follows reality and leaves it undisturbed in taking possession of it. Hence there can be science of everything, so far as things are revealed or adumbrated for us. Science is supreme, for it is another name for reality in all its forms as possessed by minds which think rightly or are attuned to reality. On the other hand, from the point of view of man, practice is all-inclusive, for the quest of truth and that of beauty, like the quest of material bodily satisfaction, are practical tendencies. Regarding man as the highest finite, his practice, which includes discovery of truth and creation of beauty, we must pronounce to represent man at his fullest. But the discovery and pursuit of truth are not truth itself, and since truth means the possession of reality by mind, we must say that while goodness is the highest manifestation of finite existence which we know, truth represents the whole of reality, while beauty is intermediate in position between the two, being that kind of existence in which neither does mind follow reality as in truth, nor is reality moulded by mind as in willing, but the two are interwoven.

CHAPTER XVI

PSYCHOLOGICAL VALUE

THE value of the highest values, the beautiful, true and good, has thus been found to lie in a relation, in the satisfaction which these creations of man give to certain specific impulses (call them desires or passions or what you will), which it has been my object to identify and to affiliate with their animal beginnings. The remainder and perhaps the most difficult part of my task is to describe the lower so-called 'values', and to ask how far we can, as we should expect, observe in them the same features of satisfaction of impulse and of object-ivity as have been manifest in the highest values. Instead of beginning as I might have done with a hypothesis about value in general and verifying it in the highest values, I have started with the more or less unhypothetical description of the highest values, and now I have to ask what is left out in tracing what corresponds to such value lower down in the scale.

In speaking of moral conduct we have seen already [1] that we may apply the predicates of value, good and bad, without moral approval or the reverse. There is a general use of the idea of value in human activities which does not carry with it moral valuation, though it leads on to such valuation wherever excess or defect may bring the agent under the direct notice of his fellow-men. Under this head come all the animal activities of men, eating and drinking, maternal de-votion or ordinary maternal care, and even, as Mr. de

---

[1] Before, Chapter XIII. p. 255 f.

Burgh has said, pursuit of beauty or knowledge, treated merely as a passion, which it is in many persons. These are all spontaneous impulses, which we may call natural, so long as we do not go on to think of moral actions as not natural, for they are as natural as the others, because the social impulse is natural however artificial in comparison with those of simpler impulses the results of its working may be. "The art itself is nature", as Polixenes says in *Winter's Tale*. In all these actions taken by themselves, that is, when they do not call for moral judgment explicitly, we do not so much approve or disapprove as accept or reject, or, in special cases, admire. Our attitude varies in different cases. We admire pursuit of knowledge, and it is difficult to keep ourselves from approbation. We accept eating and drinking, and disapprove if they become excessive and excite moral judgment. A habit like cleanliness is on the border between nature and morals. Uncleanliness we partly dislike but in the main disapprove. Yet cleanliness is a mere animal habit, which we should practise, as we do not, from infancy, if we were only born relatively late like cats and dogs, and had not to learn by drilling what they so largely come into the world possessing, or ready to acquire by mere imitation. These different attitudes arise from the extent to which our natural impulses tend to come into conflict or agreement with those of other persons. Consequently these natural or animal impulses are rarely removed from social relations, even such an animal virtue as the mother's care of the child.

Along with actions which are thus sanctioned or in some cases admired, go qualities like personal courage, kind-heartedness, even skill or talent, which Hume liked to dwell on, qualities which are useful to their possessors or to others and are agreeable or admirable.

Such qualities come under the view of morals in so far as they promote virtue or make virtue easier to the possessors.

Between the moral use of our natural tendencies and the mere animal exercise of them, and bridging over the interval between the psychological and the moral order, comes the practice of prudence which, like morality, organises the impulses into a system, but a self-regarding one, where concern for others does indeed enter but not for its own sake and only so far as others may affect the personal happiness. Prudence is an interest of man as an individual animal, and it too, like the pursuit of knowledge or the practice of the painter, enters as an item into the materials taken up into morality, and becomes as such a moral and not merely a personal virtue, because the prudent care for oneself is approved as a part of the general duty of making the best of ourselves.

Now so far as all these things are called good, it is because they satisfy impulses of the natural man, and good in the wider sense, in its application to man, what meets an interest, is the object of that interest. Its value is the relation between the object, for instance the child's welfare, and the subject, for instance in its impulse of motherly love. This is the account which Mr. Perry gave of value in general,[1] and rightly if we are confining the idea of value, as in common usage we do, to human affairs. Such value I call psychological value.

But the description is inadequate. The objects in question please because they are interesting. The interest and the pleasure are in fact one and the same thing, interest as conative, pleasure as emotional. But even psychological value is not exhausted in its pleasurable element. There is also an objective element

---

[1] R. B. Perry, *General Theory of Value*. London, 1926. Above, p. 3.

which underlies the value, though it is not the objectivity of morals. These actions or qualities are not
good merely because they please the possessor, nor
even merely because other individuals like them (as in
cleanliness), but because they are useful to the type or
kind. They have value as generic. Food and drink are
good and have value because they sustain life and maintain the kind; parental love, courage, talent are indeed
valuable to the individual, but while they *please* him
alone, they have *value* for him as representing the type.
At this lower level they are not valuable because society
demands them; they have a more elementary value, in
the requirements of the kind and the more or less overt,
more or less unconscious, feeling for the type. The
distinction of good and bad which is found here implies
a standard. It is not set by society upon this purely
natural level; nor even by prudence, though the two
things come to the same. The standard is the generic
nisus working in the individual and welcomed or liked
by other individuals. Modesty we like even before we
approve it morally; and kindness and enthusiasm in
like manner; but when they become prudishness and
sentimentality, we withhold our liking. All these cases
where we use the wider and less significant predicate of
good rather than the narrower and more intensive one
of morally good, are always on the point of adoption
into the moral judgment, because they generally are
members of a complexer situation and the moral judgment has then to be invoked. Yet even apart from this
circumstance, the value belongs to them because of the
existence of a standard, though it is not a social standard. Subjective value arises out of objective value. The
individual subject may claim value for what pleases
him, but what pleases him is not always good for
him, as when he likes unwholesome food or overmuch

alcohol. And only that is good even on this level which pleases the typical or normal or generic man.

Perhaps it is this implication of the type which makes it so difficult to settle clearly the place of art and knowledge in the human life. As passions, they resemble love or drinking. Knowledge clearly enough helps to preserve life, and there is no strain in pronouncing the pursuit of it a good apart from morals. About the pursuit of beauty, natural passion though that also is, we do not feel so sure. For it is hard to see that it helps towards the life of the kind, except on the ground that anything which enhances life may be in faith regarded as good for the species. Therefore though we think of art as good, we like also to think of it as right or morally good, for then its place seems to us securer. We tend to say knowledge is good and ignorance is bad, assuredly; but beauty is good for those that like it, and we halt in our opinion, whether it is a generic good.

There is another sort of value, according to the current use of words, which is neither morally good nor good merely in the broader sense of psychological value: namely, economic value. But it is really instrumental value. Goods have value in themselves in so far as they are exchangeable. They are subservient to the purposes of life. They touch therefore both on natural good which satisfies man's wants as normal, and on moral good which satisfies his wants as a moral being. The present process of moralising economics and the economic structure and behaviour of our affairs is an attempt to hand over economics from an old to a new master. Economics, before, was subservient to the uses of material man, who significantly was spoken of as the normal or economic man, typical though individual. This was the view of the older economics which worked wonders, and for all I know is destined still to work wonders, for I do not venture to judge what I understand so imperfectly. So far as it suffers change and becomes rather a science of consumption than one of exchange, it still remains instrumental but to the moral rather than the material life, or rather to the industrial life as moralised by conceptions of the social good. The end which industry serves is varied from mere life to good life, in the Aristotelian phrase.

Now what is the good life is a matter for morals to settle in practice and for ethics to discuss scientifically. But whether economics subserves mere life or good life, in both cases it is instrumental, and is concerned with the valuation of goods or services within the pattern to be secured. I may conclude that it is more worth while to buy a motor-car out of capital or, keeping the capital, to buy a picture every year with the interest of it. What economic value deals with is the question of exchange, what sort of pictures can be bought every year as an equivalent to the present value of a motor-car; how much food or other good thing measured in prices is equivalent to the service of a labourer; and the like. The end being set by morals, the means to the attainment of the end are the concern of economics; and it is evident that the two sets of considerations will interplay at every turn. Thus value in economics, just because it is instrumental and not intrinsic, is not the same kind of thing as value either on the moral or on the merely psychological level. Economic goods are indeed good because they satisfy human wants. But their primary value for economics is not their value in use, or directly for use, but their value in exchange, and the conception of value here has altered. Economic value satisfies impulse or wants only indirectly, so far as the satisfaction of wants involves the balancing of supply and demand so as to secure a maximum satisfaction of wants, however those wants are conceived, and so determine what rate of exchange among products conforms to the best distribution of gratified desires. Economic value thus falls indirectly under the regular rubric of value, but directly its values are, in no depreciatory sense, a part not so much of life or good life itself as of its machinery.

I may now recur to a matter left over from Chapter XIII., where, having said that I assumed right action and moral action or goodness to be coincident, I went on to contemplate the case in which right and good might be separate and distinct conceptions.

On the level of animal and, more particularly, human psychological value, the objects which satisfy are good in the wider and less intensive sense of good, in which good is less than goodness. Good is objective satisfaction of a human impulse treated as an animal one, and right is the action which is taken in order to secure good. Right has in fact here become degraded to correctness for its purpose.

Confusion arises from applying to morals and goodness what is true only at the lower level. If we begin with the impulses from which action proceeds, morally good action is the same as right action, as common usage implies and Mr. Joseph has demonstrated.[1] Thinking rather of the intention of action than of its motive as we are bidden to do by Mill, we may say that right action is action done, from whatever motive, with the right intention, and such action is not right unless the intention is morally good. Correspondingly an act is not good unless it is also right. Rightness and goodness

---

[1] H. W. B. Joseph, *Some Problems in Ethics*. Oxford, 1931.

apply to the same situation, viewed in one case from the object at which it aims and in the other case as an action. The spring of the action is impulse directed upon an object which is intended.

Now if, neglecting the impulses to action, we start with the objects secured by it, we are left with the dominating conception of good in ethics. Right then receives the meaning of being means to producing good. The good may be construed as the Utilitarians construe it, as happiness or pleasure. When this is rejected, good is left as an indefinable. On the other hand, if we deny right to be a mere means to good, right becomes separated from good, and we are credited with intuitive judgments of right and wrong.

All these confusions arise from failing to distinguish moral good and psychological or animal good. Animal good includes, when humans are concerned, not mere satisfaction of animal wants, but all human impulses so far as they are satisfied unreflectingly and without suggesting their relation to a wider and socialised system. In this way the artist who sings as the bird sings or paints because he must, secures a good as the mother does in feeding her child. But, as we have seen, any such action may become good and right as soon as it is socialised.

CHAPTER XVII

VALUE for men below the moral level is thus the satisfaction of generic interest, and mere subjective value is the interest which any individual has in an object when the individual represents the type, otherwise subjective value is only caprice arrogating value to itself. When, on the other hand, I say, for instance, that a trinket has a sentimental value for me, I do not claim a private right to my own values, but imply that my desire gratified by the possession of the trinket is consistent with objective value, as modified to suit my special case. Value then, as distinct from pleasure, is at this level, too, objective with the colouring of objectivity that is appropriate to this level.

Having recognised the extension and consequent dilution of value thus far, there is no reason why we should stop at man, and not seek to find value among animals and even lower down. The difference between us and the animals in this matter is that men do and animals do not give voice to their experience of value. Value is ascribed from the outside through our judgments to the animal's attainment of goods. Under this proviso we may call food a value for the animal, and not because it is pleasant to him, but because it is nutritious and fills his need of life. Animal value is indeed exactly parallel to human psychological value, which might have been called from the beginning animal value were it not that man proclaims his values and animals only act upon them. The point is that, even where there is only consciousness and no speech or volition, the value is still generic and in that sense objective. There is a further comment of importance to be made. The highest values owed their existence to a specific impulse, the social impulse, the constructive impulse, the impulse of curiosity. The objectivity of the values thus set up resulted from the possession of these respective impulses. But no specific impulse is needed to account for objective value below the highest level. Food is good because it satisfies hunger, and its value is not its mere pleasantness but its nutritive character. Yet hunger and thirst and maternal love and the like are all part of the general impulse to maintain life, and that impulse again is not something additional to hunger, etc., but flows through those particular channels.

In other words, value for animals, including men below the level of right and wrong, is the satisfaction of a well-founded interest, and for the individual private values are derivative. Now the objectivity of even animal value, being intimately connected with the species, exhibits itself in the process by which the species is established as a going concern. Animals whose interests do not help to maintain their existence succumb under the conditions of their existence and leave the field for those whose interests can be satisfied permanently. This is the meaning of natural selection. It is not for me to discuss how far natural selection is a sufficient account of the history by which successful types come into existence. Rightly understood, it never was proffered as a statement of how species came into existence; it never was understood to be a cause, but only a process by which types otherwise generated (by gradual accumulation of small modifications, by adaptations in the life of the individual, by sudden and sporadic genesis of new types or otherwise) establish their permanence. Consequently the doctrine of natural selection may be described as the history of how value makes its entry into the organic world. So far as it is a necessary part of the process by which species are established, it is the principle which constitutes the history of value, for it shows how the mere interests of individual organisms come to be well-founded and to be values.

Above the level of animal and mere psychological value, that is to say, in the world of socialised man, it shows itself in that experimentation by which social rules are established and with them moral values. The brute process by which inadequate species perish is here replaced by the ostracism of modes of life incompatible with social preservation. Within any society there is a suppression of unsocial modes of life through the tyranny of good persons, or rather of the moderately good persons who represent the average ideals of conduct. Such suppression does not carry with it the destruction of the recalcitrant individuals, but only of their powers of dissentient action, though hitherto it has (some think unfortunately) been thought advisable in certain cases to get rid of certain criminals altogether. Force still is needed in society to maintain its ideals, but the securing of the field to the suitable type, which among animals and plants is left to the operation of failure in the unsuitable types or individuals, is here replaced by the operation of tradition, by the education which continues the civilisation so far attained into the next generation. As we should expect, the process adopted in organic life gives way at a higher level to a modification or sublimation (if you will) of the same principle.

What is said of value in animal life, where consciousness operates at least over part of the life, applies also to plants, where consciousness is not believed to operate. Moisture is a value for plants because it satisfies an organic need, betrayed by the plant in opening the stomata of its leaves. The whole range of values from plants up to that of morals might have been called (and was so called by myself on a previous occasion) by the name of instinctive value were it not for the discredit into which the name of instinct has fallen, and were it not that the social impulse at the basis of moral distinctions may itself claim the benefit or disadvantage of that name.

Below the level of life, the phenomenon of value appears in what Mr. Laird has called by the name of 'natural election', the simple fact that one thing matters to another in an intimate manner. The magnet and the iron matter to each other, and the filings may in this sense be said to satisfy the magnet. Under the happy name of valency the chemists had long ago introduced the idea of satisfaction of the atoms by one another. A bivalent atom like oxygen needs two hydrogen atoms to 'satisfy' it. This extension by Mr. Laird of the idea of value over the inorganic world, and consequently over the whole world of things of which it is the lowest level, if indeed it is the lowest level, appears to me a most important contribution to the philosophy of value. At the same time we note that at this level the possibility of subjective value disappears; all value is objective, because the nature of the two parties to natural election is fixed or at least is supposed to be fixed. What corresponds to choice in an organism is represented here by the greater intimacy which subsists between certain things and others. I do not raise the question whether in determining the character of inorganic things there may not have been a process of experimentation corresponding to the experimentation by which types in the organic world become stable and the moral values are created in man.

Value therefore in its greatest dilution and least intension is the relation between things in virtue of which one satisfies a want of the other. In mere physical existence the application of such unavoidable metaphorical language is justified by the action of things upon one another, for, as Lotze said, things are in so far as they act. Value at this lowest stage is relation between two elements in the world. Each thing or event has need of some other; and the whole world is valuable to any one part of it, if we hold the faith that each thing is related directly or indirectly to all else, or that, in Mr. Whitehead's language, every event has the whole world for its field. This minimum of meaning becomes in the organic world the generic satisfaction of a want, and in the highest sphere it becomes the objective satisfaction of certain specific human wants. We can thus trace value upwards or downwards; downwards as I have done, by omitting complexities gradually, upwards by adding fresh elements of intensive meaning as we rise up the scale of being.

But there is no such thing as beauty or truth or virtue for the animal, or even for man considered merely as a type of animal, and still less for the atom or the molecule. We experience the highest values as things we make for ourselves in pursuance of certain wants. Such value is not experienced by the animal at all, and all we can say of the animals or plants is that they experience something corresponding to such supreme value in the only way they can, by gratification of normal wants. Not even this can be said of physical things, there is only a relation to one another in which one has need of the other to do its own work, and shows its 'need' in its actual action upon the other—preferentially, in acting

U

upon its intimate associates, as the magnet draws the iron or the iron the magnet, or hydrogen and chlorine unite to make hydrochloric acid; indirectly, in so far as all other things are implied as its support or background. There is thus in all things something which corresponds to human values, even to the supreme human values, and we have now seen that it contains the two features of satisfaction and objectivity. There is no use of metaphor here. Metaphor only enters in the use of the human word value (whether in its supreme form or in its conscious psychological form) of the animals which cannot express their sense of value, or of plants, or still more of physical things. That is why it is all-important to see exactly in what sense or under what form the value exists. It is the neglect of these provisos which has made the indiscriminate application of value to the world in every part and in the whole the source of that confusion and looseness of thought which was spoken of in the introductory chapter and has made the word value something of a reproach to present thought.

Value is pervasive in some form, but as soon as we assume that what we humans call value (even in the lower form of good, as distinct from moral good or beauty or truth) is pervasive and fundamental, we go astray and cloud wisdom with words. Throughout the world there is the relation by which one thing is intimately connected with certain things and less intimately with all. But to hold that our precious values pervade the world, is to miss the very graduation of value which makes the pervasiveness scientifically admissible and true. The confusion is still greater when the whole world is declared to be a value, a proposition which has no meaning when we inquire what value is in its simplicity. For the whole world to be a value except to its parts, would mean that the whole world satisfies its own needs, whereas value only subsists as between things which can be said to need one another.

Exactly the same sort of confusion and loose thinking as was suggested in the introductory chapter, occurs when everything and the whole world itself is said to be a mind and the world to be fundamentally spiritual. Everything, it can be shown, has a mental side, something which corresponds to mind, has a mental or subjective 'pole', again to use the language of Mr. Whitehead. But the very significance of such a statement lies in showing what sort of mind can be possessed by things on different levels of existence. There are grades of mind, as Leibniz urged. The stone has not our mind. All we are entitled to hold is that in everything something (or some aspect) exists which performs to that thing the office which our mind performs towards our body, that is to say in the thing body-mind, which we call ourselves. That is strictly true, at least it is a good philosophic hypothesis. Even in the world as a whole there is something which corresponds to mind, though to say what it is would take us further into philosophy than is desirable here. On the other hand, to call the world as a whole spiritual, as many philosophers have done, is to extend the highest form of mind or spirit outside the bounds of the beings which we know to contain spirit. The procedure is sometimes justified by the assertion that reality is known to us by the exercise of our minds and therefore has no existence apart from our mind. Even if this first step could be taken without question, we could not be justified in taking the further step, that therefore the reality which is in or before our minds is itself of the nature of mind. Not even this defence can be put up for the thoroughly confusing proposition that reality as a whole, because it involves value in all its parts, is a value as a whole.

One illustration of the confusion due to loose use of language, and what is worse loose thinking, is the growing habit of describing religion as a value. It raises so many important questions of the status of value that it deserves a special notice. Religion is a valuable thing whether we think of the beliefs and emotions called by that name, or of the object of religious worship, or of the institutions of religion; because it satisfies a human need, the need of worship. It is good and its value is its capacity of satisfying this need. Its value is expressed by calling it good, along with a multitude of other things which satisfy the human needs—food and drink, some measure of riches, flowers, health; the Greeks would have added (and Dr. Johnson would have assented to them) good looks. There is no particular harm in calling religion a value in this sense, if there were any use in doing so, except in opposition to those who deny it to be a good thing. The confusion comes when religion is numbered as a value along with truth and beauty and goodness, and when we go on to think of God or his distinctive deity as a value. Now value is always, we have seen, a relation, a relation between the object valued and the valuer or the subject for which the object has value. Neither God and his deity, nor religious beliefs, nor religious institutions, are relations. When they enter into relation, or are conceived as entering into relation with man, they become good. But their value lies in their being good and not in the religious character. Bread as bread has a constitution of its own, and being nutritious has a value, and is called consequently food. The quality of apples is to be apples. Animals eat and are fed by them and they consequently have value. Their value is the relation into which they enter and not a quality of the apples. If there were no animals to feed on them (or men to enjoy their beauty) they would not be values or valuable. Even animal value, then, is distinct from quality, and if called quality, is a tertiary quality.

When we come to the highest values, the beautiful, the true and the good, these in one respect are like wheat and apples: they are objects of a certain constitution—statues and sonatas, landscapes, generous deeds, chemistry. Their pre-eminence as values is that they have no being apart from their value. That is because they are not merely found, like apples, and their value, like the value of apples for food, then discovered, but are made to have value, come into existence along with their value. They are human inventions, made to satisfy certain impulses of men. It is quite true we discover the statue in the stone and the beautiful landscape in the natural show which is spread before our eyes. Still, to discover them we must invent. Their value lies in their being held together with the mind which values them, which they satisfy.

Now the object of religious emotion or worship is not made but discovered, or if discovered is too violent a word, is presumed or concluded to be in its own right, and the recognition of it is religion. It belongs accordingly (the simple examples are used without any irreverence) to the order of things like apples or rocks or flowers. All of these may become objects of value, the first when they are found to be food, the second in so far as they receive the impact of the waves, the third when their beauty is felt. But they are values only in these relations. The object of religion is neither supreme value, nor merely good, nor a mere object of natural election. God is a thing either in the world or transcending it; and his deity is not an instance of value, like beauty or goodness, but really *is* a quality in the sense of ordinary, secondary or primary qualities. He is not a human invention, though it may be he would not be discovered were it not that a need for him sets us seeking him, and so we seek him because, in the famous phrase of Pascal, we have found him already: and some have thought that his existence is matter rather of inference than of sight. These questions we have not to discuss. It remains that God is not a value, except in the sense of interesting us objectively, which he shares with anything that affects us.

Yet though God is a thing or being, and deity a quality, and neither of them a value, and not to be thought of under the rubric of value, even of the supreme values, and is at least regarded unscientifically and confusedly when surrounded with the sentiment which surrounds the supreme values, the intimacy of God and deity with values remains. Not strangely; for God is something higher than man or man's creations, knowledge and beauty and goodness, and in the order of significance in the scheme of things, absorbs and presupposes them and all things below them. Regarded (illegitimately as I think) as their creator he transcends them; and still transcends them if, in some becoming of the world of things, his deity is (as I think) their outcome and they are a preparation for it. Religion accordingly is in the first place so closely linked with morals that it attends upon custom and judgments of right and wrong from its beginning. So much so that some have thought it to be a device for preservation of social stability, and some treat it as in its nature practical. They forget, I believe, to ask what leads men to think of an object of worship. For considered as the outcome of goodness, the idea that there is such a being as God appears to be a pure fancy of man. Just as we should not know that other persons like ourselves exist within the bodies of men, without an experience (such as, for instance, we get in language) that we are members of a society; so we should not be able to invent a miraculous idea of a continuing supernatural being, without some experience of a need which is projected into or finds its fulfilment in the idea of such a being.

At any rate religion absorbs custom and goodness into itself, and the goodness of God may accordingly be far removed from our own present ideas of goodness; as men are, so will they fancy their God to be. Beauty is taken up into religious ceremony; and God has knowledge more than man's. The well-known account of religion given by Hoeffding defines it as the faith we have in 'the conservation of values', not only of the highest values but the values of mere life. God is the being in whom all values are conserved. The definition suffers, I think, from the inadequacy just described in relation to morals. There wants the human need of a being in whom afterwards we may have the faith that values are conserved. I mention this famous definition here because it recalls us to a problem which has already arisen when we asked how morals which are the creation of man can be regarded as pointing the way of the world's advance, when it is remembered that historical greatness and moral greatness do not always coincide. The same question arose in a still more difficult form when the creations of art claimed or had ascribed to them by philosophers direct insight into the nature of reality, especially the reality of human nature, while all the while art was an artificial interpretation of its own material reality and introduced its own interpretation of things. We fell back upon faith that it is so.

Hoeffding's definition suggests that the solution should be found in God, and that the solution is found there is declared to be matter of faith.

These reflections lead on finally to a subject which greatly occupies people's minds at the present day. In the nineteenth century, science, and especially physical science, commonly took up an attitude of aloofness, and even suspicion, towards philosophy and the humane studies with which philosophy was supposed to be especially concerned. That attitude is being abandoned; philosophy is even bidden welcome by physics, at any rate there is an approximation of the two and a disposition to live on friendly terms together, as in the earlier days in Europe in the seventeenth century, when men of science were philosophers, and philosophers often men of science. Indeed physicists in particular are so much impressed by the artificiality of their own science, that some of them have insisted on the superior directness, as they urge, of the mental sciences and suggest that in them, and in the value especially of beauty, and in the religious experience often spoken of as a value and thought also to be direct, there is a better guidance to be found to the real nature of things. The subject has been already touched on in discussing the value of knowledge.[1] But it seems necessary to return to it here. What is said, and of course rightly, is that physics does not exhaust the world of things; what is hinted is that the true nature of things is more likely to be conscious and spiritual than to be such as the physicist finds.

Now as concerns the superior directness of our acquaintance with conscious experience, it is of course true that we do have direct awareness of ourselves; but this by itself gives us no knowledge. It means only that

[1] Before, Chapter XI. p. 212.

we live the conscious life, 'enjoy' ourselves I have said elsewhere; but if we had only such direct experience to go upon we should be brutes or vegetables and have no knowledge at all, and our experience of ourselves would help us nothing towards understanding the world. On the other hand, as experience which has a meaning and which we can use, our consciousness of ourselves is no more direct than our consciousness of things, for we are aware of ourselves only in having awareness of external things, though the external thing may only be our own body; there is no awareness except an object is given with it. It would be, in Lotze's phrase, a mill working without grist. Indeed those who doubt whether reality is revealed to ourselves, in our experience of external objects must doubt equally the reality of ourselves.

In the next place, when we come to value which is thought to give us deeper knowledge, we have to observe first that knowledge itself is one of the values, and further that we have such knowledge as we can have of the other values, as the preceding chapters have attempted to show. Second, whereas science is controlled by things themselves, however artificial our procedure is with respect to them; and consequently we get this artefact knowledge only in so far as we prevent the indispensable mind from distorting the reality; in the other values we are not nearer to things than in science but remoter from them. For into beauty the mind enters as a constituent and the chief constituent, while goodness is wholly an affair of the mind under conditions set by the external world and always having ends and objects external to the mind. Instead of our being more directly in contact with reality in these values, we have made products so artificial that we were forced to ask ourselves, Do these artificial creations of ours possess any claim to insight into the real working of the world?

The belief that in religious experience we have direct experience of God goes entirely beyond the record. An experience we have, which is as direct as in other mental actions which we live through, in the language of Mr. Bergson, or as I am accustomed to say, enjoy. But what the religious experience is an experience *of* is a matter of interpretation. In the end the interpretation may be correct. But it is not direct and it is reached only after much other experience which we have learned to trust. In itself it is a craving for something we know not what, and we search in the rest of our experience for what it may tell us of the object we seek. We may start with the actual existence of a certain 'numinousness' in the world, as Mr. Otto calls it, or imagining an object to meet our need we may ask ourselves whether such an object is in keeping with the rest of our experience. Our fancy, if a true philosophy leads us to believe that the fancied object is demanded by the rest of our knowledge, may give us the assurance we need. Mr. Bergson has urged lately that on this ground we may trust the visions of mystics if they are not discordant with other truths, as having a claim to be considered probably true. Some philosophers have indeed tried to deduce the existence of God by arguments which have satisfied few. At least we can see that the object of religion is not given directly to us, though when we have accepted the idea of him, he may seem to have spoken to us directly in our conscience or in other ways. But though the object of worship has not the artificiality of value, it is not experienced as a part of the world with a force superior to the beliefs of science. On the contrary it derives part of its persuasiveness from the converging indications of the rest of our knowledge.

The artificiality of science takes us away from the consideration of particular facts and occupies us with

the universals by which we interpret them. Certainty
so far as it is attainable lies in particulars, and yet it is
these which give us least knowledge. But there is no
consolation to be found in the deliverances of consciousness, for they involve the external world at every point.

What we may, however, learn from including the
values in our survey of things is probably this. The
values of beauty, goodness and truth are the highest
creations of man, and the object of religion is still higher
in the scale than man and his works. Lower than man's
values proper we have man the animal, man with his
conscious mind, the rest of the animals and the organic
world, and life and mind are distinct stages in the
progression from physical existence upwards. But the
continuity and affinity that can be traced through all
these stages of existence suggest to us the idea that
something of what is familiar on the higher levels as
life and mind is present in appropriate form at the
lower levels. It is becoming a familiar thought to many
that there is an organic character in physical things,
and since mind and spirit are continuous with life, it
may be that these have from the beginning elements
corresponding to them in things. These elements are
plainer to us in the highly developed form which they
assume in the highest values and thereby in the object
of religion. Accordingly those who seek in something
like mind for what is fundamental in things may be
right in their conclusion, though they are mistaken in
the method by which that conclusion is reached.

INDEX

Where reference is made to a chapter, please consult Contents.

THE END

Printed in Great Britain by R. & R. CLARK, LIMITED, *Edinburgh*

BY PROF. S. ALEXANDER

SPACE, TIME, AND DEITY

GIFFORD LECTURES, 1916–1918

2 Vols. 8vo. 25s. net.

"Professor Alexander has written a book which requires more than cursory reading. It deserves careful study. For it embodies a thoroughly modern exposition of New Realism in full detail. . . . The whole book must be read. It is admirable alike in thoroughness of method and in command of material."—*Lord Haldane in "Nature."*

"A great work of philosophic speculation, nobly conceived and conscientiously carried through."—*Dr. C. D. Broad in "Mind."*

"Professor Alexander has made a most significant contribution to metaphysical science, and no discerning reader of these volumes can fail to be impressed with the striking originality of the view they present or with the subtlety of argument brought to bear in its support."—*Professor G. Dawes Hicks in "The Hibbert Journal."*

"The book has been rightly described as 'a work in the grand manner'. . . . This massive treatise may be accounted the heaviest artillery that has been brought to bear in this country of late years against the Idealist tradition in English metaphysics."—*The Times.*

"However much one may dissent from Professor Alexander's doctrine, it is impossible not to recognise in his work a remarkable effort of difficult and sustained thinking. . . . Few books are more admirable examples of the genuine philosophic temper: large, equable, fair-minded, dispassionate, with no interest in criticism except as advancing truth, no desire that the victory should be his and not another's, but only that the victory should be won."—*The Oxford Magazine.*

MACMILLAN AND CO., LTD., LONDON

WORKS ON PHILOSOPHY

THE PLACE OF MINDS IN THE WORLD. Gifford Lectures at the University of Aberdeen, 1924–1926. First Series. By Sir WILLIAM MITCHELL, K.C.M.G., Vice-Chancellor of the University of Adelaide. 8vo. 12s. 6d. net.

THE FAITH OF A MORALIST. Gifford Lectures, 1926–1928. By A. E. TAYLOR, D.Litt., Professor of Moral Philosophy, University of Edinburgh. Series I. The Theological Implications of Morality. Series II. Natural Theology and the Positive Religions. 8vo. 15s. net each series.

STUDIES IN PHILOSOPHY AND PSYCHOLOGY. By G. F. STOUT, M.A., LL.D., Professor of Logic and Metaphysics, St. Andrews University. 8vo. 15s. net.

COSMIC PROBLEMS: An Essay on Speculative Philosophy. By JOHN S. MACKENZIE, Litt.D. 8vo. 6s. net.

WHITEHEAD'S PHILOSOPHY OF ORGANISM. By DOROTHY M. EMMET, late Research Fellow of Somerville College, Oxford. Extra crown 8vo. 8s. 6d. net.

FACT: The Romance of Mind. By HENRY OSBORN TAYLOR, author of "The Mediæval Mind," etc. Extra crown 8vo. 7s. 6d. net.

ESSAYS ON THE NATURAL ORIGIN OF THE MIND. By C. A. STRONG, author of "The Origin of Consciousness: An Attempt to Conceive the Mind as a Product of Evolution." 8vo. 12s. net.

ADVENTURES IN PHILOSOPHY AND RELIGION. By JAMES B. PRATT, Ph.D., author of "The Religious Consciousness." Crown 8vo. 10s. net.

MACMILLAN AND CO., LTD., LONDON